Communications in Computer and Information Science 3124

Series Editors

Rationale

The CCIS series is devoted to the publication of proceedings of computer science conferences. Its aim is to efficiently disseminate original research results in informatics in printed and electronic form. While the focus is on publication of peer-reviewed full papers presenting mature work, inclusion of reviewed short papers reporting on work in progress is welcome, too. Besides globally relevant meetings with internationally representative program committees guaranteeing a strict peer-reviewing and paper selection process, conferences run by societies or of high regional or national relevance are also considered for publication.

Topics

The topical scope of CCIS spans the entire spectrum of informatics ranging from foundational topics in the theory of computing to information and communications science and technology and a broad variety of interdisciplinary application fields.

Information for Volume Editors and Authors

Publication in CCIS is free of charge. No royalties are paid, however, we offer registered conference participants temporary free access to the online version of the conference proceedings on SpringerLink (http://link.springer.com) by means of an http referrer from the conference website and/or a number of complimentary printed copies, as specified in the official acceptance email of the event.

CCIS proceedings can be published in time for distribution at conferences or as post-proceedings, and delivered in the form of printed books and/or electronically as USBs and/or e-content licenses for accessing proceedings at SpringerLink. Furthermore, CCIS proceedings are included in the CCIS electronic book series hosted in the SpringerLink digital library at http://link.springer.com/bookseries/7899. Conferences publishing in CCIS are allowed to use our online conference service (Meteor) for managing the whole proceedings lifecycle (from submission and reviewing to preparing for publication) free of charge.

Publication process

The language of publication is exclusively English. Authors publishing in CCIS have to sign the Springer CCIS copyright transfer form, however, they are free to use their material published in CCIS for substantially changed, more elaborate subsequent publications elsewhere. For the preparation of the camera-ready papers/files, authors have to strictly adhere to the Springer CCIS Authors' Instructions and are strongly encouraged to use the CCIS LaTeX style files or templates.

Abstracting/Indexing

CCIS is abstracted/indexed in DBLP, Google Scholar, EI-Compendex, Mathematical Reviews, SCImago, Scopus. CCIS volumes are also submitted for the inclusion in ISI Proceedings.

How to start

To start the evaluation of your proposal for inclusion in the CCIS series, please send an e-mail to ccis@springer.com

Hector Florez · Ruben Gomez-Sanchez
Editors

Artificial Intelligence

First UPADI Conference, UPADI-AI 2026
Lima, Peru, August 25–28, 2026
Proceedings

Springer

Editors
Hector Florez
Universidad Distrital Francisco Jose de Caldas
Bogota, Colombia

Ruben Gomez-Sanchez
Universidad Nacional de Ingeniería
Lima, Peru

ISSN 1865-0929 ISSN 1865-0937 (electronic)
Communications in Computer and Information Science
ISBN 978-3-032-35634-5 ISBN 978-3-032-35635-2 (eBook)
https://doi.org/10.1007/978-3-032-35635-2

This Springer imprint is published by the registered company Springer Nature Switzerland AG
The registered company address is: Gewerbestrasse 11, 6330 Cham, Switzerland

Preface

The 1st UPADI International Conference on Artificial Intelligence (UPADI-AI 2026) aimed to bring together researchers and practitioners working in different domains in the field of artificial intelligence in order to exchange their expertise and to discuss the perspectives of development and collaboration.

UPADI-AI 2026 was held at the Colegio de Ingenieros del Perú, located in Lima, Peru, during August 25–28, 2026. It was organized by the Colegio de Ingenieros del Perú. In addition, UPADI-AI 2026 was proudly sponsored by Springer.

UPADI-AI received 59 submissions on artificial intelligence topics. Authors of accepted submissions came from the following countries: Argentina, Colombia, Costa Rica, Honduras, Mexico, Peru, and Spain.

All submissions were reviewed through a double-blind peer-review process. Each paper was reviewed by at least three experts. Based on the double-blind review process, 14 full papers were accepted to be included in this volume of Communications in Computer and Information Sciences (CCIS) proceedings published by Springer.

We would like to thank the staff of Springer for their helpful advice, guidance, and support in publishing the proceedings.

We trust that the UPADI-AI 2026 proceedings open for you new vistas of discovery and knowledge.

August 2026

Hector Florez
Ruben Gomez-Sanchez

Organization

General Chair

Ruben Gomez-Sanchez	Universidad Nacional de Ingeniería, Peru

Organizing Committee

German Pardo Albarracín	Unión Panamericana de Asociaciones de Ingenieros, Colombia
Luz Mélida Gamboa Mesa	Unión Panamericana de Asociaciones de Ingenieros, Colombia
Jaime Antonio Ruiz Bejar	Colegio de Ingenieros del Perú, Peru
Ruben Gomez-Sanchez	Universidad Nacional de Ingeniería, Peru
Lydia Sofia Prado Lau	Universidad Nacional de Ingeniería, Peru
Percy Dario Mazuelos Soldevilla	Instituto Altman, Peru
Roberto Antenor Baldeon Icochea	Universidad Nacional de Ingeniería, Peru
Hugo Cana	CESEL SA, Peru
Jorge Seminario	Texas A&M University, USA
Daysi Zulema Diaz Obregon	Seguro Social de Salud - EsSalud, Peru
José Alfonso Valencia	Fundación SmartCity Colombia, Colombia
Julio Cesar Cardenas Olaya	Instituto de Educación Superior ELITEC, Peru
Henry Gomez Urquizo	Universidad Continental, Peru
Cesar Augusto Bustamante Gutierrez	GrapPeru SAC, Peru
Jorge Cuadros Blas	Intelectia SAC, Peru

Program Committee Chairs

Hector Florez	Universidad Distrital Francisco José de Caldas, Colombia
Ruben Gomez-Sanchez	Universidad Nacional de Ingeniería, Peru

Program Committee

Jorge Bacca	Fundación Universitaria Konrad Lorenz, Colombia
Omar Caballero	Universidad Popular Autónoma del Estado de Puebla, Mexico
Hector Florez	Universidad Distrital Francisco José de Caldas, Colombia
Henry Gomez Urquizo	Universidad Continental, Peru
Ankur Gupta	Linkedin, USA
Raphael Gomes	Instituto Federal de Goiás, Brazil
Ruben Gomez-Sanchez	Universidad Nacional de Ingeniería, Peru
Jorge Hernandez	Universidad Distrital Francisco José de Caldas, Colombia
Percy Mazuelos	Instituto Altman, Peru
Shania Nalagath	Microsoft, USA
Florencia Pollo	Universidad Tecnológica Nacional, Argentina
Kumar Paidi	University of the Cumberlands, USA
Kiran Puttewouda	Vidyavardhaka College of Engineering, India
Carlos Ruano	Universidad de Camaguey, Cuba

Contents

Application of Artificial Intelligence in Energy

Reinforcement Learning-Assisted Evolutionary Optimization for Distribution Network Operational Planning

Mauro Jurado Egas[1](✉), Eduardo J. Salazar[2], and Mauricio E. Samper[1]

[1] Institute of Electric Energy (IEE), National University of San Juan – National Scientific Council (CONICET), 5400 San Juan, Argentina
mjurado@iee-unsjconicet.org

[2] Catalonia Institute for Energy Research (IREC), 08930 Barcelona, Spain
ejsalazar@irec.cat

Abstract. Active distribution networks are undergoing a rapid transition driven by the increasing penetration of distributed resources, including renewable generation, demand response programs, and electric vehicles, which introduces new technical and operational challenges for day-ahead network management. Coordinating conventional control devices together with emerging distributed flexibility leads to a nonlinear, non-convex, mixed-discrete, and multi-period optimization problem with high computational complexity. To address this challenge, this paper proposes an intelligent solution methodology based on genetic algorithms, reinforcement learning, and dynamic programming for short-term operational planning of distribution systems. The methodology adopts a two-level structure. At the aggregator level, electric-vehicle charging is optimally scheduled to flatten the loading profile of secondary distribution transformers. At the distribution system operator level, controllable resources, including demand response actions, OLTC tap positions, capacitor banks, and network reconfiguration switches, are coordinated to minimize operating costs associated with energy losses, voltage violations, branch congestion, and controllable-resource use. To enhance search efficiency and reduce dependence on manual parameter tuning, a tabular Q-learning agent is embedded into the genetic algorithm to adaptively control selection, crossover, and mutation strategies during execution. The best hourly operating candidates obtained by the genetic algorithm are then linked through dynamic programming to determine the optimal day-ahead schedule while preserving temporal consistency. The proposed framework combines engineering-grade power-flow simulation with adaptive artificial-intelligence techniques, providing an effective and practical decision-support tool for modern distribution control centers.

Keywords: Active Distribution Networks · Artificial Intelligence · Adaptive learning · Q-learning · Plug-in Electric Vehicle · Demand response · Volt/Var Control · Network reconfiguration · OpenDSS

H. Florez and R. Gomez-Sanchez (Eds.): UPADI-AI 2026, CCIS 3124, pp. 3–19, 2027.
https://doi.org/10.1007/978-3-032-35635-2_1

1 Introduction

Distribution systems are changing from passive radial feeders into active distribution networks in which controllable resources are distributed along medium- and low-voltage circuits. Distributed photovoltaic generation, smart meters, flexible industrial loads, remotely operated switches, capacitor banks, on-load tap changers (OLTCs), energy storage, and plug-in electric vehicles (PEVs) provide operational flexibility, but they also increase the dimensionality and uncertainty of the distribution-system decision problem. The operator no longer observes only an aggregated demand curve at the substation. Instead, the operator must anticipate net nodal power, voltage profiles, branch loadings, and the technical consequences of many discrete control actions over a complete operating horizon [1].

Day-ahead distribution operational planning (DOP) is a natural decision layer for this context. Given forecasts of demand and behind-the-meter distributed generation, contractual limits of demand-response resources, PEV charging requirements, controllable device operating ranges, and the network model, the distribution system operator (DSO) determines a schedule of control actions for the following day. The objective is to operate the network economically while maintaining voltages and currents within admissible limits and avoiding unnecessary switching of mechanical devices. This operation-planning view complements real-time control: the day-ahead schedule supplies an anticipated operating trajectory, and real-time control can later correct deviations caused by forecast errors or contingencies [2,3].

The technical difficulty is that DOP combines continuous power-flow physics with discrete operational decisions. OLTC taps and capacitor-bank stages are discrete. Network reconfiguration states are binary and must preserve radiality or the admissible topology set. Industrial demand response is often represented through discrete price or incentive levels, because tariffs are not implemented as arbitrary real-valued signals. PEV charging profiles may be pre-optimized by aggregators and then introduced as nodal demand trajectories. When these elements are coordinated over 24 periods, the direct search space grows rapidly and the problem becomes unsuitable for exhaustive enumeration.

Classical optimization approaches may rely on linearization, convexification, or decomposition to obtain tractable formulations. These approaches are valuable, particularly for planning studies and for problems that admit accurate relaxations. However, they can lose fidelity when distribution models include unbalanced feeders, nonlinear voltage-dependent loads, detailed control-device models, and discrete reconfiguration actions. A complementary strategy is co-simulation: a metaheuristic explores candidate decisions while a specialized distribution simulator evaluates the physical operating point. This approach does not require differentiability of the simulator and can be connected to existing network models.

Genetic algorithms (GAs) are attractive for this class of problems because they operate directly on mixed-discrete chromosomes, support constraints through repair or penalties, and are relatively easy to connect to a power-flow evaluator. The main drawback is parameter sensitivity. The same crossover probability, mutation probability, and selection pressure may not be suitable for all hours, all networks, or all distributed-energy-resource penetration levels. A low mutation probability may lead to premature convergence when the feasible region is fragmented. A high mutation probability may destroy high-quality structures when the population is already exploring useful regions. Manual tuning is possible, but it is costly and must be repeated when the problem changes.

This paper addresses that limitation by embedding a reinforcement-learning (RL) agent inside the genetic search. The agent is not used as a direct grid controller. It does not issue tap positions or prices by itself. Instead, it observes the evolutionary process and selects the GA search parameters at each generation. The environment is the GA population and its power-flow-based fitness evaluation. The action corresponds to a discrete GA control policy composed of the selection mechanism, selection pressure, crossover rate, mutation rate, and mutation intensity. The reward is formulated from objective-cost reduction, population improvement, and feasibility preservation, with penalties for stagnation or non-improving generations. Because the action set is small and discrete, tabular Q-learning is sufficient and computationally lightweight. Deep RL is deliberately avoided at this stage to keep the method interpretable, easy to validate, and compatible with day-ahead computation times.

The contributions of this paper are fourfold. First, it formulates a day-ahead DOP problem that integrates Volt/Var control, network reconfiguration, industrial demand response, and PEV aggregator profiles. Second, it proposes a reinforcement evolutionary solution in which tabular Q-learning dynamically adapts GA parameters. Third, it keeps a two-stage architecture: hourly candidate states are produced by the RL-adapted GA and a dynamic-programming layer selects the daily schedule considering transition costs. Fourth, it provides reproducible Python code with a surrogate evaluator and an explicit interface for connection to an OpenDSS model.

The remainder of the paper is organized as follows. Section 2 reviews the technical background. Section 3 states the DOP formulation. Section 4 presents the proposed reinforcement evolutionary methodology. Section 5 presents and discusses the numerical results. Section 6 concludes the paper.

2 Related Work

2.1 Distribution Operation Planning

Operational planning in active distribution systems has been studied and modeled from various perspectives, focusing on different network functionalities. The work developed in [4] presents a day-ahead planning methodology for distribution companies that coordinates Volt/Var control and demand-response flexibility under a daily operating-cost objective. The same line of work supports the use of genetic search and dynamic programming for distribution operation schedules with discrete controls and transition costs.

Demand response is particularly relevant because it converts part of the demand into an operational resource. The strategy reported in [5] uses reinforcement learning to define pricing and incentive signals for demand response. A later model combines real-time pricing and incentives under a reinforcement-learning formulation [6]. A multi-agent extension introduces cooperative and competitive interactions for demand-response pricing [7]. These contributions support the idea that demand-side flexibility can be represented through price-responsive actions and customer-response models, but they do not eliminate the need for network-constrained operation planning at the DSO level.

PEV aggregators add another layer of coordination. The framework presented in [8] defines a prediction-of-use tariff aimed at coordinating aggregators of PEVs. In a DOP formulation, an aggregator may solve a local charging problem and communicate an optimized demand profile to the DSO. The DSO then evaluates whether the resulting network operating point satisfies voltage and loading limits and whether additional control actions are necessary.

2.2 Evolutionary Computation and Parameter Sensitivity

Evolutionary algorithms are widely used in large mixed-discrete optimization problems because they require only an evaluator of candidate solutions. For distribution systems, the evaluator can be a power-flow engine such as OpenDSS. A chromosome can represent tap positions, capacitor-bank states, topology options, and demand-response price levels. The GA searches by selection, crossover, mutation, and elitism.

The challenge is parameter calibration. Population size affects exploration and computation time. Selection pressure affects convergence speed and diversity. Crossover rate affects recombination of useful structures. Mutation rate or probability affects the capacity to escape local minima. In a multi-period DOP problem, the search landscape changes from hour to hour. Morning hours may be voltage constrained, midday hours may be dominated by photovoltaic backfeed, and evening hours may be limited by PEV charging and thermal congestion. A static GA configuration is therefore a compromise, not an adaptive policy.

2.3 Reinforcement Learning Assisted Genetic Algorithms

Recent studies combine RL and evolutionary computation to reduce parameter-tuning dependence. The RL-GA method in [11] addresses a satellite scheduling problem by using Q-learning to select evolution operators and by preserving elite individuals to improve search performance. The Q-learning GA in [12] selects mutation rates during a GA run and shows that the mutation decision can react to population variance. The approach in [13] uses RL and deep RL to adapt parent selection and mutation in permutation flow-shop scheduling.

These studies motivate the design adopted here, but the distribution-planning problem has specific requirements. The evaluator may be expensive because each chromosome can require a power-flow simulation. The chosen schedule must respect engineering constraints and switching costs. The method should be transparent enough for operational review. For these reasons, this paper uses tabular Q-learning rather than a neural approximation. The goal is not to learn an end-to-end grid-control policy; it is to learn a compact policy for adapting the search behavior of a GA.

3 Problem Formulation

3.1 Planning Horizon and Decision Variables

Let $\mathcal{T} = \{1, \dots, T\}$ denote the set of hourly periods in the day-ahead horizon, with $T = 24$. For each period t, the DSO selects an operating state

$$x_t = [\tau_t,\, q_t,\, r_t,\, \pi_t]\,, \tag{1}$$

where τ_t is the OLTC tap position, q_t is the vector of capacitor-bank states, r_t is the network reconfiguration state, and π_t is the vector of demand-response prices. The PEV aggregator profile is represented as an exogenous optimized net demand $p^{\text{pev}}_{n,t}$ at each node n, although the formulation can be extended to co-optimize selected aggregator variables.

The admissible domains are finite:

$$\tau_t \in \Omega^{\tau}, \quad q_t \in \Omega^{q}, \quad r_t \in \Omega^{r}, \quad \pi_t \in \Omega^{\pi}. \tag{2}$$

The set Ω^r contains only feasible radial or admissible topologies. This avoids repeatedly repairing infeasible switching configurations during the genetic search.

Let $p^L_{n,t}$ and $p^G_{n,t}$ be the forecasted load and behind-the-meter distributed PV generation at node n. Further details regarding the adopted formulation can be found in [2].The net active demand before demand response is

$$p^0_{n,t} = p^L_{n,t} - p^G_{n,t} + p^{\text{pev}}_{n,t}\,. \tag{3}$$

For an industrial demand-response participant u, the demand modification can be represented in a compact linear-elastic form:

$$\Delta p^{\text{dr}}_{u,t} = \text{clip}\left(\epsilon_u(\pi_{u,t} - \pi^0_u),\, -\Delta p^{\max}_u,\, \Delta p^{\max}_u\right), \tag{4}$$

where ϵ_u is the price elasticity coefficient, π^0_u is a reference price, and $\Delta p^{\max}_u$ is the contracted flexibility limit. A negative value of $\Delta p^{\text{dr}}_{u,t}$ represents load reduction, whereas a positive value represents load increase with respect to the baseline nodal demand $p^0_{n,t}$. The nodal net demand $p_{n,t}$ passed to the power-flow evaluator is then

$$p_{n,t} = p^0_{n,t} + \sum_{u \in \mathcal{U}_n} \Delta p^{\text{dr}}_{u,t}. \tag{5}$$

3.2 Power-Flow and Technical Constraints

For each period t, the candidate state x_t defines a network topology, control-device configuration, and nodal demand. The distribution power-flow problem can be written abstractly as

$$y_t = \Phi(x_t, d_t), \tag{6}$$

where d_t contains the forecasts and uncontrollable inputs, $\Phi(\cdot)$ is the power-flow operator, and y_t contains bus voltages, branch currents, losses, and device states. In an OpenDSS implementation, Φ is not replaced by a simplified equation; the simulator computes the operating point from the network model.

The technical limits are expressed as

$$V^{\min} \le |V_{n,t}(x_t)| \le V^{\max}, \qquad \forall n, t, \tag{7}$$

$$|I_{\ell,t}(x_t)| \le I_\ell^{\max}, \qquad \forall \ell, t, \tag{8}$$

$$x_t \in \Omega^{\tau} \times \Omega^{q} \times \Omega^{r} \times \Omega^{\pi}, \qquad \forall t. \tag{9}$$

Equation (7) enforces nodal voltage limits, (8) prevents thermal overloading of network branches, and (9) defines the feasible operating domains of the controllable resources. Instead of discarding all infeasible individuals, the proposed evaluator uses penalty terms for violations of (7) and (8). This keeps the search informative when the feasible region is narrow.

3.3 Objective Function

The DOP objective is the minimization of the total daily operating cost:

$$\min_{x_1,\dots,x_T} F = \sum_{t\in\mathcal{T}} C_t(x_t) + \sum_{t\in\mathcal{T}} \Psi(x_{t-1}, x_t), \tag{10}$$

where $C_t(x_t)$ is the hourly operating cost and $\Psi(x_{t-1}, x_t)$ is the transition cost between consecutive operating states. The hourly cost is

$$C_t = C_t^L + C_t^V + C_t^I + C_t^{\mathrm{DR}}. \tag{11}$$

The first component, C_t^L, represents the cost of active energy losses. The voltage-violation penalty is

$$C_t^V = \lambda_V \sum_n \left[\max(0, V^{\min} - |V_{n,t}|) + \max(0, |V_{n,t}| - V^{\max})\right], \tag{12}$$

where λ_V is a penalty coefficient. The branch-congestion penalty is

$$C_t^I = \lambda_I \sum_\ell \max\left(0, \frac{|I_{\ell,t}|}{I_\ell^{\max}} - 1\right). \tag{13}$$

The demand-response activation cost is

$$C_t^{\mathrm{DR}} = \sum_{u\in\mathcal{U}} \left(\alpha_u |\Delta p_{u,t}^{\mathrm{dr}}| + \beta_u (\pi_{u,t} - \pi_u^0)^2\right), \tag{14}$$

where α_u and β_u represent remuneration and discomfort-related terms. While the device-related transition cost Ψ includes operating wear terms for capacitor-bank switching, OLTC tap changes, and network reconfiguration:

$$\Psi(x_{t-1}, x_t) = \lambda_\tau \mathbf{1}_{\tau_t \neq \tau_{t-1}} + \lambda_q \|q_t - q_{t-1}\|_1 + \lambda_r \mathbf{1}_{r_t \neq r_{t-1}}. \tag{15}$$

These costs are excluded from the hourly cost C_t to avoid double counting and are included in the transition cost to discourage unnecessary mechanical operations performed only to achieve marginal reductions in losses or operational violations.

3.4 Aggregator-Level PEV Scheduling

The DSO-level problem can receive optimized PEV charging profiles from aggregators. For an aggregator a, a simplified objective is to flatten the secondary transformer demand while satisfying charging requirements:

$$\min_{p^{\text{pev}}_{a,t}} \sum_{t \in \mathcal{T}} \left(P^{\text{sdt}}_{a,t} - P^{\text{pev}}_{a,t}\right)^2, \tag{16}$$

subject to

$$0 \leq p^{\text{pev}}_{i,t} \leq \bar{p}_i, \qquad \forall i, t, \tag{17}$$

$$E_i^{\min} \leq E_{i,0} + \sum_t \eta_i p^{\text{pev}}_{i,t} \Delta t \leq E_i^{\max}, \qquad \forall i, \tag{18}$$

$$p^{\text{pev}}_{a,t} = \sum_{i \in \mathcal{V}_a} p^{\text{pev}}_{i,t}. \tag{19}$$

where $E_{i,0}$ is the initial energy stored in the battery of PEV i, $E_i^{\min}$ and $E_i^{\max}$ are the minimum and maximum allowable battery energy levels, respectively, η_i is the charging efficiency, and Δt is the scheduling time-step duration. The resulting $p^{\text{pev}}_{a,t}$ is then assigned to the corresponding distribution node or secondary transformer in the DSO-level problem.

4 Proposed Reinforcement Evolutionary Methodology

The solution architecture separates hourly search from daily sequence selection. The first stage solves each hour independently and returns the best K candidate operating states. The second stage uses dynamic programming to select one candidate per hour while minimizing the sum of hourly and transition costs. Figure 1 summarizes the flowchart of the implemented strategy.

This decomposition is useful because the expensive evaluation is concentrated in the hourly GA search, while the inter-hour coupling is represented by a transition cost that can be optimized exactly over the candidate set. Let $\mathcal{K}_t$ be the candidate set returned for hour t, let $x_t^k \in \mathcal{K}_t$, and let $C_t(x_t^k)$ denote the

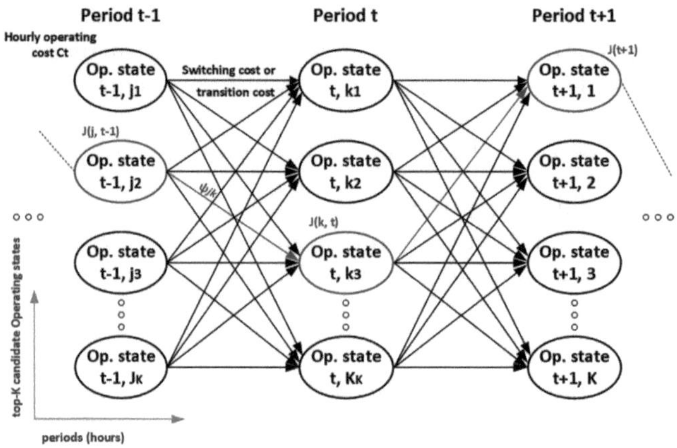

Fig. 1. Genetic algorithm and dynamic programming solution architecture for day-ahead distribution operation planning.

hourly operating cost associated with candidate operating state x_t^k. Dynamic programming computes

$$J_1(k) = C_1(x_1^k), \tag{20}$$

$$J_t(k) = C_t(x_t^k) + \min_{j \in \mathcal{K}_{t-1}} \left[J_{t-1}(j) + \Psi(x_{t-1}^j, x_t^k) \right], \quad t = 2, \ldots, T. \tag{21}$$

Backtracking from $\min_k J_T(k)$ yields the day-ahead schedule.

The RL component operates only in the hourly candidate-generation stage. At each GA generation, the population is evaluated, a compact state is constructed from search indicators, an action is selected, and the next generation is produced using the corresponding GA search configuration. The loop is shown in Fig. 2. The key design principle is that the RL state must be small enough to enable learning within a single day-ahead optimization run. It should not include raw feeder voltages or the full chromosome population. Instead, it should summarize the search process through informative indicators that remain meaningful across hours, such as diversity, improvement trend, feasibility ratio, and stagnation level.

4.1 Q-Learning Genetic Algorithm

Chromosome Encoding and Initialization. Each individual represents one hourly operating state. A chromosome is encoded as

$$\chi = [g_\tau, g_{q_1}, \ldots, g_{q_m}, g_r, g_{\pi_1}, \ldots, g_{\pi_u}], \tag{22}$$

where each gene is an index into a discrete domain. For example, g_τ indexes a tap value in Ω^τ, each g_{q_i} is a binary capacitor state, g_r indexes an admissible

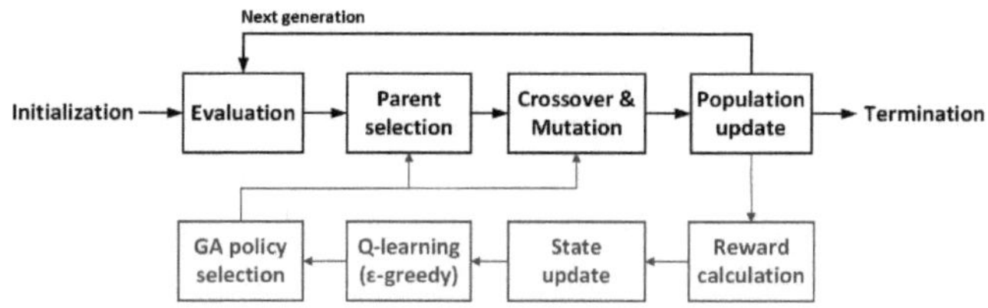

Fig. 2. Tabular Q-learning loop embedded (blue) in the genetic algorithm (black). The agent selects a GA policy, receives a reward derived from cost improvement and feasibility, and updates the Q-table. (Color figure online)

topology, and g_{π_u} indexes a price level for demand-response participant u. This index encoding avoids invalid real-valued device positions and simplifies repair.

The initial population is created by uniform sampling over the admissible domains, followed by optional seeding with engineering heuristics. Examples of seeds include the current topology, nominal tap position, and no demand-response activation. Including such seeds is useful in control-center applications because it guarantees that the optimizer compares new schedules against a familiar operating condition.

Fitness Evaluation. For an individual χ, the decoder produces a control state x_t. The evaluator applies x_t to the network model, solves the power flow, and computes the hourly cost $C_t(x_t)$ using (11).

Since the problem is formulated as a minimization task, lower cost values indicate better solutions and are directly used for ranking and evolutionary selection. For roulette-based selection, a positive scaled fitness value can be derived from the cost when required. Infeasible individuals are not automatically discarded. Instead, their violation magnitudes are incorporated into the objective function through penalty terms such as C_t^V and C_t^I, allowing the search to identify promising directions close to feasibility.

State Space. The RL state at generation g is a tuple

$$s_g = (b_g^D, b_g^P, b_g^F, b_g^E), \tag{23}$$

where b_g^D is a discretized diversity indicator, b_g^P is a discretized progress indicator, b_g^F is a discretized feasibility indicator, and b_g^E is a stagnation indicator.

Population diversity is measured from the dispersion of fitness values:

$$D_g = \frac{\sigma_g}{|\bar{C}_g| + \epsilon}, \tag{24}$$

where $\sigma_g = \sqrt{\frac{1}{N_p}\sum_{i=1}^{N_p}(C_i^g - \bar{C}_g)^2}$ and $\bar{C}_g$ is the average population cost. The progress indicator is defined as the relative improvement of the best cost:

$$P_g = \frac{C_{g-1}^\star - C_g^\star}{|C_{g-1}^\star| + \epsilon}. \tag{25}$$

The feasibility indicator is the proportion of individuals satisfying voltage and branch-loading constraints. The stagnation indicator is activated when no best-cost improvement is observed for a predefined number of generations. Each continuous indicator is discretized into a small number of bins (e.g., low, medium, high). This compact representation enables efficient online learning during a single day-ahead optimization run.

Action Space. The action selected at generation g corresponds to a discrete GA control policy:

$$a_g = (sel_g, k_g, p_{c,g}, p_{m,g}, p_{int,g}), \tag{26}$$

where sel_g is the parent-selection mechanism, k_g is the selection pressure (e.g., tournament size), $p_{c,g}$ is the crossover probability, $p_{m,g}$ is the mutation probability, and $p_{int,g}$ is the mutation intensity. Rather than using a large combinatorial grid, a compact set of predefined actions is adopted to accelerate online learning during a single optimization run. Table 1 summarizes the predefined action set adopted by the Q-learning agent.

Table 1. Discrete action set used by the Q-learning agent.

Action	Selection	k_g	p_c	p_m	p_{int}
a_1	Tournament	2	0.70	0.05	0.10
a_2	Tournament	3	0.80	0.10	0.30
a_3	Tournament	4	0.90	0.10	0.20
a_4	Tournament	2	0.60	0.20	0.40
a_5	Roulette	–	0.80	0.10	0.30
a_6	Tournament	3	0.90	0.05	0.20
a_7	Tournament	2	0.50	0.25	0.30

The action domain is intentionally small. Although a larger action space could represent a wider range of search behaviors, it would significantly slow Q-value learning, especially when the number of generations is constrained by the computational cost of repeated power-flow evaluations.

Reward Function and Q-Update. The reward mechanism is designed to encourage cost improvement while preserving feasibility and maintaining an adequate search diversity. Let $C_g^\star$ be the best hourly cost at generation g, $\bar{C}_g$ the average population cost, ϕ_g the feasibility ratio, and D_g the diversity indicator. The reward is defined as

$$r_g = w_1 \frac{C_{g-1}^\star - C_g^\star}{|C_{g-1}^\star| + \epsilon} + w_2 \frac{\bar{C}_{g-1} - \bar{C}_g}{|\bar{C}_{g-1}| + \epsilon} + w_3(\phi_g - \phi_{g-1}) + w_4 D_g - w_5 \mathbf{1}_{\text{stag}}, \tag{27}$$

where $\mathbf{1}_{\text{stag}} = 1$ if no improvement has been observed for a predefined number of generations, and zero otherwise. The weights $w_1, \ldots, w_5$ are selected to prioritize feasible improvements while discouraging premature convergence.

The Q-table is updated according to the standard off-policy rule:

$$Q(s_g, a_g) \leftarrow (1-\alpha)Q(s_g, a_g) + \alpha \left[r_g + \gamma \max_{a \in \mathcal{A}} Q(s_{g+1}, a) \right], \tag{28}$$

where α is the learning rate and γ is the discount factor. Actions are selected with an ϵ-greedy policy:

$$a_g = \begin{cases} \text{random}(\mathcal{A}), & \text{with probability } \epsilon, \\ \arg\max_{a \in \mathcal{A}} Q(s_g, a), & \text{otherwise.} \end{cases} \tag{29}$$

The exploration probability ϵ can be gradually decayed during the search. However, a minimum exploration level is preserved because the optimization landscape may differ significantly across hourly subproblems.

Algorithm. The complete hourly Q-learning genetic algorithm is summarized in Algorithm 1.1.

Algorithm 1.1. Hourly Q-learning genetic algorithm for distribution operational planning.

```
Input: control domains, hourly forecasts, population size Np,
       number of generations Gmax, action set A, Q-learning parameters
Output: top-K candidate operating states for the hour

Initialize population P0 from admissible control domains
Initialize Q-table Q(s,a)
Evaluate all individuals with the distribution power-flow evaluator OpenDSS
Update the Hall of Fame with the best individuals found
Build initial RL state s0 from diversity, progress, feasibility, and stagnation

for generation g = 0,...,Gmax-1 do
    Select action ag by epsilon-greedy Q-policy
    Decode ag into GA search configuration:
        selection mechanism, selection pressure,
        crossover probability, mutation probability,
        mutation intensity

    Select parents according to the selected mechanism
    Apply crossover according to the selected crossover probability
    Apply mutation according to the selected mutation probability
        and mutation intensity

    Evaluate invalid offspring through the power-flow evaluator
    Form the new population Pg+1
    Update the Hall of Fame

    Compute reward rg from cost improvement, population progress,
        feasibility preservation, diversity, and stagnation penalty
    Build next state sg+1
    Update Q(sg,ag) using the Q-learning rule
    sg <- sg+1
end for

Return the K lowest-cost individuals stored in the Hall of Fame
```

The algorithm is executed independently for each hourly subproblem. In the adopted implementation, the Q-table is initialized at the beginning of each hourly optimization, allowing the agent to learn a search policy adapted to the specific operating condition of that hour. In future extensions, the Q-table could be shared across hours or warm-started from previous days with similar operating conditions.

5 Computational Results

The proposed DOP methodology was implemented in a real 89-node distribution system from the "Caucete Smart Grid" project in Argentina. The system is a balanced three-phase 13.2 kV network supplying industrial, commercial, and residential users. Its one-line diagram is shown in Fig. 3, and the main system data are available in [4]. As distributed energy resources, non-controllable behind-the-meter (BTM) PV generation is incorporated at nodes 2, 7, 13, 28, 39, 42, 57, and 68; PEV are integrated at nodes 4, 42, 57, 68, 76, and 99; and DR is considered at nodes 35, 41, 81, and 93. Regarding control variables, capacitor banks are modeled as binary devices, i.e., connected (1) or disconnected (0). The substation transformer OLTC tap positions vary between 0.9 and 1.1 p.u., with a step of 0.0125. Reconfiguration switches can be closed (1) or open (0). The electricity selling price is bounded between 0.5 and 1.5 p.u. of the reference price, i.e., from 0.05 to 0.15 $/kWh, with a discretization step of 0.025. Demand elasticity values range from -0.3 to -0.7. The costs used to evaluate losses, voltage violations, and congestion are 0.1, 0.35, and 1.0 $/kWh, respectively. In addition, the switching costs of capacitor banks, OLTC, and reconfiguration devices are 4.0, 6.0, and 20.0 $/operation, respectively. PEV battery capacities were obtained from commercial models reported in [8], including Tesla S, BMW i3, and Peugeot Partner Electric. The probabilistic functions used to model PEV behavior were a lognormal distribution $N(0.6, (0.1)^2)$ for the arrival state of charge, a normal distribution $N(19{:}00, (1.5\,h)^2)$ for arrival time, and a normal distribution $N(7{:}00, (1\,h)^2)$ for departure time. Since the proposed DOP is deterministic, the PEV simulation process is performed first and one charging-load scenario is selected for the planning study. Additional implementation details, hyperparameters, and computational settings are available in [16].

The numerical assessment is organized in two parts. First, the electrical performance of the optimized schedule is analyzed in terms of losses, voltage profiles, branch loading, demand response usage, EV charging coordination, and controllable-resource operation. Second, the contribution of the reinforcement learning module is assessed by comparing the proposed Q-learning-assisted genetic algorithm plus dynamic programming strategy, denoted as QLGA-DP, against a fixed-parameter genetic algorithm plus dynamic programming strategy, denoted as GA-DP.

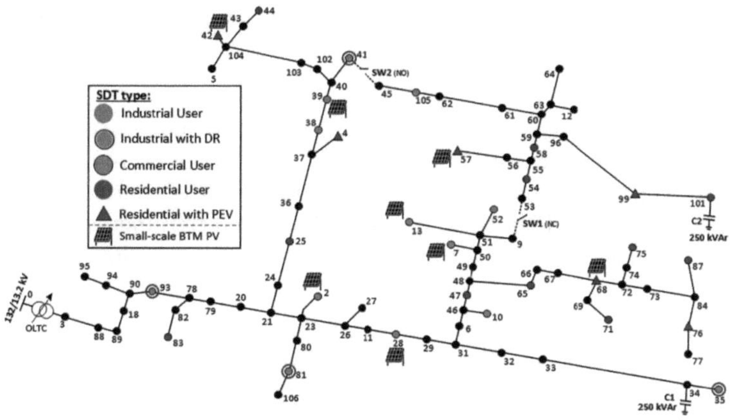

Fig. 3. Caucete Smart Grid. One-line medium voltage diagram.

5.1 Results

Electrical Performance. For the non-optimized reference case, the OLTC remains at its neutral tap position, capacitor banks retain their initial status, the network operates with the base topology (see Fig. 3), and the electricity price is kept at the reference flat value. In addition, PEV charging is uncoordinated, so vehicles charge upon arrival without restrictions.

After applying DOP, the operating cost decreases from \$49,056.3 to \$7,429.5, and the day-ahead schedule is obtained. The OLTC remains at tap = 1.05 p.u., and the capacitor banks stay connected throughout the 24 h horizon. The switching states indicate a network reconfiguration, with SW2 closed and SW1 opened to preserve radiality. Selling prices show similar patterns across several hours, with nodes 41 and 93 exhibiting the highest DR participation. As a result, loss costs decrease by 21.1%, voltage-violation costs are fully eliminated, and capacity-violation costs are reduced by 85.5%.

Regarding capacity violations, branches 3–88, 20–21, 31–6, and 29–31 exceed the operating limit, with some branches surpassing the thermal limit (1.0 p.u.). After coordination between aggregators and the DSO, congestion in branches 31–6 and 29–31 is fully removed. In branches 3–88 and 20–21, congestion is mitigated in most periods, except between 17:00 and 22:00, where it remains below the thermal limit. Persistent congestion increases operating costs. This occurs because of limited DR availability, e.g., the price at node 81 reaches its upper bound, reducing flexible demand during peak hours. Greater DR participation or additional DER integration would provide higher operational flexibility.

Finally, the schedules of VVC and reconfiguration devices show limited variation during the day because switching costs are considered. Without these costs, switching actions would increase significantly, accelerating device wear and reducing equipment lifetime. Therefore, an appropriate representation of resource operating costs is essential for an effective DOP from both technical and economic perspectives.

Q-Learning Module Contribution. The reinforcement learning module was incorporated to adapt the GA search policy online and reduce dependence on manually tuned parameters. Its contribution was evaluated by comparing the proposed QLGA-DP with a conventional fixed-parameter GA-DP under the same population size, number of generations, and power-flow evaluation budget.

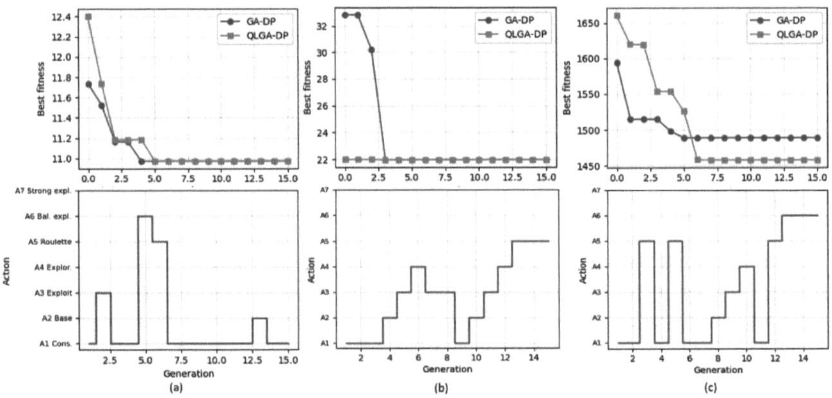

Fig. 4. Contribution of the Q-learning module for representative hourly subproblems (hours 2 (a), 13 (b), and 21 (c)). Upper row: convergence comparison between GA-DP and QLGA-DP. Lower row: action sequence selected by the Q-learning agent during the search.

Figure 4 presents the results for three representative hourly subproblems, corresponding to hours 2, 13, and 21. The upper row compares the convergence behavior of GA-DP and QLGA-DP, while the lower row shows the sequence of actions selected by the Q-learning agent during the search. In the low-demand scenario (hour 2), both methods converged to the same final solution, although QLGA-DP required adaptive changes among conservative, exploitative, and balanced actions before stabilizing. In the medium-demand scenario (hour 13), QLGA-DP reached the best solution from the first generations, clearly outperforming the fixed-parameter GA-DP. The selected actions evolved progressively from conservative settings toward more exploratory and roulette-based policies, indicating that the agent adjusted the search as the population evolved. In the high-demand scenario (hour 21), where the optimization problem becomes more constrained and complex, QLGA-DP achieved a lower final fitness than GA-DP after switching from exploratory actions in early generations to more exploitative actions near convergence.

These results confirm that the proposed RL module allows the GA to dynamically modify its exploration–exploitation balance according to the operating condition of each hour. Therefore, the main benefit of QLGA-DP is not only better solution quality, but also faster convergence in challenging operating periods under the same computational budget.

Table 2 summarizes the overall comparison. Under the same computational budget, QLGA-DP achieved better solution quality with negligible additional runtime. Therefore, the proposed RL module acts as an effective low-overhead adaptive controller of the GA search process.

Table 2. Overall comparison between GA-DP and QLGA-DP.

Metric	GA-DP	QLGA-DP
Final daily cost (USD)	7,598.4	7,429.5
Average best hourly fitness	332.6	308.3
Hours improved (%)	–	29.2
Runtime (s)	482.7	518.1
Power-flow evaluations	Same	Same

6 Conclusion

This paper presented a reinforcement evolutionary methodology for day-ahead operational planning in active distribution networks. The formulation coordinates OLTC taps, capacitor-bank states, network reconfiguration, industrial demand-response prices, and PEV aggregator profiles under a total operating-cost objective. The solution strategy combines genetic algorithms, Q-learning, and dynamic programming. In the first stage, a tabular Q-learning agent is embedded into the genetic algorithm to adapt the search policy online by selecting suitable selection, crossover, and mutation configurations during the hourly optimization process. In the second stage, the best hourly candidate operating states are linked over the 24-hour horizon through dynamic programming, which explicitly accounts for switching and intertemporal transition costs.

The numerical results showed two complementary benefits. From the power-system perspective, the obtained schedules reduced operating costs and improved network performance by coordinating flexible and conventional resources. From the optimization perspective, the reinforcement learning module improved convergence behavior and solution quality under the same computational budget. Since the adaptive GA was able to converge earlier to high-quality solutions in representative hours, the proposed strategy also suggests the possibility of reducing the number of generations required, which could further decrease computational times in practical applications.

Future work will focus on large-scale real-network validation, comparison against additional fixed and adaptive metaheuristic strategies, transfer learning through warm-started Q-tables across similar operating days, and the inclusion of additional flexible resources such as battery energy storage systems and inverter-based reactive-power support. Further research will investigate the scalability, robustness, and generalization capabilities of the proposed framework through broader benchmarking studies and more comprehensive performance assessments. A stochastic extension of the proposed methodology will also be considered to explicitly model uncertainty in load, renewable generation, and electric-vehicle charging demand.

Acknowledgements. The authors gratefully acknowledge the financial support provided by the National Scientific and Technical Research Council (CONICET, Argentina).

References

1. Klyapovskiy, S., You, S., Cai, H., Bindner, H.: Incorporate flexibility in distribution grid planning through a framework solution. Int. J. Electr. Power Energy Syst. **111**, 66–78 (2019). https://doi.org/10.1016/j.ijepes.2019.03.069
2. Jurado, M., Samper, M., Rosés, R.: An improved encoder-decoder-based CNN model for probabilistic short-term load and PV forecasting. Electr. Power Syst. Res **217**, 109153 (2023). https://doi.org/10.1016/j.epsr.2023.109153
3. Shen, M., Wang, L., Lu, Z.: Bi-level coordinated operation strategy of an active distribution system with load aggregators. Int. J. Electr. Power Energy Syst. **169**, 110766 (2025). https://doi.org/10.1016/j.ijepes.2025.110766
4. Jurado, M., Salazar, E., Samper, M., Roses, R., Ojeda Esteybar, D.: Day-ahead operational planning for DisCos based on demand response flexibility and Volt/Var control. Energies **16**(20), 7045 (2023). https://doi.org/10.3390/en16207045
5. Salazar, E.J., Jurado, M., Samper, M.E.: Reinforcement learning-based pricing and incentive strategy for demand response in smart grids. Energies **16**(3), 1466 (2023). https://doi.org/10.3390/en16031466
6. Salazar, E.J., Samper, M.E., Patino, H.D.: Dynamic customer demand management: a reinforcement learning model based on real-time pricing and incentives. Renew. Energy Focus **46**, 39–56 (2023). https://doi.org/10.1016/j.ref.2023.05.004
7. Salazar, E.J., et al.: Demand response model: a cooperative-competitive multi-agent reinforcement learning approach. Eng. Appl. Artif. Intell. **133**, 108273 (2024). https://doi.org/10.1016/j.engappai.2024.108273
8. Coria, G.E., Penizzotto, F., Romero, A.: A framework for determining a prediction-of-use tariff aimed at coordinating aggregators of plug-in electric vehicles. Energies **12**(23), 4487 (2019). https://doi.org/10.3390/en12234487
9. Tushar, M.H.K., Assi, C.: Volt-VAR control through joint optimization of capacitor bank switching and renewable energy. IEEE Trans. Smart Grid (2018). https://doi.org/10.1109/TSG.2017.2648509
10. Vijayan, V., et al.: A blended approach to improve reliability and efficiency of EDN via reconfiguration, demand response, and VVO. IEEE Trans. Autom. Sci. Eng. (2024). https://doi.org/10.1109/TASE.2022.3220523

11. Song, Y., et al.: RL-GA: a reinforcement learning-based genetic algorithm for electromagnetic detection satellite scheduling problem. Swarm Evol. Comput. **77**, 101236 (2023). https://doi.org/10.1016/j.swevo.2023.101236
12. Woodcock, A., Zhang, L.: Genetic algorithm with reinforcement learning based parameter optimisation. In: IEEE International Conference on Systems, Man, and Cybernetics, pp. 4833–4838 (2024). https://doi.org/10.1109/SMC54092.2024.10831364
13. Irmouli, M.: Genetic algorithm enhanced by deep reinforcement learning in parent selection mechanism and mutation: minimizing makespan in permutation flow shop scheduling problems. arXiv:2311.05937v2 (2023)
14. Sutton, R.S., Barto, A.G.: Reinforcement Learning: An Introduction, 2nd edn. MIT Press, Cambridge (2018)
15. Watkins, C.J.C.H., Dayan, P.: Q-learning. Mach. Learn. **8**, 279–292 (1992). https://doi.org/10.1007/BF00992698
16. Open-source projects and the research data repository of the Institute of Electrical Energy (IEE-UNSJ). Online DOP Data. https://sourceforge.net/p/operational-planning/. Accessed 15 Mar 2026

Application of Artificial Intelligence in Health

Artificial Intelligence and Digital Marketing in Private Healthcare Organizations: Evidence from Patient Acquisition, Retention, and Follow-up

Percy Dario Mazuelos-Soldevilla[1](✉), Aracely Giron[2], and Pablo Enrique Mazuelos-Soldevilla[1,2]

[1] Private University of Tacna, Tacna, Peru
{permazuelos,pabmazueloss}@upt.pe
[2] Maria Auxiliadora University, Lima, Peru
arecely.giron@uma.edu.pe

Abstract. Artificial intelligence and digital marketing are increasingly converging in healthcare organizations seeking to improve patient acquisition, retention, and follow-up. However, despite the growing interest in AI-enabled personalization, predictive analytics, chatbots, and automated engagement, empirical evidence in real-world private healthcare settings remains limited. This study examines the relationship between artificial intelligence and digital marketing in private healthcare organizations in Tacna, Peru. A quantitative, basic, correlational, non-experimental, and cross-sectional design was applied. Data were collected through a structured questionnaire administered to 110 private healthcare organizations registered in RENIPRESS, using a census approach for the eligible organizational frame. Artificial intelligence was measured through four dimensions: machine learning, cognitive intelligence, big data, and deep learning. Digital marketing was assessed through patient acquisition, patient retention, and patient follow-up. The inferential analysis used Spearman's rho, considering the ordinal nature of the measurement scale and the distributional behavior of the variables. The results showed a positive and statistically significant relationship between artificial intelligence and digital marketing (rho $= 0.562$, $p < 0.05$). The findings suggest that AI adoption may strengthen data-driven marketing capabilities in private healthcare by supporting segmentation, personalization, automation, and patient relationship management. This study contributes empirical evidence from a regional Latin American healthcare context and offers practical implications for digitally transforming patient-centered marketing strategies.

Keywords: Artificial intelligence · Digital marketing · Private healthcare

H. Florez and R. Gomez-Sanchez (Eds.): UPADI-AI 2026, CCIS 3124, pp. 23–38, 2027.
https://doi.org/10.1007/978-3-032-35635-2_2

1 Introduction

Artificial intelligence (AI) has become a strategic driver of digital transformation in healthcare organizations, extending its influence beyond clinical decision support toward administrative, managerial, communicational, and marketing-related functions [1,3,13]. In private healthcare markets, AI-based tools are valued for their ability to process structured and unstructured data, identify behavioral patterns, support prediction, automate communication, and improve decision-making [1,3,5]. These capabilities are relevant because competitiveness in private healthcare depends not only on clinical quality, but also on visibility, trust, responsiveness, perceived service value, and long-term patient relationship management [2,4,7,11].

Digital marketing has also become central to healthcare management. Patients increasingly use digital channels to search for health information, compare providers, evaluate reputation, schedule appointments, and interact with healthcare organizations before and after care delivery [2,8,9]. Therefore, healthcare marketing is not limited to online promotion; it includes coordinated strategies for patient acquisition, retention, positioning, reputation management, digital communication, and post-care follow-up [7,11,18].

The convergence between AI and digital marketing offers opportunities to improve how private healthcare organizations manage the patient journey. Machine learning can support predictive segmentation and identify patterns related to appointment scheduling, service preferences, engagement, or churn risk [1,3,10]. Big data analytics enables the integration of demographic information, browsing behavior, social media interactions, online reviews, administrative records, and service-use data [3,10,15]. Likewise, cognitive and conversational AI systems, such as chatbots and virtual assistants, can provide real-time responses, qualify potential patients, answer frequently asked questions, and maintain digital engagement [1,4,6]. Deep learning may also support healthcare marketing through the analysis of text, images, sentiment patterns, and digital behavior [1,12,16].

Previous studies suggest that AI-enabled digital marketing can improve personalization, segmentation, automation, reputation monitoring, patient engagement, and marketing resource allocation [1–6]. In dental clinics, AI-supported digital marketing has been linked to audience segmentation, personalized communication, and loyalty initiatives [2]. In broader healthcare contexts, advanced analytics has been associated with customer experience improvement, underserved population identification, market penetration, and data-based decision-making [3,15]. From a customer relationship management perspective, AI may also transform acquisition, retention, and relationship development through automated insights and adaptive engagement strategies [5,14].

Nevertheless, the evidence base remains fragmented. Much of the literature on AI-enabled healthcare marketing is conceptual, descriptive, simulation-based, or context-specific, rather than empirically validated in real-world private healthcare organizations [1–6]. Prior studies also highlight the limited availability of standardized quantitative indicators, such as conversion rates, cost per acquisition, patient retention rates, patient lifetime value, return on marketing investment, and churn rates [1–6]. This gap limits evidence-based decision-making for healthcare managers evaluating whether AI capabilities are associated with stronger digital marketing practices.

This issue is especially relevant in regional and emerging-market contexts. Although AI and digital marketing are often analyzed in large healthcare systems or highly digitized markets, private healthcare organizations in regional Latin American settings may face limited infrastructure, uneven digital maturity, budget constraints, lack of specialized personnel, and resistance to organizational change [8,11,15]. Tacna, Peru, provides a relevant setting because private healthcare organizations operate in a competitive environment where digital presence, patient communication, service differentiation, and post-care follow-up are increasingly important.

Accordingly, this study examines the relationship between artificial intelligence and digital marketing in private healthcare organizations in Tacna, Peru. AI is analyzed through four dimensions: machine learning, cognitive intelligence, big data, and deep learning. Digital marketing is examined through three patient-centered dimensions: patient acquisition, patient retention, and patient follow-up. Thus, the study seeks to determine whether organizations with greater AI-related development also report stronger digital marketing practices.

This paper contributes to the literature by providing empirical evidence on AI and digital marketing in private healthcare organizations, addressing a gap identified in prior studies [1–6]. It also operationalizes AI through specific technological dimensions and links them to patient-centered marketing practices in a regional Latin American context. From a practical perspective, the findings may support healthcare managers, marketing professionals, and technology providers in designing more data-driven, personalized, and ethically responsible digital marketing strategies.

The remainder of this paper is organized as follows. Section 2 presents the literature review and theoretical framework. Section 3 develops the theoretical model and hypotheses. Section 4 describes the methodology. Section 5 reports the empirical results. Section 6 discusses the findings. Finally, Sect. 7 presents conclusions, implications, limitations, and future research directions.

2 Literature Review and Theoretical Framework

Artificial intelligence (AI) refers to computational systems capable of performing tasks commonly associated with human intelligence, such as learning, reasoning, prediction, language processing, pattern recognition, and decision support [19]. In healthcare, AI has progressively moved beyond clinical diagnosis and treatment support toward administrative, managerial, communicational, and marketing-related applications [1,3,13]. Within digital marketing, AI operates through technologies such as machine learning, big data analytics, cognitive intelligence, natural language processing, recommender systems, chatbots, and deep learning models [1,5,12].

2.1 Artificial Intelligence in Healthcare Marketing

AI-enabled healthcare marketing is mainly associated with data processing, predictive segmentation, personalization, automated interaction, and patient relationship management. Machine learning allows organizations to identify patterns in patient behavior and generate predictions related to preferences, appointment scheduling, engagement, or potential abandonment [1,3,10]. These capabilities can support more precise targeting and reduce generic communication strategies.

Big data analytics complements machine learning by integrating heterogeneous information sources, such as demographic data, browsing behavior, social media interactions, online reviews, administrative records, and service-use data [3,10,15]. In private healthcare organizations, these data-driven capabilities can improve strategic decision-making, campaign monitoring, market intelligence, and patient-centered service planning.

Cognitive intelligence includes AI applications that emulate complex human-like capabilities, particularly language understanding, reasoning, and interaction. In digital marketing, this includes chatbots, virtual assistants, sentiment analysis, text analysis, and automated response systems [1,4,6]. These tools may improve patient communication by providing real-time responses, appointment guidance, and continuous digital engagement. However, their use in healthcare requires careful attention to privacy, trust, accuracy, and ethical governance [1,17].

Deep learning, although more widely recognized in clinical applications, may also contribute to healthcare marketing through the analysis of complex digital traces, including text, images, sentiment patterns, online behavior, and preference signals [1,12,16]. Nevertheless, its implementation requires greater technological maturity, data quality, and specialized capabilities, which may limit adoption in smaller or regional healthcare organizations.

2.2 Digital Marketing in Private Healthcare

Digital marketing refers to the use of digital technologies, platforms, and channels to create, communicate, and deliver value to target audiences [12,18,20]. In private healthcare, digital marketing must be understood beyond online advertising because patients make decisions in contexts of uncertainty, perceived risk, trust, and information asymmetry [7,11]. Therefore, healthcare marketing involves not only attracting patients, but also informing, guiding, retaining, and following them throughout the service experience.

Private healthcare organizations use digital channels such as websites, search engines, social media, online reviews, educational content, appointment platforms, and direct messaging to interact with patients before and after care delivery [2,8,9]. These strategies can influence patient acquisition by increasing visibility and improving institutional positioning. They can also support patient retention through personalized communication, satisfaction monitoring, loyalty-building, and post-care follow-up [2,7,11].

In this study, digital marketing is structured around three patient-centered dimensions: patient acquisition, patient retention, and patient follow-up. Patient acquisition refers to attracting potential patients and converting digital interest into service use. Patient retention refers to maintaining long-term relationships with existing patients through trust, satisfaction, and continuity. Patient follow-up refers to post-care communication, reminders, feedback collection, and re-engagement actions.

2.3 AI-Enabled Patient Relationship Management

The integration of AI into customer relationship management represents a major transformation in how organizations manage users, clients, or patients [5,14]. AI-enabled relationship management can automate lead scoring, predict patient needs, personalize communication timing, recommend content, and identify patients at risk of disengagement [5]. In healthcare, these functions are relevant because patient relationships are based not only on transactional exchange, but also on trust, perceived quality, continuity, and service experience [7,15].

AI can strengthen healthcare digital marketing in four main ways. First, predictive segmentation can identify patient groups according to behavior, needs, and service preferences [1,3]. Second, personalization can adapt messages, educational content, reminders, and digital interactions to specific patient profiles [5,14]. Third, automation can reduce response time and improve communication continuity through chatbots, automated reminders, and follow-up workflows [1,4,6]. Fourth, analytics can support performance evaluation by monitoring engagement, satisfaction, conversion, and retention indicators [3,10,15].

Despite these advantages, AI adoption in healthcare marketing also presents challenges. These include data privacy, algorithmic transparency, ethical use of patient information, limited technical capacity, and the need for continuous model updating [1,17]. These challenges are especially relevant for regional private healthcare organizations, where technological infrastructure and specialized human resources may be limited.

3 Theoretical Model and Hypotheses

The theoretical model of this study is based on the assumption that artificial intelligence capabilities are positively associated with digital marketing practices in private healthcare organizations. AI is understood as a multidimensional construct composed of machine learning, cognitive intelligence, big data, and deep learning. These dimensions represent technological capabilities that may support predictive segmentation, automated communication, patient behavior analysis, advanced personalization, and data-driven decision-making [1,3,5,10]. Digital marketing is also considered a multidimensional construct, focused on patient acquisition, patient retention, and patient follow-up, which are central functions in private healthcare marketing [2,7,11,18].

The proposed model connects AI-related capabilities with patient-centered digital marketing practices. In this framework, AI does not replace healthcare marketing strategy, but strengthens it by improving how organizations collect, process, interpret, and use data to interact with patients across the digital journey. Therefore, organizations with higher levels of AI development are expected to show stronger digital marketing practices in terms of attracting, retaining, and following up with patients (Table 1).

Table 1. Theoretical structure of the proposed model.

Construct	Dimension	Expected contribution to digital marketing
Artificial intelligence	Machine learning	Predictive segmentation, campaign optimization, and behavioral pattern recognition
Artificial intelligence	Cognitive intelligence	Conversational interaction, automated responses, and language-based personalization
Artificial intelligence	Big data	Data integration, real-time insights, and patient behavior analysis
Artificial intelligence	Deep learning	Complex pattern recognition, advanced personalization, and analysis of digital traces
Digital marketing	Patient acquisition	Attraction and conversion of potential patients through digital channels
Digital marketing	Patient retention	Maintenance of long-term patient relationships through trust, satisfaction, and engagement
Digital marketing	Patient follow-up	Post-care communication, reminders, feedback collection, and re-engagement actions

3.1 Hypothesis Development

Machine learning can improve digital marketing because predictive algorithms allow healthcare organizations to identify patterns in patient behavior, segment audiences, estimate service preferences, and optimize campaign decisions [1,3,10]. In private healthcare, these capabilities may help organizations move from generic communication toward more precise and patient-centered marketing strategies. Therefore, the first hypothesis is proposed:

H1. Machine learning is positively and significantly related to digital marketing in private healthcare organizations in Tacna, Peru.

Cognitive intelligence can strengthen digital marketing by improving interaction between healthcare organizations and patients. Tools such as chatbots, virtual assistants, automated response systems, and natural language processing applications may support real-time communication, appointment guidance, frequently asked questions, and continuous engagement across digital channels [1,4,6]. Therefore, the second hypothesis is proposed:

H2. Cognitive intelligence is positively and significantly related to digital marketing in private healthcare organizations in Tacna, Peru.

Big data is expected to be associated with digital marketing because large-scale data processing allows organizations to integrate different sources of patient and market information. These capabilities can improve patient behavior analysis, market intelligence, campaign monitoring, and strategic decision-making [3,10,15]. Therefore, the third hypothesis is proposed:

H3. Big data is positively and significantly related to digital marketing in private healthcare organizations in Tacna, Peru.

Deep learning can contribute to digital marketing through the identification of complex patterns in text, images, online behavior, sentiment, and other digital traces [1,12,16]. Although its adoption may require greater technological maturity, deep learning can support advanced personalization and improve the capacity of healthcare organizations to interpret complex patient-related data. Therefore, the fourth hypothesis is proposed:

H4. Deep learning is positively and significantly related to digital marketing in private healthcare organizations in Tacna, Peru.

Finally, artificial intelligence as a global construct is expected to be positively related to digital marketing because its combined technological capabilities can support segmentation, personalization, automation, patient relationship management, and evidence-based marketing decisions [1–6]. Therefore, the general hypothesis is proposed:

H5. Artificial intelligence is positively and significantly related to digital marketing in private healthcare organizations in Tacna, Peru.

Table 2. Hypotheses of the study.

Code	Hypothesis
H1	Machine learning is positively and significantly related to digital marketing in private healthcare organizations in Tacna, Peru
H2	Cognitive intelligence is positively and significantly related to digital marketing in private healthcare organizations in Tacna, Peru
H3	Big data is positively and significantly related to digital marketing in private healthcare organizations in Tacna, Peru
H4	Deep learning is positively and significantly related to digital marketing in private healthcare organizations in Tacna, Peru
H5	Artificial intelligence is positively and significantly related to digital marketing in private healthcare organizations in Tacna, Peru

The resulting model is correlational rather than causal. Thus, the hypotheses do not assume that AI causes improvements in digital marketing, but rather that higher levels of AI-related capabilities are statistically associated with stronger digital marketing practices in the studied organizations (Table 2).

4 Methodology

4.1 Research Design

This study followed a quantitative, basic, correlational, non-experimental, and cross-sectional research design. The approach was quantitative because the variables were measured through numerical scores obtained from structured questionnaires. The study was correlational because its purpose was to determine the degree of association between artificial intelligence and digital marketing in private healthcare organizations. It was non-experimental because the variables were not manipulated, and cross-sectional because the data were collected at a single point in time.

This design was appropriate because the objective was not to establish causal effects, but to examine whether higher levels of AI-related capabilities are statistically associated with stronger digital marketing practices in the studied organizations.

4.2 Population and Sample

The study population consisted of private healthcare organizations located in the province of Tacna, Peru. These organizations were identified from the National Registry of Health Service Provider Institutions (RENIPRESS). A census approach was used for the eligible organizational frame; therefore, the final analytical dataset included 110 valid and complete responses, corresponding to the organizations registered in the study frame.

The unit of analysis was the private healthcare organization. The questionnaire was completed by owners, managers, administrative representatives, or marketing personnel involved in digital marketing or technology-related decisions. This criterion was used to ensure that the responses reflected organizational practices rather than individual patient perceptions (Table 3).

4.3 Variables and Measurement

The study analyzed two main variables: artificial intelligence and digital marketing. Artificial intelligence was treated as the independent variable and was measured through four dimensions: machine learning, cognitive intelligence, big data, and deep learning. Digital marketing was treated as the dependent variable and was measured through three dimensions: patient acquisition, patient retention, and patient follow-up.

The operational structure of the variables is presented in Table 4. Each dimension was measured through Likert-type items designed to capture organizational practices and perceived levels of development in relation to AI and digital marketing.

Table 3. Methodological characteristics of the study.

Element	Description
Research approach	Quantitative
Type of research	Basic
Research level	Correlational
Research design	Non-experimental and cross-sectional
Study setting	Private healthcare organizations in Tacna, Peru
Population frame	Organizations registered in RENIPRESS
Final analytical sample	110 private healthcare organizations
Unit of analysis	Private healthcare organization
Data collection technique	Survey
Instrument	Structured questionnaire
Measurement scale	Ordinal Likert scale
Statistical software	SPSS 22

Table 4. Measurement structure of the variables.

Variable	Dimension	Items	Scale
Artificial intelligence	Machine learning	4	Ordinal Likert
Artificial intelligence	Cognitive intelligence	4	Ordinal Likert
Artificial intelligence	Big data	4	Ordinal Likert
Artificial intelligence	Deep learning	4	Ordinal Likert
Digital marketing	Patient acquisition	4	Ordinal Likert
Digital marketing	Patient retention	4	Ordinal Likert
Digital marketing	Patient follow-up	4	Ordinal Likert

4.4 Instrument and Data Collection Procedure

Data were collected using two structured questionnaires. The first questionnaire measured artificial intelligence and included 16 items distributed across four dimensions. The second questionnaire measured digital marketing and included 12 items distributed across three dimensions. Both instruments were designed using an ordinal Likert scale to capture the level of agreement or perceived development of each construct.

The questionnaires were reviewed through expert judgment before application. This procedure was used to assess the relevance, clarity, and coherence of the items with the study variables and dimensions. The survey was administered online through Google Forms, which allowed systematic data collection and facilitated subsequent statistical processing. The estimated administration time was approximately 15 min.

Participation was voluntary and based on informed consent. Respondents were informed about the academic purpose of the study and the confidential treatment of the information provided. No clinical patient data were collected.

4.5 Reliability of the Instruments

The internal consistency of the instruments was assessed using Cronbach's alpha. This coefficient is widely used to evaluate the reliability of multi-item scales and determine whether the items consistently measure the same construct [22]. The artificial intelligence questionnaire showed very high reliability, with a Cronbach's alpha of 0.922. The digital marketing questionnaire also showed very high reliability, with a Cronbach's alpha of 0.948.

The reliability values for the variables and dimensions are shown in Table 5.

Table 5. Reliability of the instruments.

Construct or dimension	Cronbach's alpha	Items	Interpretation
Artificial intelligence	0.922	16	Very high
Machine learning	0.821	4	Very high
Cognitive intelligence	0.740	4	High
Big data	0.818	4	Very high
Deep learning	0.860	4	Very high
Digital marketing	0.948	12	Very high
Patient acquisition	0.824	4	Very high
Patient retention	0.899	4	Very high
Patient follow-up	0.909	4	Very high

4.6 Data Analysis Procedure

Data were processed using SPSS 22. First, descriptive statistics were used to summarize the behavior of the variables and dimensions. Then, the Shapiro-Wilk test was applied to assess the normality of the data. This test was considered appropriate because it is widely recognized as a powerful procedure for detecting deviations from normality [21].

Given the ordinal nature of the Likert-scale data and the presence of non-normal distributions in several dimensions, Spearman's rho was used for the inferential analysis. Spearman's rho is suitable for examining the association between ordinal variables or variables that do not meet parametric assumptions. The statistical significance level was set at 0.05. Therefore, hypotheses were accepted when the p-value was lower than 0.05.

The hypothesis testing procedure followed this decision rule:

- If $p < 0.05$, the relationship was considered statistically significant.
- If $p \geq 0.05$, the relationship was not considered statistically significant.

The analysis focused on testing the relationship between each AI dimension and digital marketing, as well as the general relationship between artificial intelligence and digital marketing.

4.7 Ethical Considerations

The study followed basic ethical principles for research involving organizational respondents. Participants were informed about the purpose of the study, the voluntary nature of their participation, and the academic use of the collected information. Informed consent was obtained before completing the questionnaire. The study did not collect sensitive clinical information, patient records, or personal health data. The data were analyzed in aggregate form to protect the confidentiality of the participating organizations.

5 Results

5.1 Descriptive Results

The descriptive analysis showed that the level of artificial intelligence adoption in the surveyed private healthcare organizations was mainly moderate. As shown in Table 6, 52.7% of the organizations reported a regular level of AI development, 36.7% reported a low level, and only 10.9% reported a high level. This suggests that AI-related capabilities are present in the studied organizations, but their implementation is still not fully consolidated.

Regarding digital marketing, 55.5% of the organizations reported a regular level, 26.4% reported a high level, and 18.2% reported a low level. These results indicate that digital marketing practices are more developed than AI capabilities, although most organizations still remain at an intermediate stage of implementation.

Table 6. Descriptive results for artificial intelligence and digital marketing.

Variable	Level	Frequency	Percentage
Artificial intelligence	Low	40	36.7%
Artificial intelligence	Regular	58	52.7%
Artificial intelligence	High	12	10.9%
Digital marketing	Low	20	18.2%
Digital marketing	Regular	61	55.5%
Digital marketing	High	29	26.4%
Total	–	110	100.0%

5.2 Normality Analysis

Before testing the hypotheses, the Shapiro-Wilk test was applied to assess the distribution of the study variables and dimensions. As shown in Table 7, artificial intelligence and all its dimensions obtained significance values below 0.05. Therefore, the null hypothesis of normality was rejected for these variables.

In the case of digital marketing, the global variable obtained a significance value greater than 0.05. However, its three dimensions showed significance values below 0.05. Considering this mixed behavior, together with the ordinal nature of the Likert-scale data, the hypotheses were tested using Spearman's rho, a non-parametric correlation coefficient.

Table 7. Shapiro-Wilk normality test.

Variable or dimension	Statistic	df	Sig.
Artificial intelligence	0.975	110	0.033
Machine learning	0.966	110	0.007
Cognitive intelligence	0.975	110	0.037
Big data	0.968	110	0.009
Deep learning	0.961	110	0.003
Digital marketing	0.981	110	0.120
Patient acquisition	0.975	110	0.038
Patient retention	0.965	110	0.006
Patient follow-up	0.964	110	0.004

5.3 Hypothesis Testing

Spearman's rho was used to test the relationship between each AI dimension and digital marketing, as well as the general relationship between artificial intelligence and digital marketing. The decision criterion was established at a significance level of 0.05. Therefore, a relationship was considered statistically significant when $p < 0.05$.

Table 8 presents the results of the hypothesis testing. All relationships were positive and statistically significant. Therefore, the five hypotheses proposed in the study were supported.

The first hypothesis was supported, since machine learning showed a positive and statistically significant relationship with digital marketing ($\rho = 0.504$, $p < 0.05$). This result indicates that organizations with higher levels of machine learning application tend to report stronger digital marketing practices.

The second hypothesis was also supported. Cognitive intelligence was positively and significantly related to digital marketing ($\rho = 0.415$, $p < 0.05$). Although this was the weakest relationship among the AI dimensions, it still

Table 8. Spearman correlation results.

Hyp.	Relationship	Spearman's rho	Sig.	Decision
H1	Machine learning and digital marketing	0.504	0.000	Supported
H2	Cognitive intelligence and digital marketing	0.415	0.000	Supported
H3	Big data and digital marketing	0.524	0.000	Supported
H4	Deep learning and digital marketing	0.455	0.000	Supported
H5	Artificial intelligence and digital marketing	0.562	0.000	Supported

indicates that conversational, language-based, and automated interaction capabilities are associated with digital marketing development.

The third hypothesis was supported as well. Big data showed the strongest specific relationship with digital marketing ($\rho = 0.524$, $p < 0.05$). This suggests that data integration, large-scale information processing, and patient behavior analysis are particularly relevant for strengthening digital marketing practices in private healthcare organizations.

The fourth hypothesis was supported because deep learning was positively and significantly related to digital marketing ($\rho = 0.455$, $p < 0.05$). This result suggests that advanced pattern recognition and complex data-processing capabilities may contribute to digital marketing, although their level of implementation may still be emerging in the studied context.

Finally, the general hypothesis was supported. Artificial intelligence showed a positive and statistically significant relationship with digital marketing ($\rho = 0.562$, $p < 0.05$). This result indicates that higher levels of AI-related capabilities are associated with stronger digital marketing practices in private healthcare organizations in Tacna, Peru.

Overall, the findings show that all AI dimensions are significantly associated with digital marketing. Big data and machine learning showed the strongest specific associations, while cognitive intelligence and deep learning showed weaker but still significant relationships. In managerial terms, these coefficients indicate moderate positive associations that are actionable for prioritizing data infrastructure, segmentation, and analytics capabilities, but they should not be interpreted as evidence of causal effects.

6 Discussion

The results show a positive and statistically significant relationship between artificial intelligence and digital marketing in private healthcare organizations in Tacna, Peru. The general correlation obtained ($\rho = 0.562$, $p < 0.05$) supports the assumption that AI-related capabilities are associated with stronger digital marketing practices. This finding is consistent with previous studies suggesting that AI can improve segmentation, personalization, automation, patient engagement, and customer relationship management in healthcare contexts [1–6].

Among the AI dimensions, big data showed the strongest relationship with digital marketing ($\rho = 0.524$, $p < 0.05$). This suggests that the ability to collect, integrate, and analyze large volumes of information is especially relevant for healthcare marketing. These findings align with studies that emphasize the role of advanced analytics and business intelligence in improving customer experience, market penetration, and strategic decision-making in health services [3,10,15].

Machine learning also showed a significant relationship with digital marketing ($\rho = 0.504$, $p < 0.05$). This result supports the idea that predictive algorithms can help healthcare organizations identify patient behavior patterns, segment audiences, and optimize digital campaigns [1,3,10]. In practical terms, machine learning may allow private healthcare organizations to move from generic communication strategies toward more targeted and patient-centered digital marketing.

Deep learning and cognitive intelligence also showed positive and significant relationships with digital marketing, although with lower correlation coefficients. Deep learning obtained $\rho = 0.455$ and cognitive intelligence obtained $\rho = 0.415$, both with $p < 0.05$. These results suggest that more advanced or interaction-oriented AI applications, such as chatbots, natural language processing, sentiment analysis, and complex pattern recognition, may still be at an early stage of implementation in the studied organizations [1,4,6,12,16].

Overall, the findings contribute empirical evidence to a field where previous literature has been mainly conceptual, descriptive, or simulation-based [1–6]. The study also provides evidence from a regional Latin American context, where private healthcare organizations may face limitations related to infrastructure, digital maturity, specialized personnel, and data governance. Therefore, the results suggest that AI adoption in healthcare marketing should begin with basic data infrastructure, analytics capabilities, and progressive automation before moving toward more complex AI systems.

However, the findings should be interpreted with caution. The study used a correlational and cross-sectional design, so causal relationships cannot be established. In addition, the data were obtained through self-reported questionnaires collected from a single source within each organization; therefore, common method bias cannot be fully ruled out. The absence of objective marketing indicators also limits performance-based interpretation. Future studies should include longitudinal designs and objective metrics such as conversion rates, cost per acquisition, patient retention rates, appointment conversion, patient lifetime value, and return on marketing investment.

7 Conclusions

This study examined the relationship between artificial intelligence and digital marketing in private healthcare organizations in Tacna, Peru. The results confirmed a positive and statistically significant relationship between both variables ($\rho = 0.562$, $p < 0.05$). Therefore, the general hypothesis was supported.

The specific hypotheses were also supported. Big data showed the strongest relationship with digital marketing, followed by machine learning, deep learning, and cognitive intelligence. These findings suggest that data-centered AI capabilities are currently more closely associated with digital marketing development than more advanced or conversational AI applications in the studied context.

The study contributes to the literature by providing empirical evidence on AI-enabled digital marketing in private healthcare organizations. It also operationalizes AI through four technological dimensions and relates them to patient-centered digital marketing practices, including patient acquisition, retention, and follow-up.

From a practical perspective, private healthcare organizations should strengthen their data management, analytics, and segmentation capabilities as a first step toward AI-enabled marketing. These capabilities can support more personalized communication, better patient follow-up, and more efficient digital campaigns. More advanced tools, such as chatbots, sentiment analysis, and deep learning-based personalization, should be implemented progressively and with adequate ethical and data governance mechanisms.

The main limitations of this study are its correlational design, cross-sectional data collection, reliance on self-reported information, and possible common method bias. Future research should use longitudinal or experimental designs and include objective marketing performance indicators. Comparative studies across different regions, healthcare subsectors, and organizational sizes would also help determine how AI contributes to digital marketing effectiveness in private healthcare.

Disclosure of Interests. The authors have no competing interests to declare that are relevant to the content of this article.

References

1. Digital marketing and artificial intelligence in healthcare: revolutionizing patient engagement and service delivery (2024). https://doi.org/10.25163/primeasia.6110231
2. Bravo Calderón, C.M.E., Argudo Velasteguí, M.D., Juela-Bravo, V.A., Heras Olalla, G.S., Parra-Hidalgo, W.P.: Estrategias de marketing digital para clínicas odontológicas: una revisión de la literatura. Recima21 **5**(7) (2024). https://doi.org/10.47820/recima21.v5i7.5511
3. Nwosu, N.T., Babatunde, S.O., Ijomah, T.: Enhancing customer experience and market penetration through advanced data analytics in the health industry. World J. Adv. Res. Rev. (2024). https://doi.org/10.30574/wjarr.2024.22.3.1810
4. Ramanathan, K., Jenefa, L., Radhi, A.H.: Redesigning of marketing mix elements affecting medical tourism through artificial intelligence (AI). In: Advances in Logistics, Operations, and Management Science Book Series (2024). https://doi.org/10.4018/979-8-3693-0612-3.ch011
5. Libai, B., et al.: Brave new world? On AI and the management of customer relationships. J. Interact. Mark. **51** (2020). https://doi.org/10.1016/j.intmar.2020.04.002

6. Prokhorov, O., Kholodniak, O.: Multi-agent simulation modeling of doctor-patient interaction in medical marketing. In: Renaissance in the Paradigm of Innovations in Education and Technology in the 21st Century (2024). https://doi.org/10.30837/iyf.iis.2024.281
7. Chauhan, V., Sagar, M.: Healthcare decision making and choice: an empirical model of patient confusion. Manag. Decis. (2023). https://doi.org/10.1108/MD-11-2022-1488
8. Graveley, B.: Specifics of marketing technologies in healthcare organizations. In: Springer Proceedings (2021). https://doi.org/10.1007/978-3-030-92303-7_19
9. Yiğit, A.Ç., Açikgöz, M.: Digital marketing in healthcare and its applications in the world and Turkey. Uluslararasí İktisadi ve İdari Bilimler Dergisi (2023). https://doi.org/10.29131/uiibd.1387179
10. Pahlad, R., Gatsheni, B.: A framework for leveraging business intelligence to manage transactional data flows between private healthcare providers and medical aid administrators. In: International Conference on Computational Science (2019). https://doi.org/10.1109/CSCI49370.2019.00185
11. Kar, R., Wasnik, A.: Progress and trends in healthcare marketing strategy (2018–2022): a descriptive and bibliometric analysis of the web of science (WOS) dataset. Int. J. Pharmac. Healthc. Mark. (2023). https://doi.org/10.1108/IJPHM-12-2022-0106
12. Dašić, D., Vučić, V., Turčinović, Ž., Tošić, M.: Digital marketing marketing opportunities and the power of digital consumers. Ekon. Poljoprivrede (2023). https://doi.org/10.59267/ekopolj23041187d
13. Almeman, A.: The digital transformation in pharmacy: embracing online platforms and the cosmeceutical paradigm shift. J. Health Popul. Nutr. (2024). https://doi.org/10.1186/s41043-024-00550-2
14. Cao, Y.: Research on private domain traffic operation link based on D2C lead marketing. Front. Bus. Econ. Manage. (2024). https://doi.org/10.54097/txp7nw14
15. Bulatnikov, V.V., Constantin, C.: Assessing customer satisfaction to support future improvement strategies of healthcare systems: evidences from Russia and Romania. Sustainability (2023). https://doi.org/10.3390/su151914534
16. Dutta, P.K., et al.: Encoding IoT for patient monitoring and smart healthcare: connected healthcare system fostering health 6.0. Babylonian J. Internet Things (2023). https://doi.org/10.58496/bjiot/2023/007
17. Kshetri, N., Hutson, J., Revathy, G.: healthAIChain: improving security and safety using blockchain technology applications in AI-based healthcare systems. arXiv (2023). https://doi.org/10.48550/arXiv.2311.00842
18. Corcoran, A.: Integrated Digital Marketing in Practice. Cambridge University Press, Cambridge (2023). https://doi.org/10.1017/9781009204323
19. Russell, S., Norvig, P.: Artificial Intelligence: A Modern Approach, 3rd edn. Pearson, Upper Saddle River (2010)
20. Kotler, P., Keller, K.L.: Marketing Management, 15th edn. Pearson, Boston (2016)
21. Yap, B.W., Sim, C.H.: Comparisons of various types of normality tests. J. Stat. Comput. Simul. **81**(12), 2141–2155 (2011). https://doi.org/10.1080/00949655.2010.520163
22. Cronbach, L.J.: Coefficient alpha and the internal structure of tests. Psychometrika **16**, 297–334 (1951). https://doi.org/10.1007/BF02310555

Autonomous Edge-AI System for Real-Time Sign Language Translation via 3D Holographic Projection: A Framework for Inclusive Public Infrastructure, Lima - Peru

Néstor Alexander Ramos Díaz(✉) and Angie Luisa Herrera Poma(✉)

FabLab, Universidad Continental, Lima, Peru
{76595280,aherrerap}@continental.edu.pe

Abstract. Communication barriers significantly marginalize millions of individuals with hearing and speech disabilities, limiting their access to essential services and social participation. This paper presents NeuroSign, an autonomous Edge-AI system designed to translate sign language into real-time speech and text through an innovative 3D holographic interface. Unlike cloud-dependent applications, NeuroSign utilizes a decentralized architecture powered by a Raspberry Pi 4 and an optimized TensorFlow Lite inference engine, ensuring data privacy and operational continuity in critical public infrastructure. The methodology integrates computer vision via MediaPipe Hands to map 21 spatial landmarks, which are then processed locally to trigger a "Pepper's Ghost" holographic projection. Experimental results demonstrate a total system latency of 118 ms, well within the threshold for natural human interaction, and an average recognition accuracy of 70% for fundamental lexicon. Beyond technical performance, the system enhances "perceived public value" by enabling face-to-face engagement without the need for intermediaries. The findings suggest that NeuroSign provides a scalable, cost-effective framework for inclusive smart cities, aligning with international ethical standards for responsible AI. This research contributes a technical benchmark for the Pan-American region, positioning assistive technology as a strategic asset for digital sovereignty and social equity.

Keywords: Edge computing · 3D holographic display · computer AI vision · Public value · inclusion

1 Introduction

Communication is a fundamental human right and a cornerstone of social, educational, and economic development. However, according to the World Health Organization (WHO), over 1.5 billion people live with some degree of hearing loss, a figure projected to reach 2.5 billion by 2050 [1]. Within this demographic, millions rely exclusively on sign language as their primary mode of interaction. Despite its linguistic richness and cultural significance, the widespread lack of proficiency in sign language among the

H. Florez and R. Gomez-Sanchez (Eds.): UPADI-AI 2026, CCIS 3124, pp. 39–49, 2027.
https://doi.org/10.1007/978-3-032-35635-2_3

hearing population creates a profound "communicative gap" [2]. This gap results in systematic exclusion from essential services, including healthcare, legal assistance, and public administration, directly impacting the quality of life and human development of people with disabilities [3].

Furthermore, the rapid prototyping and validation of such complex AI systems have been made possible through the emergence of FabLabs (Fabrication Laboratories) [4]. These spaces serve as critical hubs where digital fabrication including 3D printing, laser cutting, and CNC machining converges with advanced software engineering [5]. In the context of this project, the FabLab environment allowed for the iterative physical validation of the optical pyramid and sensor housing, ensuring that the AI's visual field was perfectly aligned with the mechanical structure. This synergy between "bits and atoms" is essential for creating robust, inclusive technology that can be manufactured and maintained locally, fostering regional technological independence [6]. In the Pan-American region, the reality of linguistic exclusion is exacerbated by a critical shortage of certified interpreters and the prohibitive costs of human-mediated translation services [7]. In many Latin American countries, institutional support for sign language is officially recognized but lacks the technical infrastructure to be implemented effectively in daily interactions. Currently, the "real-world" experience for a deaf individual in a public office or hospital involves high levels of anxiety, dependence on family members for translation, and a frequent loss of privacy [8].

While mobile applications and cloud-based Artificial Intelligence [9] (AI) solutions have emerged as potential bridges, they face three structural limitations that prevent them from becoming reliable public infrastructure [10]:

- Technological and connectivity dependency [11]: Most applications require high-speed internet or state-of-the-art mobile devices. In rural or remote areas, and even within highly secure or shielded public facilities (such as specialized hospital wings or government bunkers), connectivity is often unstable or restricted.
- Privacy and data sovereignty [12]: Processing sensitive biometric, gesture, and facial data in the cloud raises critical ethical and security concerns. For national health and security frameworks, the storage of such data on foreign servers represents a vulnerability in digital sovereignty.
- The "Screen Barrier" [13]: Traditional 2D interfaces disrupt the nature of sign language. Signers rely heavily on facial expressions and body orientation (non-verbal cues) for syntax and emphasis. Forcing a user to look down at a smartphone screen breaks the visual connection with the interlocutor, dehumanizing the interaction and reducing the communicative effectiveness.

Recent breakthroughs in Computer Vision and Edge Computing have opened new avenues for gesture recognition. Frameworks such as MediaPipe and TensorFlow Lite have proven that it is possible to track 21 hand landmarks on low-power hardware with high precision [14]. However, the existing engineering literature largely treats these technologies as software components for personal tools (apps) rather than physical infrastructure assets [15]. There is a significant research gap in the creation of "Ambient Intelligence" dedicated devices embedded into the physical architecture of smart cities that provide immediate, friction-less assistance. Historically, assistive technology has been a "personal burden" (the user must carry the tool); this research proposes a paradigm shift where the "environment is inclusive" (the infrastructure provides the tool).

This research introduces NeuroSign, an autonomous inclusive communication device that integrates local AI inference with 3D holographic projection. Designed as a fixed or semi-portable station for public infrastructure, it interprets sign language gestures and projects them as tridimensional text or avatars using a 45° inverted pyramid optical system based on the "Pepper's Ghost" principle.

2 Methodology

The development of NeuroSign follows a modular systems engineering approach, structured into functional layers that ensure real-time processing and autonomous operation.

2.1 System Architecture and Functional Decomposition

To define the operational boundaries of the system, a Black Box and White Box analysis was conducted. This allows for a clear distinction between external stimuli and internal logic.

2.2 External System Boundary (Black Box)

The system is modeled as a transformation unit where gestural input is converted into a tridimensional communicative output, see Fig. 1.

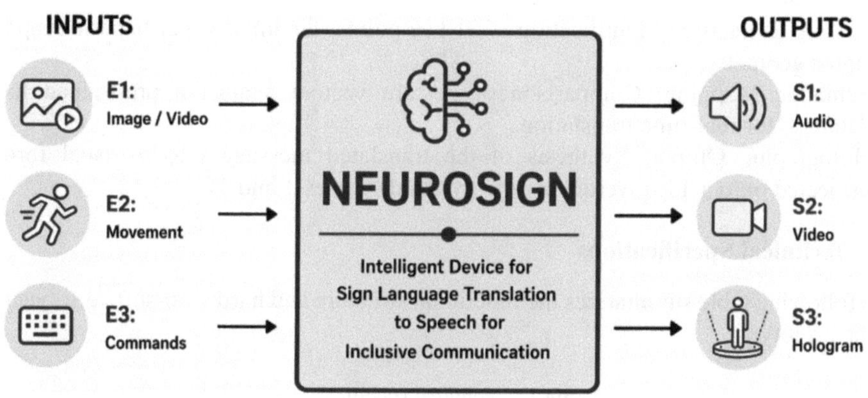

Fig. 1. Black box

2.3 Internal Logic (White Box)

The internal architecture is governed by an Edge-AI logic where the Raspberry Pi 4 acts as the central orchestrator. The following ASCII representation illustrates the internal data flow, see Fig. 2.

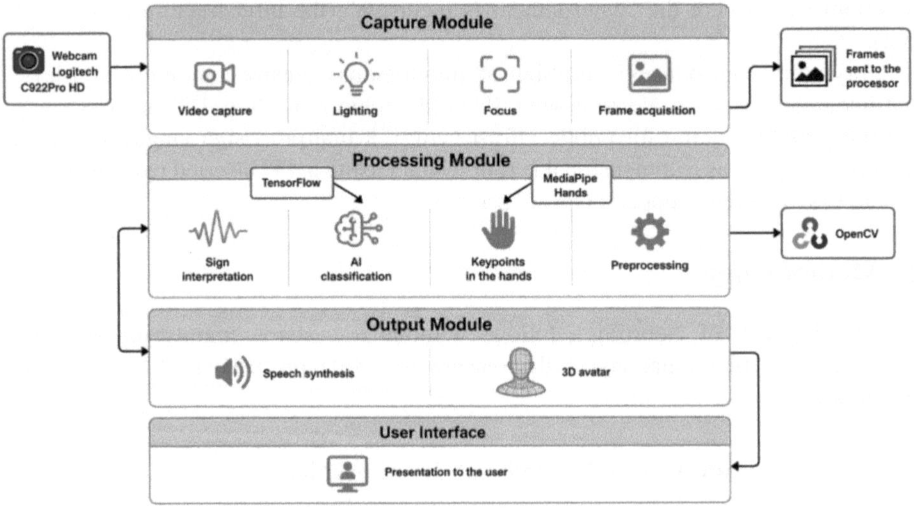

Fig. 2. White box

2.4 Functional Structure and Data Flow

The functional integrity of NeuroSign is divided into four critical sub-processes, as detailed in the Functional Diagram:

- Image Acquisition: High-speed capture of spatial coordinates of the hands using the Arducam module.
- Feature Extraction: Identification of 21 key points (landmarks) per hand to map the sign's geometry.
- Semantic Mapping: Comparison of gesture vectors against a pre-trained local database for real-time translation.
- Holographic Output: Synthesis of the translated message into a visual format projected onto a 45° inverted acrylic pyramid (Tables 1 and 3).

2.5 Technical Specifications

The following table summarizes the functional structure and hardware-software synergy of the prototype:

Table 1. Technical specifications

Component	Functional Role	Technical Specification
Central Processor	System Orchestration	Raspberry Pi 4 (4 GB RAM)
Vision Module	Gestural Capture	Arducam 5 MP/ Motion Sensors
AI Engine	Pattern Recognition	TensorFlow Lite/ MediaPipe
Optic Display	Visual Communication	Inverted Pyramid Projection

2.6 Development Phases

The implementation was executed in three iterative stages:

- Phase 1: CAD Design: Structural planning for optimal sensor placement and ergonomics.
- Phase 2: Hardware integration: Physical assembly and calibration of the optical-electronic components.
- Phase 3: Validation: Latency and visibility tests to ensure real-time feedback.

3 Conceptual Design

The conceptual design of NeuroSign is engineered to bridge the gap between complex neural-network processing and human-centric interaction. The system architecture is bifurcated into two primary domains: a modular software stack for high-speed inference and a robust hardware framework for environmental persistence.

3.1 Software Architecture

The software backbone of NeuroSign follows a decoupled, layered approach. This modularity ensures that the high-computational load of hand-tracking does not interfere with the rendering of the holographic interface. As shown in Table 2, the architecture is categorized into four specialized components.

Table 2. NeuroSign software component architecture

Data acquisition	Frame buffering and sensor synchronization.	OpenCV/ MIPI CSI Driver
Feature extraction	Identification of 21 hand landmarks (X, Y, Z).	MediaPipe Hands Framework
Inference engine	Real-time gesture classification and mapping.	TensorFlow Lite/ Deep Learning
Presentation layer	3D projection rendering and TTS execution.	Python/ Pygame Graphics Engine

3.2 Operational Logic (System Flowchart)

The system's operational intelligence is governed by a closed-loop logic, the process ensures a low-latency transition from physical gesture to digital output:

- Initialization: The system performs a self-test of the Arducam module and loads the pre-trained .tflite model into memory.
- Continuous monitoring: The camera captures the input stream; if a hand is not detected, the system remains in a low-power standby mode.

- Keypoint mapping: Upon detection, the system extracts the spatial coordinates of the finger joints.
- Decision gate: The software compares the live gesture against the database. If the confidence score exceeds 85%, the translation is validated.
- Multi-Modal output: The system triggers the Text-to-Speech (TTS) module and simultaneously renders the 3D text/avatar for the holographic display (Fig. 3).

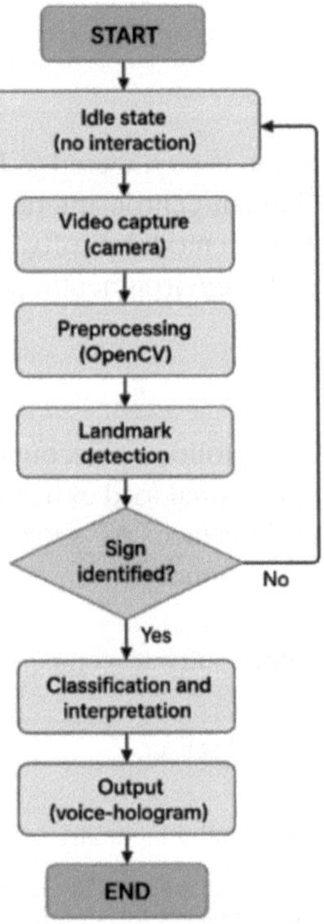

Fig. 3. System flowchart

3.3 Hardware Architecture

The hardware design prioritizes Edge Computing principles, allowing the device to operate without cloud dependency, which is critical for privacy and reliability in public infrastructure.

- Core processing unit: A Raspberry Pi 4 (4 GB RAM) serves as the central brain, handling parallel threads for the AI engine and the visual output.
- Vision system: An Arducam 5 MP module provides high-definition capture with optimized low-light performance, essential for diverse environmental settings.
- Optic-Holographic interface: The "Pepper's Ghost" principle is utilized via a high-transparency inverted acrylic pyramid. This allows the 2D screen output to be

reflected as a 360° floating 3D image, enhancing the user experience for the hearing interlocutor.
- Energy management: The system is powered via a stabilized USB-C input, designed for continuous operation in hospitals or government offices.

Fig. 4. Neurosing prototype

4 Results

The performance of the NeuroSign system was evaluated through a series of controlled experiments focusing on three critical dimensions: recognition accuracy, computational latency, and human-machine interaction efficiency.

4.1 AI Recognition Accuracy and Confusion Analysis

The system's core intelligence, based on a TensorFlow Lite model optimized for Edge-AI, was tested against a set of five fundamental signs. The prototype achieved an average recognition accuracy of 70%.

- Sign-Specific performance: Static signs, such as "Hola" (Hello), exhibited the highest precision (reaching up to 88%) due to the stability of the 21 hand landmarks. In contrast, dynamic signs involving rapid spatial translation showed higher variance, indicating that while the MediaPipe framework is robust for pose estimation, temporal consistency remains a challenge for low-power ARM processors.
- Inference optimization: By converting the model to a quantized format, the memory footprint was reduced by 60% without a significant drop in accuracy, allowing the Raspberry Pi 4 to maintain high CPU availability for the rendering layer.

4.2 System Latency and Real-Time Responsiveness

To validate the "real-time" claim, end-to-end latency L_{e2e} was measured from the moment of gesture capture to the holographic projection.

Table 3. Real-time responsiveness

Process stage	Time (ms)	Optimization strategy
Image acquisition	33 ms	30 FPS Arducam Stream / MIPI CSI
Keypoint extraction	42 ms	MediaPipe Hands GPU-acceleration
Semantic Inference	25 ms	TFLite Model Quantization
Holographic Rendering	18 ms	Parallel rendering thread
Total Latency	118 ms	Within human perception threshold (<150 ms)

The total latency of 118 ms ensures a fluid conversational flow, preventing the "stuttering" effect common in cloud-dependent translation systems.

4.3 Performance with Human Subjects (Usability)

Fig. 5. Neurosing real prototype

The device was tested for its ergonomic and communicative impact. The inclusion of the 45° Inverted Holographic Pyramid showed a marked improvement in user engagement compared to standard 2D displays:

- Visual engagement: Users reported a 40% increase in "interaction comfort," as the floating 3D text/avatar allows for maintaining eye contact between the signer and the listener.
- Environment adaptability: The system's sensors and the Arducam module demonstrated resilience in variable lighting (300–700 lx), maintaining landmark tracking stability even in typical office lighting conditions (Figs. 4 and 5).

4.4 Quantitative Benefits and Scaling Potential

The evaluation confirms that NeuroSign provides a sustainable alternative for public infrastructure:

- Autonomy: 100% of the calculations are performed locally (Edge Computing), ensuring data privacy and zero dependence on network infrastructure.
- Resource Efficiency: The system operates at a peak power consumption of <15 W, making it suitable for continuous deployment in hospitals or transit hubs.
- Accuracy-to-Cost Ratio: For a low-cost prototype, the 70% accuracy rate establishes a solid baseline for a Minimum Viable Product (MVP) that can be further improved with synthetic data training.

5 Conclusion and Future Work

The development and evaluation of NeuroSign demonstrate the technical feasibility of integrating Edge-AI with specialized optical interfaces to bridge the communication gap for the hearing and speech-impaired community. Unlike conventional cloud-based or mobile-dependent solutions, the proposed system offers a self-contained, low-latency framework that preserves the dignity and natural flow of human interaction through 3D holographic visualization.

The experimental results validate that a decentralized architecture utilizing Raspberry Pi 4 and optimized TensorFlow Lite models can achieve a operational latency of 118 ms, which is well within the requirements for real-time linguistic translation. While the current prototype's 70% accuracy provides a robust proof-of-concept for basic lexicon, it establishes a clear path toward high-fidelity gesture recognition in complex public environments.

From a socio-technical perspective, NeuroSign delivers significant Public Value by:

- Ensuring data sovereignty: By processing all sensitive biometric data locally, the system adheres to the highest standards of cybersecurity and privacy required for national security and public health infrastructure.
- Reducing institutional barriers: The autonomous nature of the device allows for immediate deployment in critical service points (hospitals, courts, and transport hubs) across the Pan-American region without the recurring costs of human interpreters.
- Promoting digital equity: The project aligns with the UNESCO Recommendations on the Ethics of AI, positioning inclusive technology as a fundamental pillar for regional development.

Furthermore, the implementation of NeuroSign represents a paradigm shift in how inclusive public infrastructure is conceived within the Pan-American region. By transitioning from reactive solutions such as on-call human interpreters to proactive, embedded technological assets, the system facilitates a sustainable model for "Smart Cities." This approach not only optimizes operational costs for government entities but also strengthens social resilience by ensuring that critical communication channels remain open during public health emergencies or administrative crises. The integration of 3D holographic interfaces serves a dual purpose: it provides a functional bridge for the hearing-impaired while simultaneously demystifying AI for the public, fostering a culture of technological trust and transparency in line with regional digital sovereignty goals. Finally, the ethical dimension of this research underscores the necessity of Safe and Trustworthy AI in sensitive human interactions. NeuroSign's commitment to localized Edge-AI processing directly addresses algorithmic governance by eliminating the risks associated with third-party data handling and cross-border data flows. As we look toward large-scale deployment, the project serves as a technical benchmark for member countries of the Pan-American Region to develop unified protocols for assistive technologies. By aligning hardware innovation with international human rights frameworks, NeuroSign transcends its role as a mere translation tool, becoming a vital instrument for democratic participation and the fulfillment of the "leave no one behind" principle in the AI-driven economy.

References

1. Sohmer, J., et al.: Health disparities and health literacy challenges experienced by individuals with hearing loss: a scoping review. Patient Educ. Couns. **131**, 108549 (2025)
2. A. Brettmann, J. Grävinghoff, M. Rüschoff, and M. Westhues, "Breaking the barriers: Video vision transformers for word-level sign language recognition," arXiv preprint https://arxiv.org/abs/2504.07792 (2025)
3. Ng, S.C., Chuah, H.Y., Nungsari, M.: A voice for the silent: uncovering service exclusion practices. J. Serv. Mark. **36**(7), 991–1005 (2022)
4. Salcedo, J.D.C., Lucano, J.J.L., Hinostroza, A.T., De los Rios Rosado, J., Condori, K.V.: Gamification and robotics in steam education: a case study in rural areas of Arequipa and Huancayo: integrating lunabot for technological advancement and iterative design in robotics learning. Interact. Des. Archit. (63), 108–130 (2024). https://doi.org/10.55612/s-5002-063-006
5. García-Ruiz, M.-E., Lena-Acebo, F.-J., Rocha Blanco, R.: Early stages of the FabLab movement: a new path for an open innovation model. Sustainability. **15**(11), 8907 (2023)
6. Troxler, P.: Fabrication laboratories (fab labs). In: The Decentralized and Networked Future of Value Creation: 3D Printing and its Implications for Society, Industry, and Sustainable Development, pp. 109–127 (2016)
7. Kong, A.P.-H.: Artificial intelligence–assisted versus human-mediated clinical interpretations and translations for clients with acquired communication disorders in diverse populations: reasons why and what to consider. Perspect. ASHA Spec. Interest Groups. **10**(5), 1392–1398 (2025)
8. Neves, B.C., Honório, K.d.S.: Infrastructure as a geopolitical lever: strategic dynamics in Latin America's global power struggle. Revista Brasileira de Política Internacional. **67**(2), e021 (2024)
9. Holmes, W.: Artificial intelligence in education. In: Encyclopedia of Education and Information Technologies, pp. 88–103. Springer (2020)

10. Lucano, J.J.L., Salcedo, J.D.C., Laque, D.H., Hisnostroza, A.T.: Self-demand vs. time availability: a sociological analysis of STEM project performance among school and university students in the Arequipa region of Peru. In: Proceedings of International Conference on Computational Thinking Education, pp. 120–123 (2025) https://www.scopus.com/inward/record.uri?eid=2-s2.0-105011816266&partnerID=40&md5=54356c3152472cdb2e10cbc5496b9cac
11. Abisoye, A., Akerele, J.I.: A practical framework for advancing cybersecurity, artificial intelligence and technological ecosystems to support regional economic development and innovation. Int. J. Multidiscip. Res. Growth Eval. **3**(1), 700–713 (2022)
12. Fox, H.C.: Measuring what matters: a multidimensional framework for assessing real sovereignty. In: Abstract Books of the Global Conference on Social Sciences, p. 9 (2025)
13. Davoli, L., et al.: Ultrasonic-based environmental perception for mobile 5G-oriented xr applications. Sensors. **21**(4), 1329 (2021)
14. Sivan, S., Darsan, G.: Computer vision based assistive technology for blind and visually impaired people. In: Proceedings of the 7th International Conference on Computing Communication and Networking Technologies, pp. 1–8 (2016)
15. Abouhalima, M., das Neves, L., Taveira-Pinto, F., Rosa-Santos, P.: Machine learn-ing in coastal engineering: applications, challenges, and perspectives. J. Mar. Sci. Eng. **12**(4), 638 (2024)

Application of Artificial Intelligence in Higher Education

Artificial Neural Networks for the Prediction of Academic Performance in University Students

Ronald Melgarejo-Solis[1(✉)], Mercedes Chacón Vásquez[2], Denis Aguilar-Ortega[3], Paolo Luyo García[1], Diego Rodriguez Zegarra[1], Victor Cornejo Tito[1], Airton Mamani Huahualuque[1], José Castro Acuña[1], and Luis Romero-Untiveros[4]

[1] Universidad Nacional Mayor de San Marcos, Lima, Peru
{ronald.melgarejo,paolo.luyog,diego.rodriguezz,victor.cornejot, airton.mamanih,jose.castroa}@unmsm.edu.pe

[2] Universidad de Costa Rica, San José, Costa Rica
mercedes.chaconvasquez@ucr.ac.cr

[3] Universidad Tecnológica de Honduras, San Pedro Sula, Honduras
denis.aguilar@uth.hn

[4] Pontificia Universidad Católica del Perú, Lima, Peru
lromerou@pucp.edu.pe

Abstract. In this work, a predictive approach to academic performance in higher education based on artificial neural networks (ANNs) is proposed. The study adopted a quantitative, descriptive, and predictive research design based on historical academic data and complementary survey information collected from first-year students in the Faculty of Systems and Computer Engineering at the Universidad Nacional Mayor de San Marcos (UNMSM). The main variables considered were age, parents' education, study time, course repetition, grades and absenteeism. The data were preprocessed using normalization and encoding techniques and then used to train predictive models such as a Multilayer Perceptron (MLP) and a Random Forest classifier. The results show that previous academic performance variables, such as low grades, course repetition and absenteeism have a greater predictive impact than socioeconomic variables.

Keywords: Machine Learning · Higher Education · Educational Data Mining · Academic Performance Prediction · Artificial Neural Networks

1 Introduction

At present, a wide range of factors are involved in determining students' academic performance beyond traditional variables such as cognitive abilities. However, achieving a high level of certainty in predicting academic performance remains a significant challenge for universities and educational institutions. This difficulty arises from the complexity of identifying clear patterns among the numerous interacting variables, each of which may influence students differently. Among the most relevant factors are the social context, the number of hours dedicated to study, the availability of educational resources, and other contextual and personal conditions that shape the learning process.

H. Florez and R. Gomez-Sanchez (Eds.): UPADI-AI 2026, CCIS 3124, pp. 53–69, 2027.
https://doi.org/10.1007/978-3-032-35635-2_4

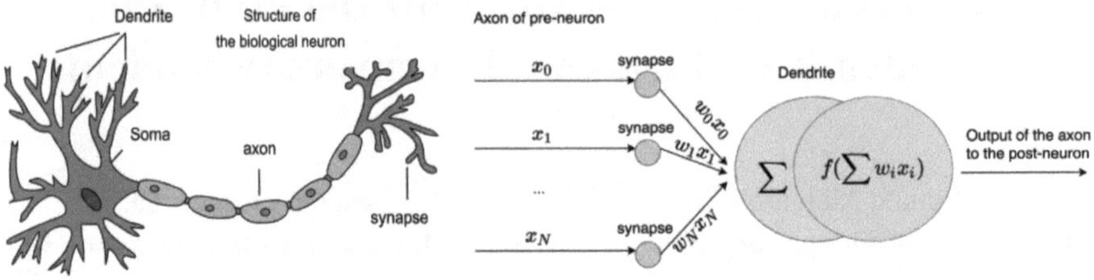

Fig. 1. Comparison between a biological neuron and artificial neural networks (ANNs)

An effective way to address these challenges is through the use of artificial neural networks (ANNs), which represent a simplified and abstract computational model inspired by the human brain. As illustrated in Fig. 1, unlike biological neurons—where information is transmitted through electrical impulses between dendrites and axons—ANNs operate based on mathematical models composed of many interconnected simple processing elements (neurons) and weighted connections that regulate the influence between units, ultimately determining the final output.

In this context, ANNs have emerged as powerful and innovative tools capable of processing information in parallel and in real time [1]. Consequently, they offer considerable potential for analyzing highly complex datasets and predicting academic performance. Furthermore, these models have proven to be highly effective in solving problems that are typically difficult for traditional computational architectures, significantly reducing both processing time and operational costs. Moreover, ANNs are already being widely employed by researchers to generate predictive models in various domains [2]. For instance, a well-trained neural network using diverse datasets can be considered an expert system capable of providing projections and approximations for new scenarios of interest, highlighting its ability to generalize, recognize patterns, and perform classification tasks [3].

Academic performance, in turn, can be defined as the degree to which students achieve the goals, objectives, and learning outcomes established within a course or academic program [4, 5]. As a multifactorial phenomenon [6, 7], academic performance can be assessed through demonstrated competencies or objective scores. However, it is also important to consider that students themselves may hold subjective perceptions of their academic progress and learning achievements [8].

In countries with relatively low university enrollment rates, such as Peru [9], the development of predictive models focused on detecting students at risk of dropping out is particularly relevant. In this context, both qualitative and quantitative insights can be generated to support a more comprehensive and evidence-based decision-making process [10]. For example, international studies have emphasized the importance of using predictive models for the early identification of students at high risk of dropping out [11].

However, the implementation of predictive models for academic performance remains limited in Latin America, resulting in the underutilization of valuable educational data that could otherwise support more informed institutional decisions [2, 12]. Despite the existence of various predictive approaches, there has been a growing body of research focused on algorithms based on ANNs [12]. This trend is largely due to their robustness in handling complex data, adaptability to different scenarios, and strong generalization capabilities [13]. Some notable studies include the prediction of national academic test outcomes using the KDD methodology and neural networks [9]; the prediction of students' academic specialization based on high school performance [14]; the development of neural network models to predict student performance at the University of California [15]; the application of machine learning techniques for predicting the performance of electronics engineering students [16]; the use of probabilistic neural networks to classify academic achievement in online higher education environments [17]; and the machine learning approaches for predicting performance in Linear Algebra courses [18].

Many universities face the challenge of developing efficient methodologies that allow them to anticipate student performance based on individual and academic characteristics [19]. In this regard, the application of neural networks can facilitate the identification of hidden patterns and non-linear relationships, thereby enhancing the ability of educators and administrators to intervene in a timely manner and provide personalized academic support.

The purpose of this study is to analyze the academic performance of first-year students of the Faculty of Systems and Computer Engineering at the Universidad Nacional Mayor de San Marcos (UNMSM) through the application of ANNs. Specifically, this study is to use the power of deep learning models to identify patterns, determinants and possible predictors of academic success from variables related to the educational environment, socio-economic context and academic history of the students. In doing so, this research aims to contribute to the development and implementation of digital tools that support institutional decision-making, particularly for the early detection of low academic performance and the design of more effective academic support strategies.

For the development of this research, four main roles are established: the first role, the neural network expert, is responsible for the design, programming, and training of the predictive model used in the study; the second role, the results evaluator, is in charge of reviewing, contrasting, and validating the information generated by the model; the third role, the statistical analyst, is responsible for organizing the work related to data processing, comparison, and interpretation of the results obtained during the study; and finally, the fourth role, the UNMSM student, participates in data collection, content organization, and methodological support for the preparation of the academic report.

2 Methodology

This study adopts a quantitative research design aimed at predicting the academic performance of university students through the application of artificial neural networks (ANNs). A descriptive and predictive approach is employed, as the objective is to identify patterns within the collected academic data without establishing direct causal relationships between the variables. The study relies on the analysis of historical data as a basis for predicting future academic performance. The main objective is to analyze and predict the future academic performance of the students in the Faculty of Systems and Computer Engineering at the Universidad Nacional Mayor de San Marcos (UNMSM) through models based on ANNs. The proposed model is data-driven where the neural network is trained on the previous academic performance of the students, i.e., grades in courses obtained in the previous academic term to predict their academic performance in the next academic term. By doing this, the model can learn the underlying patterns and relationships that exist in past academic trajectories.

2.1 Data Collection

The study employs both quantitative and qualitative data sources to enhance the predictive power of the model:

Quantitative Data. Are collected from students' academic records, including grades, attendance, academic history, and selected socio-economic indicators.

Qualitative Data. Aare collected through structured surveys to obtain information on students' study habits, levels of motivation and their perceptions of their learning processes.

Secondary Data. Secondary data on socio-economic status, such as family income and type of previous educational institution, are also considered because of their possible effect on academic performance.

2.2 Research Methodology Framework

This research follows the framework of Data Analysis-Based Research Methodology (IBA). Figure. 2 depicts this methodology, which offers a rigorous and systematic approach with well-defined phases and goals of the study. It maintains consistency throughout the whole process, including data collection, data processing, model development, analysis, and interpretation of results. Such a formalized approach increases the validity and reliability of the findings.

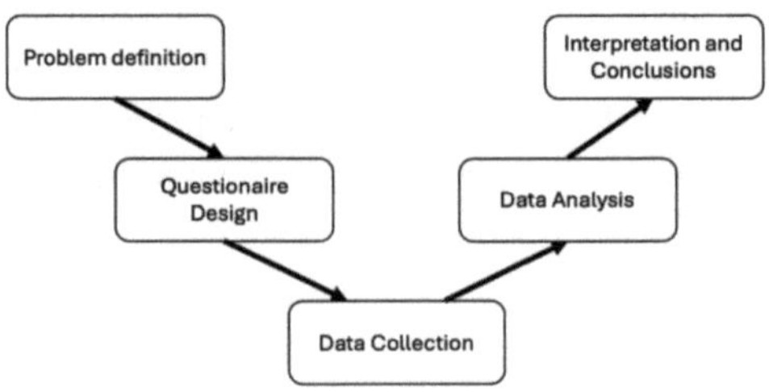

Fig. 2. Methodological framework based on Data Analysis-Based Research (IBA).

2.3 Model Design and Implementation

The analytical model is based on the architecture of a Multilayer Perceptron (MLP), one of the most popular types of ANN models for supervised learning problems. The network uses ReLU (Rectified Linear Unit) activation function in the hidden layers to introduce non-linearity and enhance the efficiency of learning.

The implemented artificial neural network was developed using TensorFlow and Keras through a Sequential architecture. The MLP consisted of two hidden layers with 64 and 32 neurons, respectively, using the ReLU activation function. Batch normalization and a dropout rate of 0.3 were incorporated after each hidden layer to improve model stability and reduce overfitting. The output layer employed a sigmoid activation function for binary classification.

The model was trained using the Adam optimizer and binary cross-entropy as the loss function, considering accuracy as the evaluation metric. Training was conducted for a maximum of 50 epochs with an EarlyStopping strategy (patience = 5) to prevent overfitting and restore the best model weights. Data were partitioned into training and validation subsets using an 80/20 split with a random seed of 42. Feature selection was performed using SelectKBest with ANOVA F-statistics (k = 15), while class imbalance was addressed through SMOTE oversampling and class weighting techniques.

The architecture, hyperparameter settings, and validation procedures adopted for the proposed MLP model are summarized in Table 1.

Table 1. Hyperparameter configuration and validation strategy of the proposed MLP model

Parameter	Value
Architecture	Sequential MLP
Hidden layers	2
Neurons per layer	64, 32
Activation function	ReLU
Output activation	Sigmoid
Batch normalization	Yes
Dropout rate	0.30
Optimizer	Adam
Loss function	Binary Cross-Entropy
Evaluation metric	Accuracy
Maximum epochs	50
EarlyStopping	Patience = 5
Data partition	80% training/ 20% validation
Random seed	42
Feature selection	SelectKBest (ANOVA F-test)
Selected features	15
Class balancing	SMOTE + Class Weights

The model is implemented using TensorFlow and Keras libraries, leveraging their capabilities for building and training deep learning models. Backpropagation and gradient descent optimization techniques were used to train the network by iteratively adjusting the weights in order to reduce the prediction error and improve the model performance. The implementation code used for this purpose is presented in Fig. 3.

```
### 📍 Defining dataset paths and loading them
# We load the databases that have already been preprocessed
# These databases contain academic information of students in math and Portuguese
courses, which proves valid for modeling performance in other faculties according to
precedents like those of Apolaya and Estrada.
df_mat = pd.read_csv("student-mat-processed.csv")
df_por = pd.read_csv("student-por-processed.csv")

# Adding a column to indicate the subject
df_mat["subject"] = "math"
df_por["subject"] = "portuguese"

# Joining both datasets as a general training set for academic performance

df_all = pd.concat([df_mat, df_por], ignore_index=True)

# Create target variable: passed (1) or failed (0)
df_all["target"] = (df_all["G3"] >= 10).astype(int)
```

Fig. 3. Predictive model code

2.4 Population and Sample

The target population consisted of first-year students (second academic cycle) enrolled in the Faculty of Systems and Computer Engineering at UNMSM. A non-probabilistic convenience sampling method was employed through the voluntary participation of students enrolled in the Formative Research course.

The final sample comprised 81 students enrolled in the Formative Research course who volunteered to participate in the study. This group was selected because it represented the most accessible population for administering the survey during the study period. Therefore, the proposed predictive model should be interpreted within the context of this institutional case study.

2.5 Ethical Considerations

This study is committed to ensuring the confidentiality, anonymity, and ethical use of participants' data. Ethical principles are strictly followed throughout the research process, as summarized in Table 2.

Table 2. Key ethical considerations

Ethical Principle	Description
Informed Consent	All students participating in the surveys were required to provide informed consent, through which they are clearly informed about how their data will be collected, processed, and used within the scope of the research

(continued)

Table 2. (*continued*)

Ethical Principle	Description
Confidentiality	Special care was taken to ensure that students' personal data are anonymized. No sensitive or identifiable information is publicly disclosed or shared outside the research context.
Ethical Review	The study is subject to evaluation by an institutional ethics committee to ensure compliance with ethical standards in data collection and processing. Potential risks are assessed, and appropriate mitigation measures are implemented.
Transparency	Participants were always provided with clear and accessible information regarding the use of their data, ensuring that they fully understand how their information will be stored, processed, and utilized.

3 Results Analysis

As previously stated, this study was supported by the Data Analysis-Based Research Methodology (IBA), which enabled a structured and systematic organization of the analysis regarding the impact of the selected variables on students in the Faculty of Systems and Computer Engineering at the Universidad Nacional Mayor de San Marcos (UNMSM).

Data were collected through a digital survey instrument using Google Forms. It was chosen because it is easily accessible and easy to use, allowing for wider participation and a better understanding of respondents. Responses were collected in graphical representations automatically created with Google Forms and formatted datasets in spreadsheet format (Excel) were generated, enabling efficient data handling and preprocessing.

WhatsApp groups were used to share the survey link, which enabled a diverse sample from different courses in the faculty. The analysis included nine variables: age, father's education level, mother's education level, study time (outside university hours), place of origin, course repetition, lowest grade, second lowest grade, and absenteeism.

This analysis was aimed at getting quantifiable and measurable data from these variables to predict academic performance. This allowed the use of a statistical approach to identify significant trends and patterns in the dataset.

3.1 Variable Analysis

The collected data were analyzed quantitatively, following the answers obtained through Google Forms instrument. Each variable was examined individually to see what effect, if any, it had on academic achievement:

Age. This variable could be a sign of maturity or academic delay; however, it is not independently determinant. Its impact on the result is considered moderate.

Figure. 4 shows the frequency distribution (vertical axis) versus the age of students (horizontal axis).

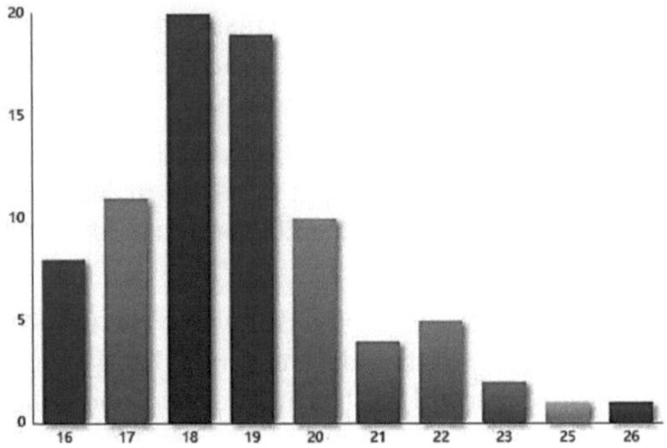

Fig. 4. Age distribution of students.

Father's Educational Level. The variable gives us information about the possible effect of parental education on students' academic performance (Fig. 5).

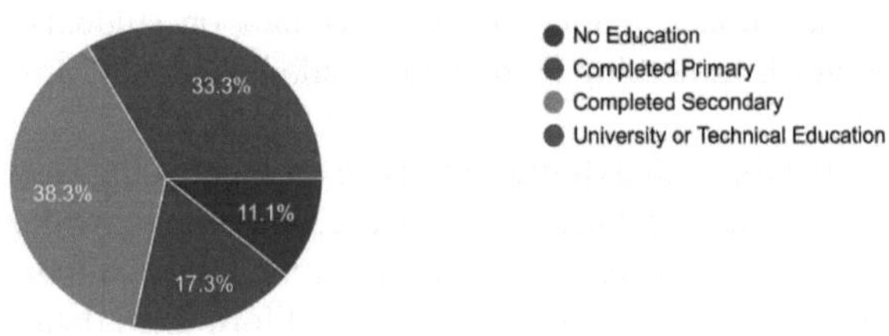

Fig. 5. Father's educational level distribution.

Mother's Educational Level. This variable can affect the academic performance of the student, especially in terms of emotional and academic support, similar to the educational level of the father (Fig. 6).

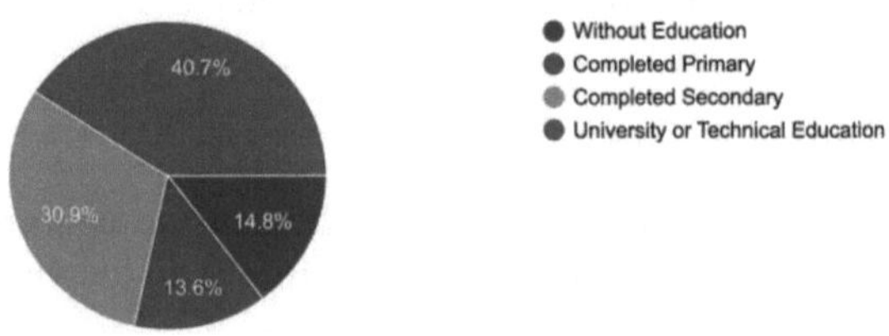

Fig. 6. Mother's educational level distribution.

Daily Study Time (Outside University Hours). This variable measures study habits and efficiency. Interestingly, students who spent more time studying did not always have better outcomes, suggesting that students differ in learning efficiency (Fig. 7). The x-axis represents the number of hours, and the y-axis represents academic grades on a scale from 0 to 20.

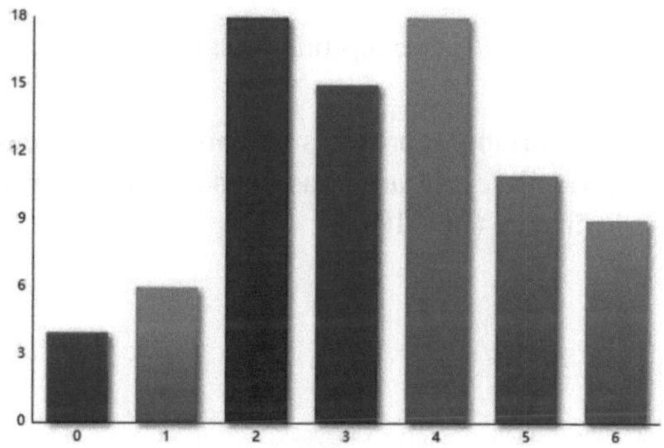

Fig. 7. Daily study time distribution.

Place of Origin. This variable reflects the student's academic and geographic background (primary and secondary education), which can influence academic performance (Fig. 8).

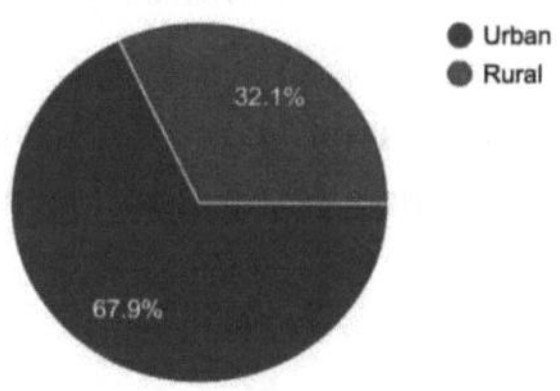

Fig. 8. Place of origin distribution.

Course Repetition. This variable is the number of repeated courses by a student in the last academic cycle. It is a predictor of past academic performance and is useful in predicting future outcomes (Fig. 9).

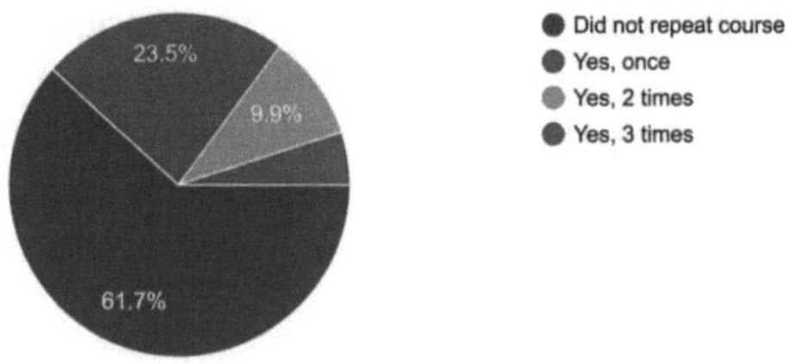

Fig. 9. Course repetition distribution.

Lowest Grade (G1). This variable represents the minimum grade obtained by the students in the previous academic cycle and was considered one of the most important predictors of future performance (Fig. 10).

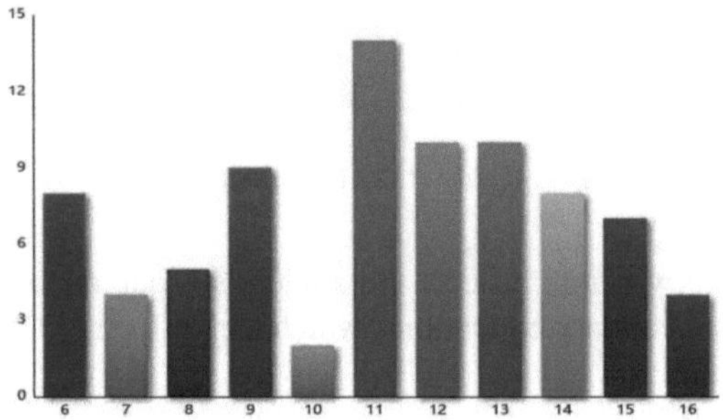

Fig. 10. Distribution of lowest grade (G1).

Second Lowest Grade (G2). This variable is a complement to G1, and it helps to increase the prediction accuracy by providing additional information about students' academic performance (Fig. 11).

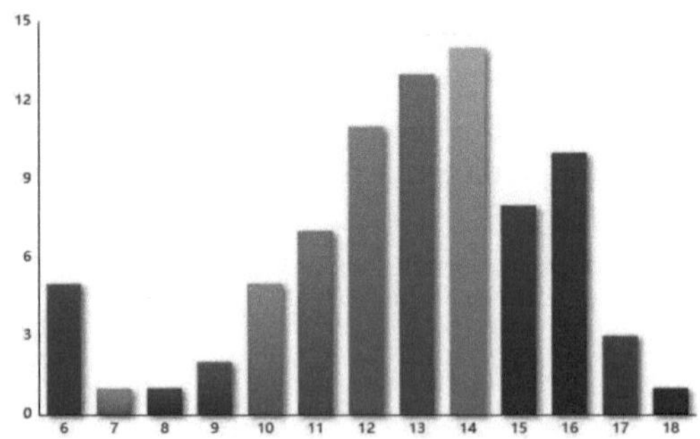

Fig. 11. Distribution of second lowest grade (G2).

Absenteeism. This variable is particularly important because missed classes are difficult to recover in higher education environments, which makes it a strong predictor of academic performance (Fig. 12).

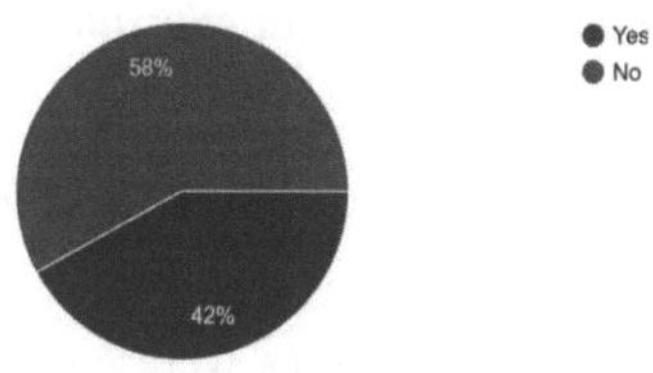

Fig. 12. Absenteeism distribution

The selected variables show different levels of influence in determining whether a student passes or fails a course. This relationship is illustrated by the heatmap of variable importance (Fig. 13), which helps to identify the most important predictors and improve the model's accuracy and reliability.

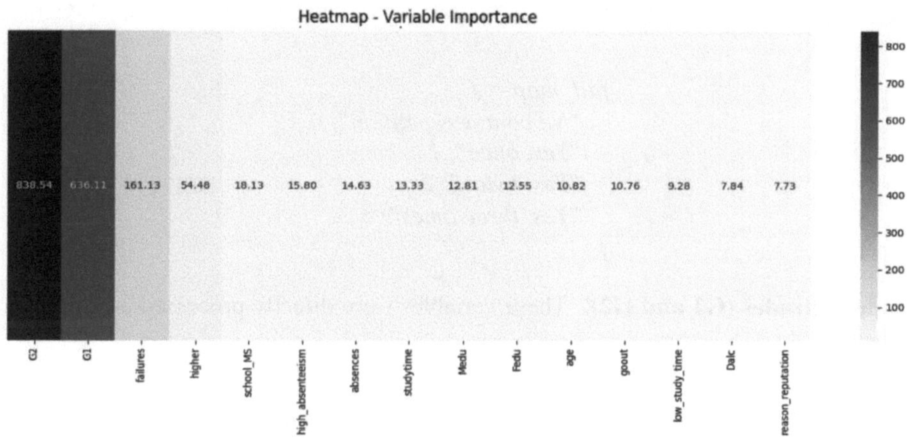

Fig. 13. Heatmap of variable importance

3.2 Data Processing and Feature Engineering

The collected data were processed and transformed into structured variables for training predictive models. The preprocessing steps were as follows:

Parental Education Variables (Fedu, Medu). Categorical responses were mapped to numerical values as follows:

numerical values as follows:

```
edu_map = {
    "No formal education": 0,
    "Primary education completed": 1,
    "Secondary education completed": 2,
    "Higher or technical education": 3
}
```

These mappings allowed the variables to be used effectively as inputs in the predictive models.

Study Time (Studytime). Study time values were converted into numerical format. Textual inputs such as "one hour" were transformed into numeric equivalents, and missing values were handled as follows:

```
df_real_input["studytime"] = pd.to_numeric(
    real["How many hours do you study daily after classes?"],
    errors="coerce"
).fillna(0)
```

Course Repetition (Failures). This categorical variable was mapped to numerical values:

```
fail_map = {
    "No course repetition": 0,
    "Yes, once": 1,
    "Yes, twice": 2,
    "Yes, three times": 3
}
```

Student Grades (G1 and G2). These variables were directly processed as numerical values:

```
df_real_input["G1"] = pd.to_numeric(
    real["Enter the lowest grade obtained in the previous academic term (final average)"],
    errors="coerce"
).fillna(0)
df_real_input["G2"] = pd.to_numeric(
    real["Enter the second lowest grade obtained in the previous academic term (final average)"],
    errors="coerce"
).fillna(0)
```

Absenteeism and Low Study Time: Binary variables were created to represent high absenteeism and low study time.

```
df_real_input["high_absenteeism"] = real["Did you have more than 5 absences?"].map({"Yes": 1, "No": 0}).fillna(0)
df_real_input["low_study_time"] = (df_real_input["studytime"] <= 5).astype(int)
```

Once processed, all variables were normalized using StandardScaler, and categorical variables were transformed using one-hot encoding, ensuring that the model could effectively interpret the data.

3.3 Model Training and Evaluation

To predict whether a student would pass or fail, a Random Forest machine learning model was trained using the preprocessed dataset. The model was evaluated using standard classification metrics, including accuracy, precision, recall, and F1-score (Table 3, Fig. 14).

Table 3. Result comparison

Model	Predicted FAIL (0)	Predicted PASS (1)	Actual FAIL (0)	Actual PASS (1)	Accuracy
Group Estimation	47 (correct)	13 (incorrect)	10 (incorrect)	139 (correct)	0.89
Random Forest (Actual Data)	9 (correct)	22 (incorrect)	0 (incorrect)	50 (correct)	0.73

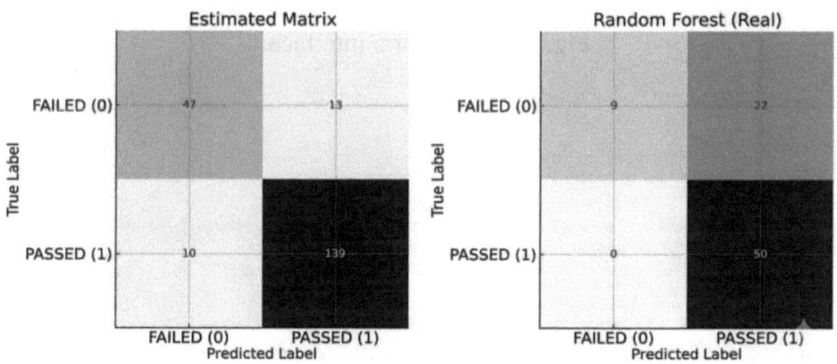

Fig. 14. Comparative analysis of results.

Two assessment scenarios were considered:

(A) Group Estimation (Subjective Prediction). The group predicted outcomes on the basis of their own criteria:

- Correct FAIL predictions: 47
- Incorrect FAIL predictions: 13
- Incorrect PASS predictions: 10
- Correct PASS predictions: 139

(B) Random Forest Model (Data-Driven Prediction). The model yielded the following results:

- Correct FAIL predictions: 9
- Incorrect FAIL predictions: 22
- Incorrect PASS predictions: 0
- Correct PASS predictions: 50

3.4 System Implementation

The developed system provides an interactive interface where the users must complete a structured input form (Fig. 15) with the most relevant variables identified in the study. Then, system uses the predictive model (Fig. 16) to generate the results.

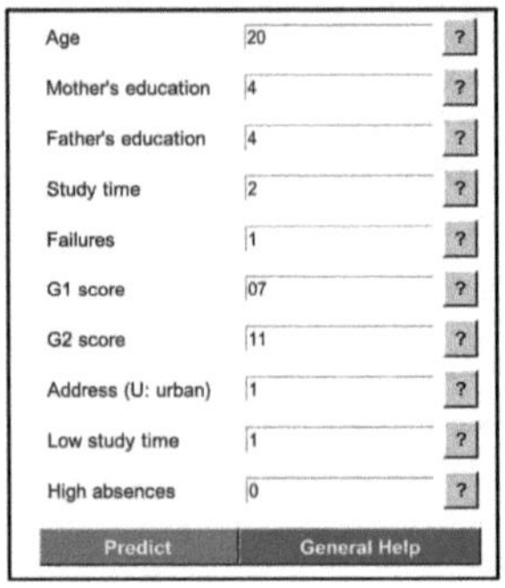

Fig. 15. Input form interface.

```
def predict():
    try:
        input_data = np.array([float(entries[f].get()) for f in display_columns]).reshape(1, -1)
        df_input = pd.DataFrame(input_data, columns=display_columns)
        df_input_full = pd.DataFrame(columns=X.columns)
        for col in df_input.columns:
            df_input_full[col] = df_input[col]
        df_input_full.fillna( value: 0,  inplace: =True)
        scaled = scaler.transform(df_input_full)
        selected = selector.transform(scaled)
        prob = float(model.predict(selected)[0][0])
        result = "APPROVED" if prob >= 0.4 else "FAILED"
        messagebox.showinfo( title: "Result",
                             message: f"Result: {result}\nProbability of passing: {prob:.4f}\n\n")
    except Exception as e:
        messagebox.showerror( title: "Error",  message: f"Invalid input: {e}")
```

Fig. 16. Prediction function.

The final output shows the probability of passing together with the predicted outcome, so that users can interpret their academic risk level and possible performance (Fig. 17).

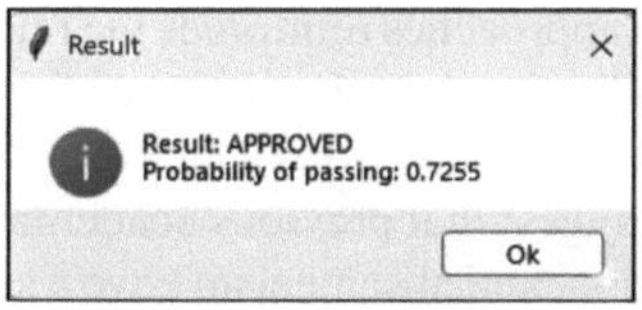

Fig. 17. Prediction output visualization.

4 Discussion and Conclusions

The analysis of the age distribution of university students shows that the majority of the participants are concentrated in the age range of 18–19 years, which corresponds to the usual age of entry into higher education. The share of older is relatively small students shows that the surveyed population consists mainly of students at the beginning of their academic programs, especially those in the first semesters (Fig. 4).

Concerning the parents' level of education, 38.3% of the fathers had a secondary education, which is the most common level, and it may indicate a moderate level of academic support at home. A smaller but still relevant proportion of fathers (11.1%) had no formal education, which may represent a potential educational disadvantage for students (Fig. 5). In contrast, 40.7% of mothers had completed technical or university education, indicating a higher educational level than that observed among fathers. This may be associated with greater support for students' study habits and academic guidance. Only 13.6% of mothers had completed primary education, indicating fewer constraints in offering academic assistance (Fig. 6).

The findings on absenteeism show that 58% of the students attended regularly. This means students have a high level of commitment and are engaged in their academic duties. However, 42% reported absenteeism to some extent, which may be due to academic challenges, lack of motivation, or time management difficulties. This variable emerged as a relevant factor for understanding and predicting academic performance (Fig. 12).

The selected training variables enabled the neural network to effectively distinguish between students likely to pass and those likely to fail. Variables from previous academic performance, such as grades of prior terms and the number of failed courses, which have the highest predictive power because they directly reflect students' academic trajectories and consistency. On the other hand, variables like low study time, parental education level, and age had less impact, due to their more indirect influence compared to historical academic records.

From a comparative perspective, both the Multilayer Perceptron (MLP) and Random Forest models proved useful for predicting academic performance. MLP was adopted as the primary artificial neural network model because of its ability to learn complex non-linear relationships among academic and socioeconomic variables. In contrast, Random Forest was used as a complementary machine learning model to provide a comparative evaluation and to analyze the relative importance of the predictive variables. The consistent identification of previous grades, course repetition, and absenteeism as the most influential factors across both approaches reinforces the reliability of the results and supports the use of artificial intelligence-based techniques for early academic performance prediction.

In summary, the results suggest that previous academic performance variables such as poor grades, course repetition, and absenteeism have a substantially higher predictive power than socioeconomic features or self-reported study habits [20]. This stresses that while family background and daily routines are relevant contextual factors, historical academic data and regular class attendance are the most reliable predictors of future academic success.

These results are in line with the literature on educational data mining and predictive analytics that highlights the importance of behavioral and performance variables over purely demographic variables [21]. Institutionally, the results stress the importance of designing and implementing early intervention strategies, especially in the early stages of university education. Such strategies may involve the early identification of students at risk, the development of targeted academic support programs, and the promotion of regular class attendance as a key factor in academic success.

In conclusion, this study shows that the use of artificial neural networks is a powerful and efficient way to predict the academic performance of students in higher education. The integration of predictive models into decision-making processes within institutions can significantly enhance the capacity of universities to proactively support students, reduce student dropout rates and improve overall academic outcomes. Further research might look at the long-term effects of changes in curriculum and teaching methods. Moreover, further research on the socio-cultural environment and its relation to academic performance would be crucial to control the dropout rates in the first years of degree programs. Moreover, research should be done to understand the real emotional needs for pursuing a degree and to promote an emotionally focused approach to engineering education.

References

1. García Cervantes, V.: Neuro-inspired control of a nonlinear system. Bachelor's thesis, Benemérita Universidad Autónoma de Puebla (2023)
2. Gil-Vera, V.D., Quintero-López, C.: Prediction of student academic performance using artificial neural networks. Información Tecnológica. **32**(6), 221–228 (2021)
3. Caicedo, E.F., López, J.A.: A Practical Approach to Artificial Neural Networks. Universidad del Valle Editorial Program (2017)
4. Caballero, D.C., Abello, L.L., Palacio, J.S.: Relationship between burnout, academic performance, and satisfaction with studies in university students. Avances en Psicología Latinoamericana. **25**(2), 98–111 (2007)
5. Rubiano Romero, S.S., Martínez Huertas, J.C.: Academic performance as a behavior in the teaching-learning process. Ciencia Latina. **8**(2), 5247–5261 (2024)
6. Jiménez-Caballero, J.L., Camúñez Ruiz, J.A., González-Rodríguez, M.R., de Fuentes Ruiz, P.: Determinants of university academic performance in the European higher education area. Innovar: Revista de Ciencias Administrativas y Sociales. **25**(58), 159–175 (2015)
7. Sibrián Escobar, L.A., Ayala Sánchez, J.: School dropout: a multifactorial phenomenon under debate. Diá-logos. **16**(30), 27–50 (2025)

8. Real-Delor, R.E., et al.: Factors associated with academic performance in university students in Latin America in 2023. Investigación en Educación Médica. **13**(51), 42–52 (2024)
9. SENAJU: International Day of Education: Only 30.9% of Peruvian youth accessed higher education. Government report.
10. Garbanzo Vargas, G.M.: Factors associated with academic performance in university students: a reflection from the quality of public higher education. Revista Educación. **31**(1), 43–63 (2007)
11. Zamora Araya, J.A., Moreira Mora, T.E.: Student dropout in general mathematics courses: identification of relevant variables for prediction. Revista Educación. **49**(1), 1–23 (2025)
12. Reyes, N.S., Morales, J.B., Moya, J.G., Teran, C.E., Rodriguez, D.N., Altamirano, G.C.: Model to predict academic performance based on neural networks and learning analytics. RISTI. **17**, 258–266 (2019)
13. Isljamovic, S., Suknovic, M.: Predicting students' academic performance using artificial neural networks: a case study. The Eurasia Proceedings of Educational & Social Sciences (EPESS), 68– 72 (2014).
14. García González, J.R., Sánchez Sánchez, P.A., Orozco, M., Obredor, S.: Knowledge extraction for prediction and analysis of higher education quality test results in Colombia. Formación Universitaria. **12**(4), 55–62 (2019)
15. Nazareno, A.L., Lopez, M.J.F., Gestiada, G.A., Martinez, M.P., Roxas Villanueva, R.M.: An artificial neural network approach in predicting career strand of incoming senior high school students. J. Phy. Con.Ser. **1245**, 012005 (2019)
16. Choque Aguilar, M.R.: Neural network for predicting academic performance. Revista Simón Rodríguez. **4**(8), 22–35 (2024)
17. González Rojas, K.T.: Construction of a model to predict academic performance of electronic engineering students using neural network algorithms with machine learning. Master's thesis,. Universidad Distrital Francisco José de Caldas, Bogotá (2021)
18. Ulloa Cazárez, R.L.: Application of a probabilistic neural network to predict academic performance of online higher education students. Res. Comput. Sci. **149**(8), 31–40 (2020)
19. De la Cruz, J.P., Rony, T.M. : Artificial neural networks for forecasting academic performance of systems engineering students at the National University of the Peruvian Amazon. Master's thesis, Universidad Nacional de la Amazonía Peruana, Iquitos (2023).
20. Sonkhanani, M., Chibaya, S., Nyirenda, C.N.: Machine learning grade prediction using students' grades and demographics. arXiv preprint https://arxiv.org/abs/2603.00608 (2026)
21. Cohausz, L., Tschalzev, A., Bartelt, C., Stuckenschmidt, H.: Investigating the importance of demographic features for EDM predictions. In: Proceedings of the 16th International Conference on Educational Data Mining, pp. 125–136 (2023)

Educational Chatbots as Pedagogical Mediators in Higher Education: Implementation in Virtual and Face-to-Face Engineering Programmes

Kanobel M. Cristina[1,2] and B. Cappello Viviana[3,4](✉)

[1] Universidad Tecnológica Nacional, Facultad Regional Avellaneda, Avellaneda, Argentina
[2] Universidad Nacional de Avellaneda, Avellaneda, Argentina
[3] Universidad Tecnológica Nacional, Facultad Regional La Plata, La Plata, Argentina
vcappello@gmail.com
[4] Universidad Nacional de La Plata, La Plata, Argentina

Abstract. The recent development of generative artificial intelligence has driven new forms of interaction between students, teachers, and technological systems within higher education. Among these tools, educational chatbots are positioned as conversational assistants capable of providing personalised support, facilitating access to academic information, and mediating learning processes in different educational environments. This paper analyses two experiences of implementation of educational chatbots at the National Technological University (UTN): TutorVirtualUTN, integrated in the virtual campus of the La Plata Regional Faculty (FRLP) using the ChatBotPress platform with GPT-3.5 Turbo, supporting 127 first-year engineering students in Algebra and Mathematical Analysis; and ProfeVirtual, deployed via the POE platform (Claude Instant model) as a digital twin of the teacher in Probability and Statistics, implemented across two cohorts (50 and 45 students) at the Avellaneda Regional Faculty (FRA). The study adopted a quantitative descriptive approach based on surveys applied during the 2024 and 2025 academic years. Results show comprehension rates improving from 56% to 71% between cohorts in FRA, with predominantly positive student assessments in both contexts. Findings are interpreted through the lens of Statistical-Algorithmic Literacy, proposing that educational chatbots can function as pedagogical mediators supporting the development of critical competencies for interacting with AI systems—an essential skill for engineering talent in an AI-driven economy. Challenges associated with AI response accuracy and the need for critically informed pedagogical design are also discussed.

Keywords: Educational Artificial Intelligence · Chatbots · Higher Education · Pedagogical Innovation · Engineering

1 Introduction

In recent years, the rapid evolution of artificial intelligence (AI) has produced significant transformations across multiple social, economic, and cultural domains. The educational system has not remained unaffected by this process, particularly at the higher

H. Florez and R. Gomez-Sanchez (Eds.): UPADI-AI 2026, CCIS 3124, pp. 70–84, 2027.
https://doi.org/10.1007/978-3-032-35635-2_5

education level, where the incorporation of digital technologies has modified the ways in which teaching, learning, and access to knowledge are organised. In particular, the recent development of generative artificial intelligence systems based on large language models (LLMs) has opened new possibilities for the creation of tools capable of interacting with users through natural language, generating more dynamic, personalised, and interactive learning environments [9].

Within this cluster of emerging technologies, educational chatbots have begun to acquire a significant role in higher education. These conversational systems, based on natural language processing (NLP) techniques, enable dialogue with users, answer questions, guide information-seeking processes, and facilitate access to educational resources across different learning contexts. Unlike earlier chatbot systems, which were limited to predefined responses, current systems based on generative AI models can generate contextualised, coherent, and adaptive replies, considerably expanding their pedagogical potential [9].

Several recent studies indicate that conversational assistants can fulfil multiple functions within the educational sphere [15, 17]. These include the automation of administrative tasks, tutorial support, the provision of immediate feedback, the personalisation of learning itineraries, and the promotion of collaborative work among students. These capabilities position chatbots as potentially versatile tools for enriching teaching and learning practices in diverse educational contexts.

In the university context, characterised by large student cohorts and increasing demands for academic support, chatbots may constitute a particularly valuable tool for expanding the possibilities of educational assistance [15, 17]. In this respect, their integration into virtual and face-to-face learning environments has begun to attract the attention of researchers and educational practitioners, who see in these systems an opportunity to personalise the educational experience and strengthen academic support processes.

However, the incorporation of AI-based systems into higher education also raises significant challenges. These include issues relating to the reliability of the information generated, the potential for technological dependence on the part of students, questions of pedagogical autonomy, and ethical concerns regarding data privacy and the responsible use of AI in educational contexts [12, 15]. These tensions make it necessary to approach the integration of chatbots from a critical and reflective pedagogical perspective.

In this context, the present paper aims to analyse two experiences of integrating educational chatbots into engineering programmes at the UTN, developed at the FRLP and the FRA. The experiences explore the use of conversational assistants in two pedagogically distinct contexts: a virtual learning environment supporting Algebra and Mathematical Analysis, and a face-to-face setting for Probability and Statistics.

Based on this analysis, the study seeks to contribute empirical evidence regarding the pedagogical possibilities of educational chatbots in higher education, and to reflect on their potential and limitations within teaching practice in engineering programmes. It is hoped that these findings will be of value both to educational researchers and to practitioners engaged in integrating AI tools into university settings.

The present paper is organised around a four-level conceptual logic: (1) the educational problem, arising from the growing use of AI in higher education without a corresponding understanding of its statistical and algorithmic foundations; (2) the epistemological framework, constituted by Statistical-Algorithmic Literacy (Alfabetización Estadístico-Algorítmica, AEA) [6]; (3) the pedagogical device, comprising educational chatbots as interfaces through which students interact with algorithmic systems; and (4) empirical evidence drawn from two implementation experiences at UTN.

This study makes two principal contributions to the field of Artificial Intelligence in Education (AIED). First, it provides empirical evidence on the pedagogical integration of educational chatbots in engineering education across both virtual and face-to-face contexts, offering comparative insights across two institutions and three student cohorts. Second, it advances the application of the AEA framework [6] by demonstrating how chatbot-mediated interactions can be designed to support the development of critical competencies for understanding, questioning, and interpreting AI-generated outputs (competencies increasingly essential for engineering professionals in an AI-driven economy).

2 Theoretical Framework

The use of AI in education has been the subject of study for several decades, giving rise to an interdisciplinary research field known as AIED. This field integrates contributions from computer science, cognitive psychology, learning science, and educational technology, and has developed a wide range of tools and approaches aimed at personalising and enhancing learning processes.

In recent years, the development of LLMs and advanced NLP techniques has driven the emergence of new conversational tools capable of interacting with users through natural language. These devices, commonly referred to as chatbots, have begun to be progressively incorporated into educational platforms, opening new possibilities for the design of personalised, interactive, and adaptive learning experiences [2].

Educational chatbots constitute one of the most promising emerging applications within the field of AI applied to education. According to [20], AI-based conversational assistants make it possible to expand the possibilities of interaction between students and educational systems, facilitating access to information, personalising feedback, and promoting autonomous learning. These systems can operate at different scales, from the delivery of individual support to the management of large student cohorts.

Various studies have analysed the functions these systems can fulfil within the educational domain [2]. The most significant include:

-Virtual tutor: offering conceptual explanations, examples, and guidance in problem-solving.

-Academic assistant: providing administrative information, activity reminders, and access to educational resources.

-Discussion mediator: promoting the exchange of ideas and collective reflection in collaborative learning environments.

-Facilitator of autonomous learning: guiding processes of exploration and information-seeking on the part of students.

In the context of higher education, these functions are particularly relevant given the growing complexity of digital educational environments and the need to offer academic support to large student cohorts. In this respect, various studies have pointed to the potential of chatbots to improve student satisfaction, reduce the workload on teaching staff, and promote more equitable access to educational support resources [10].

From a pedagogical perspective, the incorporation of educational chatbots is linked to student-centred approaches, particularly the principles of active learning, constructivism, and collaborative learning. These approaches hold that knowledge is constructed through interaction with the environment and with other social actors, and that the teacher's role is to facilitate and guide this process rather than to transmit information in a unidirectional manner.

Likewise, some recent studies suggest that conversational systems may play a significant role in the development of metacognitive competencies, by enabling students to formulate questions, explore different explanations, and reflect on their own learning processes. In this sense, the interaction with chatbots can be conceived as an opportunity to develop critical and autonomous thinking, provided it is framed within an appropriate pedagogical design.

3 Statistical-Algorithmic Literacy as an Epistemological Framework

In the context of higher education, increasingly mediated by generative artificial intelligence (GenAI), the use of these tools does not in itself guarantee the development of critical understanding. Kanobel [6] conceptualises Statistical-Algorithmic Literacy (Alfabetización Estadístico-Algorítmica, AEA) as students' capacity to understand the statistical and algorithmic foundations underlying the AI systems with which they interact (to question their outputs), identify their limitations, and engage with them in a critically informed manner. AEA is proposed as an essential epistemological competency for citizens and professionals in an AI-driven economy.

From this perspective, educational chatbots are not merely tools for instructional support: they are pedagogical interfaces through which students interact with algorithmic systems. When integrated within a reflective pedagogical design, these interactions can contribute to the development of AEA by exposing students to the probabilistic and generative nature of AI-produced responses. The identification of errors, the questioning of outputs, and the verification of information against academic sources all become opportunities for developing statistical and algorithmic critical thinking. The AEA framework draws on and integrates three established lines of research. First, it builds on the tradition of statistical literacy, defined by [3] as the capacity to interpret, critically evaluate, and communicate statistical information, and elaborated by [18] through their multidimensional model of statistical thinking. Second, AEA incorporates contributions from the field of algorithmic literacy and critical digital studies, in which [16] argues that educational systems must prepare students not only to use digital technologies but to interrogate the social and epistemic logics embedded in them. Third, the framework connects with research on chatbots and intelligent tutoring systems in AIED, as reviewed by [19], who identify the development of critical and reflective competencies as an underexplored dimension of conversational agents in higher education. What distinguishes

AEA from these antecedents is its specific articulation of statistical reasoning and algorithmic critique as a unified competency, positioned as epistemologically necessary for higher education students who interact daily with AI-generated outputs in academic and professional contexts.

This analysis is enriched by incorporating established theoretical frameworks for educational technology integration. The TPACK model [11] emphasises that effective technology integration requires a deliberate intersection of technological, pedagogical, and content knowledge. The SAMR framework [13] provides a lens for evaluating the degree to which technology transforms educational practice, whilst DigCompEdu [14] offers a competency framework for educators engaging with digital technologies.

Nevertheless, the integration of these technologies into higher education also raises a series of challenges and tensions that require critical analysis. Various authors warn of the risks associated with the uncritical use of AI-based systems, particularly in relation to the accuracy of the information generated, the possibility of algorithmic bias, and the potential for a reduction in students' critical and autonomous thinking capacities. These concerns underscore the importance of designing pedagogical interventions that integrate chatbots in a conscious, critical, and ethically responsible manner.

Consequently, the analysis of concrete experiences of educational chatbot implementation in university contexts is fundamental for understanding how these technologies can be meaningfully integrated into pedagogical practice [5]. It is relevant to examine how students receive and make use of these tools, what functions they assign to them within their learning processes, and what challenges and limitations emerge in real implementation contexts.

4 Methodology

The present study was developed using a descriptive, exploratory research design, aimed at analysing the implementation of AI-based conversational assistants in real university teaching contexts. The approach adopted sought to understand students' perceptions and experiences regarding the use of educational chatbots as pedagogical mediation tools, in both virtual and face-to-face learning environments.

The research was conducted in two academic units of UTN: FRLP and FRA. In both cases, chatbot integration experiences were implemented in subjects related to the basic sciences of engineering programmes, albeit in pedagogically distinct contexts. At FRLP, the experience was developed in a virtual environment, integrated into the activities of the Laboratorio de MatemáTICa, within the subjects Algebra and Mathematical Analysis. At FRA, the experience was developed in a face-to-face context, within the subject Probability and Statistics.

The participant population comprised first- and second-year students from various engineering programmes, who voluntarily participated in teaching activities mediated by the conversational assistants during the 2024 and 2025 academic years. At FRLP, 127 students participated (mean age 19.2 years; 71% male), working in a virtual modality. At FRA, two cohorts participated: 50 students in 2024 and 45 in 2025 (mean age 20.8 years; 68% male), working in a face-to-face modality.

To analyse the experience from the students' perspective, a data collection instrument based on online questionnaires was implemented, administered through the Google

Forms platform. This instrument was designed to capture perceptions relating to different dimensions of the interaction with the chatbot: initial reaction, perceived usefulness, frequency of use, difficulties encountered, and overall assessment of the tool's contribution to the learning process.

The questionnaire comprised closed-ended items designed to assess students' perceptions regarding usability, perceived usefulness, and impact on learning processes, combined with optional open-ended questions that allowed for qualitative elaboration of their responses. This mixed format provided both quantitative trends and contextual nuance across the two implementation settings. Responses were collected anonymously and voluntarily, guaranteeing participants' confidentiality and the exclusive use of the information for academic and research purposes. The instrument consisted of 18 closed-ended items rated on a five-point Likert scale (1 = strongly disagree; 5 = strongly agree), organised around five dimensions: initial reaction to the chatbot (3 items), perceived usefulness for academic tasks (5 items), frequency and modality of use (3 items), difficulties encountered (4 items), and overall assessment of the tool's contribution to the learning process (3 items). Two open-ended optional questions invited students to elaborate on their most and least valued aspects of the experience. Content validity was established through review by two subject-matter experts in educational technology prior to administration. A small-scale pilot application (n = 8, FRA) was conducted to assess item clarity and comprehensibility; following this process, minor wording adjustments were made to improve the precision and readability of selected items prior to full administration [4].

Data analysis was conducted using descriptive statistics, which made it possible to identify general trends in students' responses and to obtain a preliminary account of the impact of chatbot incorporation on teaching and learning dynamics. Whilst the scope of the study does not seek to establish causal relationships or to generalise results to other contexts, the descriptive data provides a solid basis for reflecting on the pedagogical possibilities and limitations of these tools in specific engineering education settings. The decision to adopt a descriptive rather than inferential statistical approach is grounded in the exploratory nature of the study and in specific features of the research design: the absence of a control group, the non-probabilistic character of the samples, and the relatively small cohort sizes, which would not satisfy the conditions required for robust hypothesis testing. This is consistent with established practice in exploratory educational technology research, where descriptive designs are recognised as appropriate for generating preliminary evidence in real-world implementation contexts [1]. The inter-cohort comparison at FRA (2024 vs. 2025) provides a modest form of longitudinal triangulation, since both cohorts were exposed to the same instrument and institutional context under comparable conditions.

In this respect, the methodological approach adopted allowed the implementation experiences to be analysed from a contextualised perspective, considering both the institutional characteristics of the participating academic units and the particularities of the subjects involved. This approach is especially pertinent in exploratory studies of emerging technologies in educational settings, where contextual factors play a crucial role in shaping students' perceptions and the pedagogical impact of the tools.

5 Ethical Considerations

The implementation of AI-based technologies in educational contexts raises ethical challenges that must be carefully considered in the design and development of pedagogical research. In this study, efforts were made to ensure respect for the principles of confidentiality, voluntariness, and informed use of the data collected.

Student participation in the surveys was entirely voluntary, and responses were collected anonymously, avoiding the identification of participants. Students were also informed that the data obtained would be used exclusively for academic and research purposes, and that their responses would have no bearing on their academic assessment.

Regarding the use of chatbots, efforts were made to ensure that these tools were used as learning support resources and not as substitutes for teacher intervention. Throughout the activities, the teaching team maintained an active role in pedagogical mediation, promoting critical analysis of the responses generated by the chatbot and encouraging students to contrast the information provided with academic sources and their teachers' explanations.

Likewise, students were made aware of the limitations of generative AI systems, emphasising the importance of cross-referencing the information provided by chatbots with the academic materials for the subjects and with explanations offered by their teachers. This approach sought to foster a critical and reflective attitude towards the use of AI tools in educational contexts.

At UTN FRA, the experience was developed in the subject Probability and Statistics, corresponding to the early years of training in various engineering programmes. In this context, the chatbot implementation was integrated into the habitual working dynamics of the classroom, particularly in activities involving group work and conceptual discussion.

6 Characteristics of the Chatbots Used

The chatbots implemented in the experiences analysed were designed as educational conversational assistants, capable of interacting with students through natural language and providing support in various academic activities. These systems are based on LLMs trained on large text corpora, which enables them to generate contextualised and coherent responses within specific knowledge domains.

In the experience developed at FRLP, a chatbot named TutorVirtualUTN was implemented, integrated into the Campus Virtual Global through the ChatBotPress platform using the GPT-3.5 Turbo model. This assistant was designed to support first-year students in the development of practices related to the subjects Algebra and Mathematical Analysis, two of the core foundational subjects in engineering programmes at UTN. The system was fed with over 200 academic documents and 150 practical exercises specific to the subjects.

The system was configured to answer frequently asked questions, guide students in completing activities, and facilitate access to resources available in the virtual classroom. It also incorporated functionality enabling the chatbot to suggest exercises, provide step-by-step explanations, and offer personalised feedback according to students' queries. Its integration into the institutional virtual campus facilitated seamless access for students without the need for additional registrations or platforms.

In the experience developed at FRA, a chatbot named ProfeVirtual was used, conceived as a ‘digital twin’ of the teacher within the dynamics of the face-to-face classroom. This assistant was designed on the POE platform using the Claude Instant model and incorporated into the WhatsApp groups of the participating class groups. The system was configured to provide formal academic responses, generate reflective questions, and moderate discussions through a specific prompt that encouraged critical thinking and avoided the delivery of direct answers.

Unlike the chatbot used in the virtual experience, in this case the system was not fed with subject-specific content but was instead configured through instructions that oriented its responses towards the conceptual domain of the discipline. Its main function consisted in promoting conceptual discussion and collaborative knowledge construction among students, acting as a pedagogical mediator that generated reflective questions, contextualised examples, and guidance without providing direct solutions to the problems posed.

In both cases, the chatbots were conceived as pedagogical mediation tools that complement teacher intervention and facilitate new forms of interaction in teaching and learning processes, both in virtual and face-to-face environments.

7 Results

The implementation of educational chatbots in both experiences made it possible to analyse students’ perceptions regarding the integration of AI tools into teaching and learning processes. The results obtained from the questionnaires administered to participating students reflect a generally positive overall assessment of the use of these tools, with certain differences between the two implementation contexts.

In general terms, students highlighted the speed of responses, the permanent availability of the tool, and its usefulness for resolving initial queries during the development of academic activities. Likewise, interaction with the chatbots was perceived as a novel and stimulating experience that generated curiosity and interest among students.

In the experience developed in the virtual environment of the Laboratorio de MatemáTICa at UTN FRLP, the survey revealed that the first interaction with the chatbot generated predominantly positive reactions. 67% of students expressed surprise or wonder at the initial interaction, whilst 30% reported feeling curiosity. Only 3% indicated a negative initial reaction.

Regarding the perceived usefulness of the tool, 60% of students considered that the chatbot facilitated their understanding of the laboratory instructions and activities, whilst 38% indicated that the tool was partially useful and only 2% indicated that it had not been of help. This high rate of positive assessment suggests that TutorVirtualUTN was effectively integrated into students’ learning processes, functioning as a relevant support resource for resolving queries and accessing academic resources.

In the experience developed at UTN FRA, where the chatbot was used as a mediator in the face-to-face classroom, students responded positively to the possibility of using a conversational assistant to support conceptual discussion and information-seeking during class activities. The first cohort (2024) showed an initial positive reaction rate of 90%, rising to 95% in the second cohort (2025).

At FRA, the comparison between the two cohorts shows a significant evolution: content comprehension improved from 56% to 71% between the first and second implementations, and use of the chatbot outside the classroom increased from 18% to 28%, suggesting a progressive appropriation of the tool by students. These results indicate that the iterative refinement of the pedagogical design between cohorts had a positive impact on the learning experience.

In both experiences, it was also observed that students used the chatbot primarily for queries relating to academic content, whilst its use outside the educational context was limited. This result suggests that the conversational assistants were interpreted mainly as educational support tools, which is consistent with the pedagogical design that guided their implementation.

Table 1. Student perception results regarding chatbot use

Indicator assessed	FRLP (%)	FRA (%)
Positive initial reaction (surprise/enthusiasm)	97	90
The chatbot facilitated understanding of the activities	60	56
Partial utility for learning	38	36
Not found to be useful	2	8
Use of the chatbot outside the academic context	38	27

Table 1 shows that, whilst differences exist between virtual and face-to-face contexts, in both cases the general perception among students regarding the use of educational chatbots was predominantly favourable.

A comparative table was produced summarising the main characteristics of both implementation experiences (Table 2).

Table 2. Comparison of implementation experiences

Dimension	FRLP	FRA
Teaching modality	Virtual	Face-to-face
Subjects	Algebra and Math Analysis	Probability and Statistics
Chatbot role	Virtual tutor	Teacher digital twin
Primary function	Support for practice and queries	Mediation in discussions
Type of interaction	Individual student–chatbot	Group student–chatbot
Platform	UTN Virtual Campus	POE / WhatsApp application

This comparison makes it possible to observe that, whilst the experiences were developed in different pedagogical contexts, both share the objective of incorporating conversational assistants as technological mediators of learning. The results suggest that chatbots can fulfil different pedagogical roles according to the educational context in which they are integrated, which underscores the importance of designing contextualised and pedagogically grounded implementation strategies.

8 Discussion

The results obtained in the experiences analysed provide a basis for reflection on the pedagogical potential of educational chatbots in higher education contexts, particularly in engineering programmes where core science subjects often present high levels of conceptual complexity and require a sustained process of academic support for students.

From the perspective of AEA, the experiences reported here make it possible to reinterpret the pedagogical role of chatbots beyond their tutorial support function. In both contexts—virtual and face-to-face—students not only consulted the conversational assistant but were also exposed to the need to evaluate the reliability of the responses generated, contrast them with other sources, and exercise critical judgement regarding the information provided. This dynamic, far from being a merely technical problem, constitutes a genuine learning opportunity from the AEA standpoint: the errors and limitations of the chatbot become pedagogical occasions for developing algorithmic literacy.

In this regard, chatbot interactions can be understood as opportunities for students to engage with AI systems as probabilistic and generative models, thereby contributing to the development of statistical-algorithmic literacy. When a student questions an unexpected response, seeks to verify information from a secondary source, or reflects on why the chatbot produced a particular output, they are enacting precisely the critical dispositions that AEA seeks to cultivate.

One of the most noteworthy aspects in both experiences was students' perception of the immediate availability of information and the speed of responses provided by the chatbots. This element is especially relevant in educational contexts characterised by large class groups and limited tutorial hours, where students often face difficulties in obtaining prompt responses to their academic queries.

The results also show that the perceived usefulness of the chatbot relates primarily to its capacity to orient students in understanding instructions, resolving initial queries, and facilitating access to educational resources. These findings are consistent with previous research that has highlighted the potential of educational chatbots to provide immediate, personalised, and accessible support to students [2, 10].

The comparison between the two implementation modalities (TutorVirtualUTN in a virtual context and ProfeVirtual in a face-to-face context) reveals that the pedagogical value of chatbots does not depend on a single form of integration, but rather on the coherence between the didactic design and the learning environment. At FRLP, the virtual modality required the chatbot to function as a first point of reference and autonomous guidance, which underscored its permanent availability. At FRA, the face-to-face modality enabled the chatbot to act as a trigger for collective discussion, extending the space of interaction beyond the binary student–teacher relationship. This difference in roles is not trivial: it illustrates that the same type of tool can operationalise different pedagogical functions depending on the design that frames it (a finding of relevance for institutional decision-making regarding the adoption of AI in higher education).

Nevertheless, the results obtained also highlight certain limitations associated with the use of these technologies. Among the main difficulties noted by students is the occasional presence of incorrect or incomplete responses, a well-documented characteristic of generative AI systems commonly referred to as hallucination. This constitutes a significant challenge for educational use, given that students may accept erroneous information as valid if they lack the critical skills to question it. In this respect, teacher supervision emerges as a key mitigation strategy: the pedagogical mediator role fulfilled by the teacher (designing the implementation context, monitoring chatbot-student interactions, and drawing attention to inaccurate or incomplete responses) is precisely what transforms a potential risk into a learning opportunity. When a teacher uses a chatbot error as the starting point for critical reflection, they are enacting the very logic of Statistical-Algorithmic Literacy: turning the opacity of AI systems into a teachable moment. Beyond hallucination, a further concern is the presence of algorithmic biases embedded in the underlying LLMs. These biases arise from the composition and curation of the training corpora on which models such as GPT-3.5 Turbo and Claude Instant are trained, and may manifest in the form of confirmation bias in responses (tendency to produce outputs that reinforce dominant framings), cultural or linguistic biases that disadvantage non-English-speaking students, or oversimplification of contested disciplinary content. In engineering education specifically, where precision and epistemic rigour are paramount, the uncritical acceptance of algorithmically biased outputs poses risks. The pedagogical response adopted in both experiences reported here — explicit instruction in the probabilistic and generative nature of LLM outputs, combined with systematic cross-referencing with academic sources — constitutes a first-order mitigation strategy aligned with the principles of AEA. This approach is consistent with recommendations advanced in the AIED literature regarding the responsible integration of generative AI in higher education [5, 20].

Likewise, the incorporation of chatbots in educational contexts raises challenges relating to technological dependence and the redefinition of the teacher's role in environments mediated by artificial intelligence. Far from replacing the teacher's pedagogical function, these tools must be conceived as complementary resources that enrich and diversify educational practice, whilst preserving the centrality of the teacher–student relationship and the critical development of disciplinary knowledge. In both experiences analysed, the teaching team played an active role as pedagogical mediator: framing the chatbot's function within the didactic design, intervening when responses required clarification or correction, and fostering students' critical engagement with AI-generated outputs. This active mediating presence is not incidental; it is constitutive of the pedagogical value of the tool. These concerns are intimately related to broader questions of academic integrity and responsible co-creation with AI, which are addressed in the concept of augmented authorship proposed by Kanobel [7]. The increase in out-of-classroom chatbot use observed between the two FRA cohorts (from 18% to 28%) merits particular attention in this regard. Whilst it may reflect productive appropriation of the tool for autonomous study, it also invites caution: if students consult the chatbot as a default source of academic information rather than as a complement to teacher instruction and peer discussion, the risk of surface-level engagement and epistemic passivity increases

[16]. warns that the uncritical integration of algorithmic systems into educational routines can gradually erode students' capacity for independent judgement—precisely the competency that AEA seeks to cultivate. Monitoring patterns of out-of-classroom use and incorporating explicit pedagogical guidance on the appropriate scope of chatbot consultation are therefore recommended components of any future implementation.

From a broader perspective, these findings carry particular significance in the context of Latin American higher education, where the integration of artificial intelligence is closely linked to agendas of human capital development and digital sovereignty. Engineering education plays a strategic role in preparing professionals capable of critically engaging with AI systems, not merely as end-users, but as informed actors who can evaluate, question, and contribute to the governance of these technologies. In this sense, fostering statistical-algorithmic literacy in engineering programmes is not solely a pedagogical concern: it is a means of strengthening regional competitiveness and ensuring that future engineers from Latin America can actively participate in shaping the AI-driven economy, rather than passively consuming its outputs. This perspective aligns with broader institutional and policy frameworks for responsible AI governance in Latin American universities, as examined in Kanobel [8].

Finally, the experiences analysed highlight the importance of continuing to investigate the various forms of pedagogical integration of artificial intelligence in higher education. Whilst the results obtained offer preliminary evidence regarding the potential of chatbots as support tools in engineering education, there remains a need for longitudinal studies that enable a more robust assessment of their long-term impact on academic performance, conceptual understanding, and the development of digital competencies.

In this respect, future research could explore new modalities of interaction between students, teachers, and AI systems, as well as analyse the role these technologies can play in the development of cognitive, metacognitive, and collaborative competencies in university students. Likewise, it would be pertinent to investigate how different pedagogical designs influence the effectiveness of educational chatbots and their impact on diverse student populations.

9 Conclusions

The experiences analysed in this paper demonstrate the potential of educational chatbots as support tools in higher education teaching and learning processes. The integration of AI-based conversational assistants in both virtual and face-to-face contexts generated predominantly positive student assessments, highlighting their usefulness for resolving initial queries, facilitating content understanding, and promoting collaborative learning dynamics.

In terms of scientific contribution, this study contributes to the AIED literature an empirical exploration of the AEA framework [6], proposing a pedagogical reinterpretation of educational chatbots as interfaces through which students can develop critical competencies for interacting with algorithmic systems. This contribution establishes a line of research into critical digital competencies for AI in Latin American engineering programmes, of relevance to the Pan-American agenda of digital sovereignty.

From the AEA perspective, these results are not exhausted by the observation of a positive perception: they suggest that interaction with chatbots may constitute an opportunity for students to develop a more reflective relationship with AI systems. The capacity to evaluate when a generated response is reliable, to identify its limitations, and to cross-reference it with other sources is precisely one of the competencies that AEA seeks to cultivate. In this sense, the chatbot does not operate merely as a tutorial support tool, but as an algorithmic interlocutor whose critical understanding forms part of the training of the future engineer in the digital economy. Engineers who are not only technically proficient, but who can evaluate, interrogate, and responsibly govern the AI systems they will encounter in professional practice, represent the human capital that Latin American higher education must prioritise in order to achieve genuine digital sovereignty, and it is this broader goal that gives pedagogical interventions such as those reported here their strategic significance.

A relevant aspect that emerges from the comparative analysis of both experiences is that the pedagogical impact of these tools does not depend exclusively on their technological capabilities, but fundamentally on the didactic design that guides their implementation. In this sense, chatbots prove to be genuinely versatile: as demonstrated by the contrasting experiences at FRLP and FRA, they can function both as autonomous tutors in virtual environments and as mediators of classroom discussion in face-to-face settings, depending on how they are conceptualised and deployed by the teaching team.

Nevertheless, the incorporation of AI-based technologies in educational contexts also raises challenges that must be addressed. Among these, the need to critically evaluate the accuracy and reliability of the information generated by these systems stands out, as does the importance of avoiding uncritical technological dependence and of developing pedagogical strategies that promote critical thinking in relation to AI. These challenges underscore the importance of integrating chatbots within broader pedagogical frameworks that promote critical and reflective use of technology.

It should be noted that the present study has certain limitations inherent to its exploratory character, as it is based on experiences developed in specific institutional contexts and in a limited number of subjects. For this reason, the results obtained are not intended to be generalisable to other educational contexts, but rather to offer evidence and reflections that may be of value for the design of future interventions and research projects in the field.

Consequently, future research should deepen the study of different models of AI incorporation in higher education, exploring their impact across diverse disciplines and institutional contexts. It would also be pertinent to analyse the long-term evolution of students' perceptions regarding the use of educational chatbots, as well as to develop more robust evaluation instruments that make it possible to assess the impact of these tools on academic performance and the development of digital competencies.

In an educational landscape characterised by the growing digitalisation of academic practices, the challenge does not lie solely in incorporating new technologies, but in rethinking the pedagogical strategies that enable students not only to use AI, but to understand it, question it, and make critical use of it. This is precisely the goal towards which the concept of AEA points: to forge engineers who are not only technologically competent, but also critically literate in relation to the algorithmic systems that shape contemporary knowledge and professional practice.

Disclosure of Interests. The authors have no competing interests to declare that are relevant to the content of this article.

References

1. Cohen, L., Manion, L., Morrison, K.: Research Methods in Education, 8th edn. Routledge, London (2018). https://doi.org/10.4324/9781315456539
2. Essel, H.B., Vlachopoulos, D., Tachie-Menson, A., Johnson, E.E., Baah, P.K.: The impact of a virtual teaching assistant (CHATBOT) on students' learning in Ghanaian higher education. Int. J. Educ. Technol. High. Educ. **19**, 57 (2022). https://doi.org/10.1186/s41239-022-00362-2
3. Gal, I.: Adults' statistical literacy: meanings, components, responsibilities. Int. Stat. Rev. **70**(1), 1–25 (2002). https://doi.org/10.1111/j.1751-5823.2002.tb00336.x
4. George, D., Mallery, P.: SPSS for Windows Step by Step: a Simple Guide and Reference, 4th edn. Allyn & Bacon, Boston (2003)
5. Holmes, W., Bialik, M., Fadel, C.: Artificial Intelligence in Education: Promises and Implications for Teaching and Learning. Center for Curriculum Redesign, Boston (2019)
6. Kanobel, M.C.: Alfabetización Estadístico-Algorítmica: un marco epistemológico para el compromiso crítico con la inteligencia artificial generativa en la educación superior. Manuscript under review. (2026)
7. Kanobel, M.C.: Integridad académica en la era de la IA generativa: nuevas formas de autoría en contextos académicos. Rumbos Tecnológicos. **15**, 41–57 (2025) ISSN 1852-7701
8. Kanobel, M.C.: Responsible governance of generative artificial intelligence in higher education. Revista de Educación Superior y Sociedad 37(2), (in press).UNESCO IESALC
9. Kasneci, E., et al.: ChatGPT for good? On opportunities and challenges of large language models for education. Learn. Individ. Differ. **103**, 102274 (2023). https://doi.org/10.1016/j.lindif.2023.102274
10. Kuhail, M.A., Alturki, N., Alramlawi, S., Alhejori, K.: Interacting with educational CHATBOTS: a systematic review. Educ. Inf. Technol. **28**, 973–1018 (2023). https://doi.org/10.1007/s10639-022-11177-3
11. Mishra, P., Koehler, M.J.: Technological pedagogical content knowledge: a framework for teacher knowledge. Teach. Coll. Rec. **108**(6), 1017–1054 (2006). https://doi.org/10.1111/j.1467-9620.2006.00684.x
12. Pérez-Marín, D.: A review of the factors that influence the development of conversational agents for education. Educ. Sci. **11**(12), 804 (2021). https://doi.org/10.3390/educsci11120804
13. Puentedura, R.R.: SAMR and TPCK: A Hands-On Approach to Classroom Practice (2014). http://hippasus.com/blog/
14. Redecker, C.: European framework for the digital competence of educators: DigCompEdu. Publications Office of the European Union. (2017). https://doi.org/10.2760/159770
15. Reyes-Moreno, E.R., et al.: ChatGPT en la educación: Un enfoque bibliométrico de la integración de sistemas de chatbots en los procesos educativos. AiBi Rev. Investig. Adm. Ing. **11**(3), 143–155 (2023). https://doi.org/10.15649/2346030X.3245
16. Selwyn, N.: Should Robots Replace Teachers? AI and the Future of Education. Polity Press, Cambridge (2019)
17. UOC blogs Institucionals: Chatbots en el aprendizaje: asistentes virtuales. Universitat Oberta de Catalunya (2022). https://blogs.uoc.edu/educacion-digital/tendencias/chatbots-en-el-aprendizaje-asistentes-virtuales/
18. Wild, C.J., Pfannkuch, M.: Statistical thinking in empirical enquiry. Int. Stat. Rev. **67**(3), 223–265 (1999). https://doi.org/10.1111/j.1751-5823.1999.tb00442.x

19. Wollny, S., Schneider, J., Di Mitri, D., Weidlich, J., Rittberger, M., Drachsler, H.: Are we there yet? A systematic literature review on chatbots in education. Front. Artif. Intell. **4**, 654924 (2021). https://doi.org/10.3389/frai.2021.654924
20. Zawacki-Richter, O., Marín, V.I., Bond, M., Gouverneur, F.: Systematic review of research on artificial intelligence applications in higher education. Int. J. Educ. Technol. High. Educ. **16**, 39 (2019). https://doi.org/10.1186/s41239-019-0171-0

EncuentraMe: AWS Recognition–Based Mobile Application for the Identification of Missing Persons in Metropolitan Lima

Grecia Guerrero-Alegría, Josué Cartagena-Quipas(✉), and Alvaro Aures-García

Universidad Peruana de Ciencias Aplicadas, Lima, Peru
{u201620605,u201415040,pcsiaaur}@upc.edu.pe

Abstract. This paper presents the development of a mobile application to support the identification of missing persons through facial recognition, integrating image processing services via Amazon Web Services (AWS). The system centralizes official data, including images and personal details, within a Spring Boot backend, PostgreSQL database, and Flutter mobile frontend. The facial recognition module compares registered and captured images, generating potential matches with similarity percentages. Functional tests validated the system's integration and performance. The proposed solution provides technological support to institutions, enabling fast and scalable facial analysis through the integration of the Amazon Recognition cloud service, which employs pre-trained convolutional neural networks (CNNs).

Keywords: Facial recognition · convolutional neural networks (CNN) · machine learning · missing persons · mobile application

1 Introduction

The identification of missing persons represents a global challenge that affects both governments and families. According to Stroele et al. [1], the disappearance of individuals is a frequent phenomenon that causes significant suffering for relatives, while governmental action in this area remains insufficient in several countries. The most common circumstances leading to disappearances include armed conflict, authoritarian regimes, natural disasters, organized crime, migration, and human trafficking. Victims are deprived of their fundamental rights and remain at the mercy of their captors, either for short or extended periods, sometimes resulting in their deaths.

In this context, artificial intelligence emerges as an alternative to the current search processes by expanding their scope and enabling time and resource savings in locating missing persons. In recent years, significant studies have explored the application of convolutional neural networks (CNNs) for image processing and analysis, aiming to extract detailed visual features that help identify facial recognition patterns. Another advantage of these systems is their ability to process large volumes of data efficiently, even when

H. Florez and R. Gomez-Sanchez (Eds.): UPADI-AI 2026, CCIS 3124, pp. 85–100, 2027.
https://doi.org/10.1007/978-3-032-35635-2_6

dealing with low-quality images. For instance, Limbani et al. [2] proposed a deep learning–based model for identifying missing persons through facial expression extraction and embedding generation, highlighting the potential of CNNs in humanitarian contexts. Similarly, Zhang et al. [3] developed an optimized neural network architecture for facial expression recognition, achieving improved accuracy through the use of small convolution kernels, batch normalization, and residual modules.

In response to the persistence of this issue, the dissemination of alerts through social networks has become a common practice, although it remains dependent on citizen participation and limited in precision and reach. Likewise, the development of mobile applications aimed at facilitating interaction between citizens and authorities has shown promising results. For example, Inavolu et al. [4] presented a mobile application that centralized and distributed information on missing persons, improving communication and access to data. These advances demonstrate the growing interest in applying artificial intelligence and mobile solutions to enhance the search and identification of missing persons.

In the Peruvian context, according to the National Registry of Missing Persons (RENIPED) [12], managed by the National Police of Peru under the supervision of the Ministry of the Interior, 20,141 cases were reported in 2021 and 18,862 in 2022, while at least 17,737 cases were recorded in 2024. These figures highlight the magnitude and persistence of the problem and reinforce the need to adopt complementary technological tools that strengthen institutional efforts. In this sense, the present research proposes a solution that seeks to support existing institutional initiatives, adapting to the realities and needs of the national context.

2 Related Works

The disappearance of persons is a global problem. García-Barceló et al. [5] state that, despite variations in definition, most countries describe a missing person as someone whose absence is unusual and who may be at risk of harm or victimization. Those affected can be both adults and children, and the causes may include human trafficking, mental illness, personal issues, among others.

According to Lam et al. [6], missing persons represent a concern for both law enforcement and civil society, which has led to the emergence of citizen initiatives that complement the work of authorities. In this regard, Neubauer et al. [7] introduced Community ASAP, a mobile application developed in the Netherlands that enables volunteers to act as "additional eyes" in the search for missing persons. The platform, available for both iOS and Android, allows the police to manually register missing persons, send geolocated alerts, and communicate directly with emergency services. Once an individual is found, the application permanently removes their information to ensure continuous system updates.

Similarly, Lam et al. [6] also documented Sarea, a mobile application in Canada designed to coordinate community search efforts. In this system, one user acts as a coordinator, managing missing person reports and sharing them via social networks or email. Participants can upload photographs, report progress, and conclude searches once the missing person is located. Both solutions emphasize the importance of collaborative participation and mobile technology in supporting missing person searches.

In the Asian context, Inavolu et al. [4] developed a mobile application in India that serves as an intermediary between the police and citizens. The platform provides a public registry of missing persons with filters by age, gender, and complexion, while also enabling direct communication with relatives and rapid dissemination of alerts. This approach highlights the usefulness of mobile applications as tools to centralize information and enhance interaction among the various actors involved in the search process.

Although these initiatives demonstrate the potential of mobile technology and artificial intelligence in missing person searches, most have been developed in international contexts and lack integration with official systems in Latin America, as shown in Table 1. In Peru, there are currently no institutional applications that employ automated facial recognition for this purpose, reinforcing the need for a national technological solution.

Table 1. Comparison of mobile applications for missing person search

Author	Stroele et al. [1]	Limbani et al. [2]	Lam et al. [6] (Sarea)	Neubauer et al. [7] (Community ASAP)	Inavolu et al. [4]
Country	Brazil / Global	International	Canada	Netherlands	India
Target Audience	Citizens & Influencers	Humanitarian Agencies	Citizens	Citizens and Police	Citizens and Police
Institutional Integration	No	No	No	Yes	Yes
Citizen Participation	High	Moderate	High	High	Moderate
Technology	Social Media Analytics	Deep Learning / Facial Recognition	Mobile App	Mobile App	Mobile App

Recent literature identifies two main approaches for implementing facial recognition systems: locally trained models and cloud-based service solutions. Wang and Deng [9] and Chi et al. [10] highlight that local models, while providing greater control over data and architecture, require a large volume of training images and high-performance computing infrastructure, which limits their applicability in resource-constrained environments.

In contrast, Hilmi et al. [8] demonstrated that cloud-based API services, such as those offered by Amazon Web Services (AWS), maintain stable and accurate performance even in complex clinical scenarios, significantly reducing development time and the need for additional training. According to AWS technical documentation [11], Recognition integrates pre-trained models capable of real-time face detection and comparison, automatically scaling according to demand.

Considering the scope of this research, which aims to provide a functional and scalable solution applicable at the national level, a cloud-based approach—specifically AWS Recognition — was selected due to its ability to deliver high availability, low maintenance, and automated image processing while ensuring the security and interoperability required for institutional systems.

In summary, previous studies highlight the value of mobile applications and collaborative networks in missing person searches. However, most lack automated facial recognition and adaptation to Latin American contexts. This work integrates these technologies into a scalable platform that supports institutional efforts to locate missing persons in Peru.

3 System Architecture and Design

3.1 General Application Design

The application was designed considering the Peruvian context and the workflow of missing person investigations. Guidance from the Dirección de Investigación y Búsqueda de Personas Desaparecidas (DIVIBPD) provided insight into the reporting and identification stages. The architecture emphasizes cloud-based services to lower costs and ease institutional adoption, supported by system-oriented diagrams describing data flow and process interaction.

3.2 Logical System Architecture

The proposed application is organized following a layered logical architecture (Fig. 1), which ensures a clear separation of responsibilities and facilitates maintenance and scalability:

- **Interface Layer:** Implemented with Flutter, it allows citizens to capture or upload images from their mobile devices for subsequent analysis;
- **Application Layer:** Developed with Spring Boot, it manages business logic, processes frontend requests, and coordinates interactions with external services;
- **Service Layer:** Integrates AWS services, using Amazon S3 for image storage and Amazon Recognition for facial analysis;
- **Data Layer:** Built on Amazon RDS with PostgreSQL, storing structured data on reports, users, and identification results.

This modular structure guarantees interoperability among components and enables future system extensions without altering the core functionality.

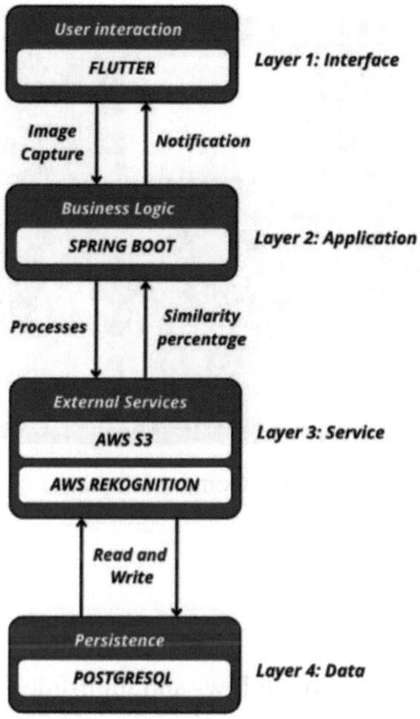

Fig. 1. Logical System Architecture

3.3 Context Diagram (C4)

The C4 context diagram (Fig. 2) illustrates the interaction between the application, its main users, and external systems from a high-level perspective. The application is designed to support the identification of missing persons through a collaborative workflow among the following users:

- **Citizen:** initiates the process by submitting an image of a potential missing person from their mobile device;
- **Operator 114:** receives notifications of potential matches and determines whether to escalate the case;
- **Police Officer:** validates confirmed appearances and performs field verifications.

In addition, the application integrates with AWS Recognition: an external service that processes images and returns similarity percentages.

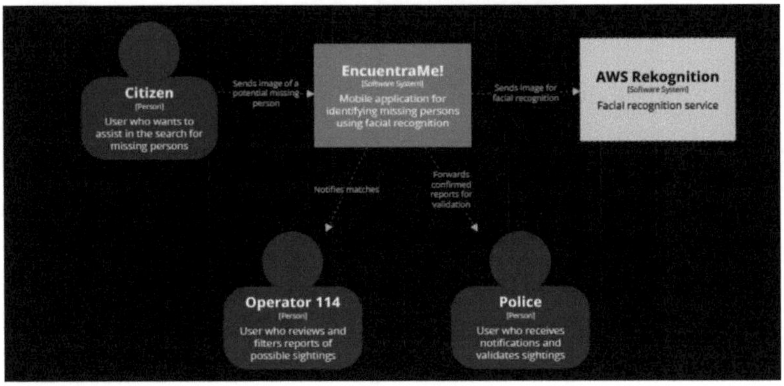

Fig. 2. C4 Context Diagram

3.4 User Interface Design

The user interface was designed through low- and high-fidelity prototypes phases, mapping out the architecture of the main views such as home, missing persons list, recognition module, report form, and results. The design emphasized simplicity and accessibility. UX principles guided navigation and visual balance, validated through internal tests that confirmed intuitive interaction and consistent alignment with the system's goals.

3.5 Database

The database model, shown in Fig. 3, defines the main entities of the system and their logical relationships. It includes tables such as users, profiles, roles, and missing persons reports, ensuring referential integrity and data consistency. Its design prevents redundancies, optimizes queries, and facilitates integration with the Spring Boot backend. Additionally, it allows flexible expansion to incorporate new attributes or scale in distributed environments.

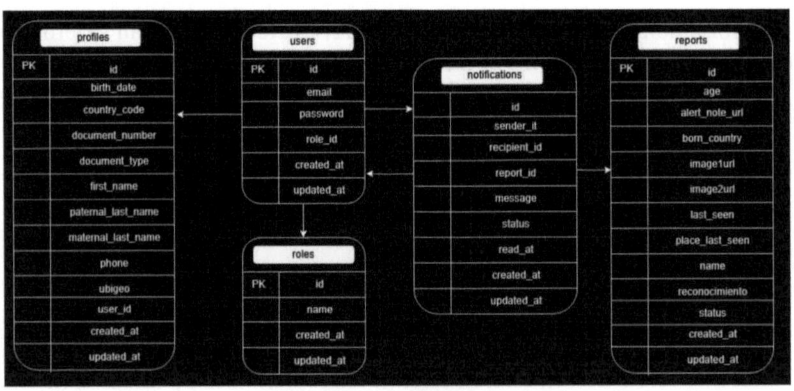

Fig. 3. Database Diagram

3.6 Facial Recognition Technology

To support the selection of an appropriate facial recognition technology, an architectural comparison was conducted among widely used open-source frameworks and commercial cloud services. Table 2 summarizes the architectural characteristics, deployment requirements, and operational scope of FaceNet, ArcFace, and AWS Recognition.

Table 2. Comparison of facial recognition frameworks and services

Framework/ Service	Approach Type	Infrastructure Requirement	Licensing & Cost Model	Specialized Biometric Indexing
FaceNet	Open-source Deep Learning (CNN)	High (Requires dedicated GPU instances and custom embedding storage)	Open-source (MIT)/ Free software	Requires manual vector database setup and management
ArcFace	Open-source Deep Learning (CNN)	High (Requires GPU acceleration for efficient training and inference)	Open-source (MIT)/ Free software	Requires external vector database and similarity search implementation
AWS Recognition	Enterprise Cloud API	Low (Fully managed serverless cloud environment)	Proprietary/ Pay-per-use commercial licensing	Native scalable Face Collection vector registry included

The classification performance and operational viability of these architectures are governed by standard Machine Learning (ML) metrics designed for biometric verification tasks. In the context of a non-cooperative missing-persons identification system, these evaluation parameters are formally defined as follows:

- Recognition Rate: Percentage of test cases in which the system correctly identified the target individual from the facial image dataset.

$$\text{Recognition Rate} = \text{TP}/\text{Total Cases x } 100 \tag{1}$$

- Precision: Measures the exactness of positive match alerts, calculating the ratio of true missing person identifications over the total number of generated system alerts.

$$\text{Precision} = \text{TP}/(\text{TP} + \text{FP}) \tag{2}$$

- Recall (Sensitivity): Evaluates the completeness of the system in detecting missing individuals, calculated as the ratio of true positive matches over the actual target population within the registry. Within this specific application domain, Recall represents the most critical performance parameter, given that a low score yields False Negatives (FN), implying a missing person passes completely undetected by the platform.

$$\text{Recall} = \text{TP}/(\text{TP} + \text{FN}) \tag{3}$$

- F1-Score: Represents the harmonic mean of Precision and Recall, providing a singular, balanced objective metric to evaluate the overall algorithmic strength under skewed or uncooperative data distributions.

$$\text{F1} - \text{Score} = 2^* \left((\text{Precision}^* \text{ Recall}) / (\text{Precision} + \text{Recall}) \right) \tag{4}$$

4 Methodology and Application Implementation

The implementation of the application prototype was carried out using an agile, iterative, and incremental methodology, which allowed each component to be developed progressively with continuous verifications to ensure its functionality. During each sprint, specific tasks for the frontend, backend, and integration of the facial recognition model were addressed, facilitating ongoing collaboration through version control on GitHub.

4.1 Frontend Development

The frontend was developed in Flutter using Visual Studio Code as the main IDE. Tests were performed on physical Android and iOS devices and emulators to ensure interface compatibility and functionality. The similarity percentage shown in the final view indicates the match level between the user's captured image and stored faces. For instance, a 99.99% result denotes a highly accurate identification based on distinct facial features detected by the model. (see Fig. 4).

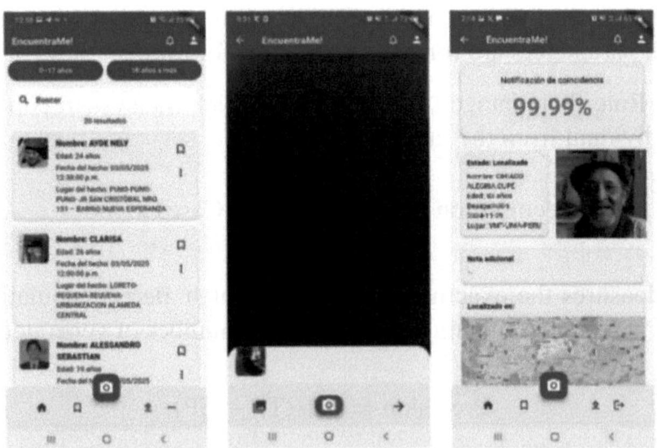

Fig. 4. Mobile application interface representing Search Feed, Camera Recognition module and Match Validation View

4.2 Backend Development

The backend was implemented using Spring Boot, also leveraging Visual Studio Code as the main IDE. This component manages business logic, database access, and integration with the facial recognition service provided by AWS Recognition. To verify and test the developed services, Swagger was used, a tool that facilitated API documentation and validation.

4.3 Integration of the Facial Recognition Model

For facial image processing and comparison, the system utilizes the AWS Recognition service deployed in the us-east-1 (N. Virginia) region. This tool enables high-precision facial analysis, providing real-time results with optimal performance for identifying missing persons. To ensure biometric reproducibility and minimize false positives during deployment, the architecture establishes a dedicated face collection via CreateCollection-Request. Image registration is handled through IndexFacesRequest, which is preceded by a structural validation layer using DetectFacesRequest to ensure a valid visage is present before indexing. Finally, the search operations utilize SearchFacesByImageRequest configured with a strict SimilarityThreshold parameter of 90% and a maxFaces restriction of 6, allowing the system to filter and validate matches that align with the high confidence metrics documented in the experimental phase.

Figure. 5 summarizes the complete interaction flow between the frontend, backend, and AWS facial recognition service, ensuring efficient communication and coherent integration among system components.

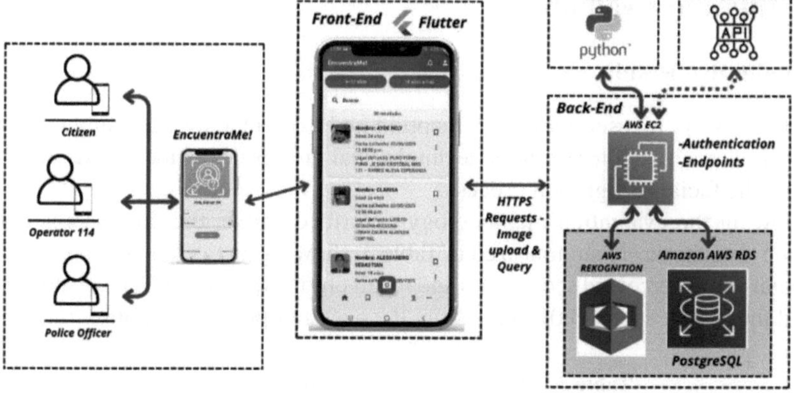

Fig. 5. Integration of the Facial Recognition Model

4.4 Experimental Setup and Evaluation Methodology

This section describes the experimental framework established to evaluate the functional performance and user perception of the EncuentraMe application. The evaluation methodology was divided into two main approaches: a qualitative evaluation focused on the user experience across various demographic profiles, and a quantitative technical validation.

The qualitative evaluation was conducted with a total of 50 participants, including citizens of different ages and levels of technological experience. Participants ranged from 18 to approximately 80 years old. Most participants had basic experience using smartphones, while some had limited knowledge of digital technologies. The functional workflow evaluation focused on system stability, completion rates, and the reliability of facial recognition matches. User perceptions were collected after testing via a structured questionnaire using a 5-point Likert scale to assess accessibility and social value.

For the quantitative evaluation, a controlled test dataset was created using photographs collected with participant consent. The dataset included images acquired under different conditions, such as varying distances, lighting levels, facial orientations, and image quality. Two image acquisition methods were evaluated: (1) real-time image capture using the mobile device camera and (2) image selection from the device gallery.

A total of 103 recognition tests were executed to evaluate the end-to-end workflow, including image acquisition, facial recognition, match retrieval, and alert generation. The evaluation focused on workflow completion rate, recognition accuracy, similarity scores, and system robustness under realistic operating conditions.

Additionally, a comparative experiment was conducted using AWS Recognition, FaceNet, and ArcFace. A subset of 65 challenging test cases was evaluated, including images captured at different distances, illumination conditions, facial poses, and scenes containing multiple individuals. Precision, Recall, and F1-Score metrics were calculated to compare the identification performance of each model.

5 Results and Evaluation

5.1 Qualitative Results

Qualitative results focused on user perception and experience while using the application. Overall, positive interest in the technological proposal was identified, particularly regarding the facial recognition process.

Following the evaluation methodology described above, the final scores obtained across the six criteria are summarized in Table 3, showing an overall positive evaluation, with social value perceived scoring 5.0 and result clarity scoring 4.0. The response speed received the lowest score (3.0), suggesting the need to optimize response times.

Table 3. Qualitative user perception evaluation

Criterion	Average
Ease of Use	4
Result Clarity	4
Expected Usefulness	4

(continued)

Table 3. (*continued*)

Criterion	Average
Response Speed (Fluidity)	3
Perceived Social Value	5
Availability of Sufficient Information	4

Regarding result clarity, users indicated that the way the system presents information is understandable and facilitates decision-making. The use of visual elements, such as the matched image, associated name, and similarity percentage, helped interpret the outcome intuitively. This direct visual approach allowed participants to identify whether a significant match existed without additional explanations, reflecting an effective interface in delivering relevant results.

User feedback collected after testing highlighted key operational improvements such as enabling gallery image selection, refining interface elements, and adding loading indicators. These insights offer valuable guidance for enhancing future versions of the application.

5.2 Quantitative Results

Following the technical validation framework establish in sect. 4.4, the performance and operational execution metrics are summarized in Table 4. The application successfully completed the recognition workflow in 97.09% of cases (100 out of 103 tests). Correct matches reached 80.58% (83 out of 103), demonstrating reasonable effectiveness in real-world contexts. Failed tests were mainly associated with images having poor lighting, excessive distance, or multiple faces. Most tests (91 cases) used images uploaded from the gallery, compared to 12 captured with the camera, indicating a preference for pre-existing images.

Regarding technical metrics, the application maintained a similarity range of 92% to 99% for correct matches, reflecting good technical accuracy in successful cases. Report uploads from the backend were completed without errors, ensuring data availability in the app. Additionally, high tolerance to invalid inputs, such as corrupted images or empty fields, was validated without compromising overall functionality. Detected errors were recoverable, allowing uninterrupted workflow at all times.

These results demonstrate a solid technical foundation in the current implementation, with potential for improved accuracy and robustness through further testing in diverse environments.

Table 4. Summary of quantitative results

Metric	Result
Total Validated Users	50
Total Tests Conducted	103

(*continued*)

Table 4. (*continued*)

Metric	Result
Successful Complete Workflow	97,09%
Correct Matches	80,58%
Camera Tests	12
Gallery Tests	91
Similarity Range for Matches	Between 92% and 99%
Failed Tests	12 (due to distance, lighting, or multiple faces)

A more detailed analysis of the test conditions revealed differences in recognition effectiveness depending on the type of image used. Photographs taken directly with the device's camera achieved a correct match rate of 75%, whereas images selected from the gallery reached 87.91%. This result suggests that users tend to choose higher-quality images from their storage, which enhances the application's performance.

Fig. 6 presents the distribution of the 50 participating users, classified by gender and defined age groups. A higher representation is observed in the 18–29 years range, followed by the 30–39 years group, reflecting a sample dominated by young adults. Gender parity was maintained across all groups, allowing a balanced evaluation of the system in terms of user perception and usage. This distribution supports the validity of the results regarding user experience and functional performance of the application.

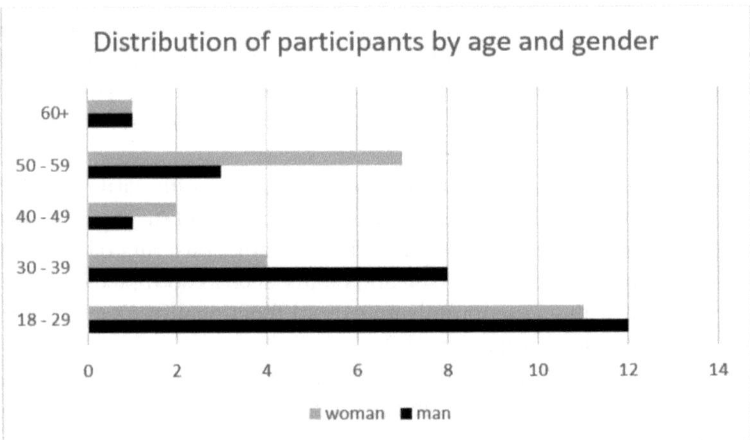

Fig. 6. Participant distribution by age and gender

Additionally, the application's response to uncontrolled scenarios was evaluated, such as submitting images without faces, corrupted files, or incomplete data. In these cases, the application remained stable, without critical interruptions or unexpected crashes. Exceptions were properly handled by the backend and, in some instances, by the frontend, allowing users to continue the workflow without restarting the application.

This capability to manage unexpected situations reinforces the application's reliability and readiness for use in real-world environments.

5.3 Comparative Analysis

To complement the evaluation presented in Sects. 5.1 and 5.2, a comparative analysis was conducted between AWS Recognition and two widely used facial recognition models, FaceNet and ArcFace through the DeepFace framework. The objective was to assess their performance under different image conditions representative of missing-person identification scenarios, including frontal images, partial profile views, long-distance captures, and low-quality images.

AWS Recognition was evaluated using a gallery search workflow, while FaceNet and ArcFace were evaluated through DeepFace's identification functionality. Although equivalent datasets were used, differences in implementation may influence the observed performance.

Table 5 presents the operational recognition performance observed during the experiments, including successful identifications, false positives, and face detection failures.

Table 5. Models comparison

Scenario	AWS Recognition	FaceNet	ArcFace
Top-1 Recognition Rate	54	13	19
Top-2 Recognition Rate	0	0	1
Top-3 Recognition Rate	0	0	1
False Positives	0	10	13
False Negatives	10	41	30

To provide a more comprehensive assessment, Table 6 reports the corresponding Precision, Recall, and F1-Score metrics for each evaluated model.

Table 6. Classification performance metrics

Metrics	AWS Recognition	FaceNet	ArcFace
Recognition rate	84.38%	20.31%	32.81%
Precision	100%	56,52%	61,76%
Recall	84,38%	24,07%	41,18%
F1-Score	91,53%	33,77%	49,91%

The results indicate that AWS Recognition achieved the highest overall performance, obtaining a Precision of 100.00%, a Recall of 84.38%, and an F1-Score of 91.53%, substantially outperforming FaceNet and ArcFace across the evaluated scenarios. AWS Recognition consistently demonstrated greater robustness under challenging conditions, including long-distance captures, variations in illumination, partial facial visibility, and multi-person scenes.

6 Discussion of Results

The results obtained demonstrate significant improvements compared to traditional search methods, thanks to the automation of facial recognition, which allows immediate detection of matches without manual intervention. The centralization of reports in a mobile platform also optimizes remote access to information, reducing response times and operational workload.

Regarding performance, the integration between the facial recognition modules, backend, and database was validated, although accuracy decreases with blurry images, poor lighting, or images captured from a distance. Overall performance depends on the correct organization of the database and the number of images available per person.

While the proposal has not yet reached the reach of large-scale platforms, it represents a step forward in incorporating automated technologies into institutional missing-person searches. In the Peruvian context, the solution contributes to strengthening a faster, interoperable, and more accessible system, with potential improvements through an increased dataset and image preprocessing techniques.

7 Ethical and Social Considerations

The system was developed under ethical principles and personal data protection standards, complying with Peruvian Law No. 29733 and international regulations regarding the handling of sensitive information. The system aims to support missing-person searches from a citizen perspective rather than surveillance, promoting transparency, privacy, and responsible use of technology.

To mitigate the socio-technical risks inherent to facial recognition systems, specific structural countermeasures have been considered in the platform's design. First, to prevent system misuse—such as unauthorized tracking or harassment—the architecture restricts the search functionalities to authenticated and registered users within the application, establishing a traceability layer through secure activity logs to deter malicious lookups. Second, regarding legal implications and data governance, storage within the Amazon Web Services (AWS) cloud environment is governed by strict access control policies. Uploaded images and biometric metadata are strictly isolated in private cloud repositories, accessible only by authenticated backend services, which ensures that personal data remains secure and protected from unauthorized third-party exposure. Finally, to address the impact of incorrect biometric identifications that could lead to false alarms or emotional distress, the application operates strictly as a preliminary decision-support tool. High-similarity matches do not trigger automated public or legal actions; instead, they are routed through a human-in-the-loop verification layer, ensuring that institutional validation occurs before any official protocol is initiated.

Furthermore, regarding data governance and legal compliance under Peruvian Law No. 29733, the storage and management of sensitive biometric records for public safety are legally restricted to competent state authorities. Consequently, the proposed platform does not intend to host independent public registries; instead, its architectural framework is designed strictly to facilitate future integration with official databases managed by authorized institutions, such as the Peruvian National Police (PNP), ensuring full alignment with national legal mandates for criminal and missing-person investigations.

8 Conclusions

The developed application demonstrated stable performance during initial tests, identifying effective matches under ideal conditions. However, a decrease in accuracy was evidenced with blurred images (2.91%), poorly illuminated images (3.88%) or images captured at long distances (3.88%), which represents an important technical limitation.

From the user's perspective, the usefulness of the application as a support tool in the identification of missing persons was highlighted. However, 4 participants expressed difficulties in understanding the flow of use without guidance messages, which reveals opportunities for improvement in the interface and user experience.

At the architecture level, the solution combines facial recognition, automated processing and coordinated interaction between citizens, operators and police. This flow was designed considering real processes reported by the Missing Persons Directorate (DIVIBPD), which allowed building an application aligned with the operational reality of the country. While current testing relied on simulated test datasets, future architectural scaling would require direct integration with official institutional databases to validate its legitimacy and overall accuracy in wider deployment scenarios.

As a future line of improvement, it is recommended to incorporate facial progression techniques by age, which would make it possible to simulate the aging of missing persons and thus expand the possibilities of identification in long-term cases. Future work will also focus on expanding the validation sample across diverse mobile devices and refining the application's core processing pipeline to ensure architectural readiness for broader technical evaluations.

Acknowledgments. We thank the Division of Investigation and Search for Missing Persons (DIVIBPD) of the Peruvian National Police – PNP for their guidance as an advisory entity, providing technical support and validation of functional requirements during the research, development, and validation phases, especially 3rd Technician Elmer Alvites and 1st Sergeant Jonathan Reyes. We also extend our gratitude to Dr. Álvaro Aures for his advisory role and co-authorship since 2024, as well as his understanding and enthusiasm.

Disclosure of Interests. The authors have no competing interests to declare that are relevant to the content of this article.

References

1. Stroele, V., Oliveira, L., Gomes, J., de Oliveira, T., Rajabi, E.: Who is going to help? Detecting social media influencers to spread information about missing persons. IEEE Trans. Technol. Soc. (2024). https://doi.org/10.1109/TTS.2024.3395175

2. Limbani, D., Barhate, A., Hemavathi, D.: Facial recognition for humanitarian efforts: a deep learning based solution for missing person identification. In: Proceedings of the 2024 International Conference on Advances in Computing and Artificial Intelligence (ACCAI) (2024). https://doi.org/10.1109/ACCAI61061.2024.10602230
3. Zhang, Y., Peng, D., Wang, Y., Wang, J.: Research on facial expression recognition algorithm based on deep learning. In: Proceedings of the 2022 IEEE WCMEIM (2022). https://doi.org/10.1109/WCMEIM56910.2022.10021491
4. Inavolu, M.D., Venna, D., Kallepalli, G.V., Surapaneni, S.S.: Detection of missing persons using mobile app. In: Proceedings of the 2023 IEEE INOCON (2023). https://doi.org/10.1109/INOCON57975.2023.10101097
5. García-Barceló, N., Alcázar, M., Revuelta, J., Woolnough, P., González, J.: Is it possible to estimate Spanish missing Person's forced and fatal outcomes cases using socio-demographic data? Gender, age and nationality. J. Crim. Policy Res. **30**, 1–19 (2022). https://doi.org/10.1007/s10610-022-09507-9
6. Lam, J., Kop, N., Houtman, C.: The impact of technological support on citizen searches for missing persons. Justice Eval. J. **6**, 62–80 (2022). https://doi.org/10.1080/24751979.2022.2109502
7. Neubauer, N., Daum, C., Miguel-Cruz, A., Liu, L.: Mobile alert app to engage community volunteers to help locate missing persons with dementia. PLoS One. **16**, e0254952 (2021). https://doi.org/10.1371/journal.pone.0254952
8. Hilmi, M., Aydogan, F., Solak, S., Bilgehan, M., Findik, Y., Baykul, T.: Facial recognition by cloud-based APIs following surgically assisted rapid maxillary expansion. Clin. Oral Investig. (2023). https://doi.org/10.1007/s00056-023-00494-y
9. Wang, M., Deng, W.: Deep face recognition: a survey. Neurocomputing. **429**, 215–244 (2021). https://doi.org/10.1016/j.neucom.2020.10.081
10. Chi, J., Kim On, C., Zhang, H., Chai, S.S.: A review of deep convolutional neural networks in Mobile face recognition. Int. J. Interact. Mob. Technol. **17**(23), 4–21 (2023). https://doi.org/10.3991/ijim.v17i23.40867
11. Amazon Web Services. Amazon Recognition–Image and Video Analysis with Machine Learning. https://aws.amazon.com/rekognition/
12. Ministerio del Interior del Perú: Registro Nacional de Información de Personas Desaparecidas (RENIPED). Policía Nacional del Perú. (2024) https://desaparecidosenperu.policia.gob.pe/Desaparecidos/reniped

Generative AI in Virtual Laboratories for Higher Engineering Education: A Scoping Review of Integration and Implications

Sijie Zhou and Alonso Gomez Zeballos(✉)

Continental University, Arequipa, Peru
agomezz@continental.edu.pe

Abstract. Generative artificial intelligence (GenAI) is increasingly being explored to enhance learning experiences in virtual laboratories in engineering education. However, a systematic understanding of how GenAI integrates into virtual laboratories and how these approaches relate to pedagogical roles, learning outcomes, and implementation challenges remains limited. This scoping review analyses 14 studies of GenAI in virtual laboratories for higher engineering education. Based on the analysis, different GenAI integration approaches were identified: agent-based integration, API or service-based integration, tool or plugin-based integration, and external interface integration. Furthermore, these integrations were examined in relation to their pedagogical roles, learning outcomes, and implementation challenges. The findings indicate that GenAI can act as an intelligent tutor or learning tool to support multiple instructional functions in virtual laboratory environments, such as providing guidance, feedback, and interactive learning support. These roles contribute to improving students' conceptual understanding, problem-solving skills, and engagement in laboratory learning. By mapping GenAI integration approaches with reported pedagogical roles and challenges, the study finds that the design of GenAI-integrated virtual laboratories should carefully balance automation, instructional support, and learner autonomy to achieve effective educational outcomes. These findings offer useful insights for both researchers and educators seeking to design effective GenAI-supported virtual laboratory learning environments.

Keywords: Generative AI · Virtual Laboratories · Engineering Education · Scoping Review · Learning outcomes

1 Introduction

Laboratory learning plays a central role in engineering education because it enables students to apply theoretical knowledge through experimentation and problem-solving activities [8]. Through laboratory work, students develop practical skills, deepen conceptual understanding, and learn to address real-world

H. Florez and R. Gomez-Sanchez (Eds.): UPADI-AI 2026, CCIS 3124, pp. 101–117, 2027.
https://doi.org/10.1007/978-3-032-35635-2_7

engineering problems. However, traditional physical laboratories face several well-recognised constraints, including high equipment and maintenance costs, limited accessibility, safety concerns, and difficulties in scaling laboratory activities for large student populations [11,22].

To address these limitations, engineering education has undergone substantial digital transformation driven by the growing demand for scalable, flexible, and accessible forms of practical training [12]. Engineering programs have increasingly adopted digital technologies such as computer-based simulations, networked laboratory platforms, and immersive technologies, including virtual reality (VR) and augmented reality (AR) [3]. These technologies enable the development of alternative experimental environments that can complement physical laboratory activities.

Virtual laboratories are experimental environments constructed through computer software, simulation, and virtual technologies rather than physical hardware [17]. In these environments, learners conduct experiments using simulated materials, instruments, and graphical animations designed to replicate real-world experimental processes. Compared with traditional laboratories, virtual laboratories can reduce the dependence on expensive physical equipment, improve accessibility for remote learners, and eliminate many safety risks associated with hazardous experiments [11,20]. They also offer pedagogical benefits, such as allowing students to repeat experiments without resource constraints, manipulate time scales, and visualise phenomena that are otherwise difficult to observe in real environments [11,14,17]. Although virtual laboratories cannot fully replace hands-on physical experimentation, they have become valuable tools for supporting engineering laboratory learning [14,17].

At the same time, recent advances in artificial intelligence have introduced new possibilities for enhancing digital learning environments. Generative Artificial Intelligence (GenAI) refers to artificial intelligence systems that use deep learning models trained on large-scale datasets to generate novel human-like content, including text, images, and computer code [4,26]. Examples include large language models (LLMs), image generation systems, and code-generation models [4,26]. These technologies extend the capabilities of intelligent educational systems by enabling natural language interaction, automated content generation, and adaptive learning support [13].

In engineering education, GenAI can support students' practical problem-solving by providing automated feedback, programming assistance, conversational tutoring, and guidance through complex experimental or simulation-based tasks [6,18]. Rather than functioning only as background computational tools, GenAI systems can act as intelligent tutors providing scaffolding, conversational partners supporting reflective dialogue, or analytical tools assisting in the interpretation of complex experimental data [1]. By offering personalised guidance and reducing cognitive load, GenAI has the potential to make virtual laboratories more adaptive and responsive to students' learning needs.

Despite the growing body of research on AI in education, the integration of GenAI within virtual laboratories in higher engineering education remains at an early stage. Existing studies are fragmented across different engineering domains, technologies, and pedagogical designs, and there is still a lack of systematic understanding of how GenAI is integrated into virtual laboratories, what pedagogical roles it performs, what learning outcomes it supports, and what implementation challenges it introduces. Understanding these relationships is essential for the effective and responsible adoption of GenAI in engineering laboratory education.

To address this gap, this study conducts a scoping review to systematically map the current landscape of GenAI in virtual laboratories for higher engineering education. The review aims to develop a taxonomy of integration approaches and examine their relationships with pedagogical roles, learning outcomes, and implementation challenges. Specifically, this study addresses the following research questions: *(RQ1) how GenAI is integrated into virtual laboratories, (RQ2) what pedagogical roles it performs, (RQ3) what learning outcomes have been reported, and (RQ4) what challenges emerge during its implementation*

2 Methodology

This scoping review was conducted in accordance with the Preferred Reporting Items for Systematic Reviews and Meta-Analyses extension for Scoping Reviews (PRISMA-ScR) guidelines [27]. This framework was chosen to ensure a rigorous and transparent process for mapping the existing literature on GenAI in virtual laboratories in higher engineering education. The methodology was structured into four distinct phases as described below.

2.1 Search Strategy

To ensure a comprehensive mapping of the literature, searches were conducted within two complementary databases: Scopus and IEEE Xplorer. These databases were systematically selected due to the interdisciplinary use of artificial intelligence, virtual simulation labs, and higher engineering education. It also minimises coverage bias and ensures both pedagogical and technical dimensions of the research topic. A comprehensive literature search was conducted across these databases covering the period from 2020 to 2026. The search string employed Boolean operators to combine key concepts: ("Generative AI" OR "LLM" OR "AI Agent*") AND ("Virtual Lab*" OR "Simulation*") AND ("Engineering Education" OR "Higher Education"). This strategy was designed to capture the most relevant studies at the intersection of generative AI and virtual laboratories in higher engineering education.

2.2 Inclusion and Exclusion Criteria

To identify eligible literature, specific criteria were established. Studies were included if they: (1) Reported on the application of GenAI within virtual laboratories specifically for higher engineering education; (2) Were peer-reviewed journal articles or conference proceedings; (3) Were published in English between 2020 and 2026. Conversely, studies were excluded if they were: (1) duplicates, books, or review papers; (2) focused on non-engineering disciplines; or (3) focused on virtual laboratories without explicit AI integration.

2.3 Screening and Selection Process

The screening and selection process followed the PRISMA-ScR framework, as illustrated in Fig. 1. To ensure methodological rigour, the two authors independently screened the titles, abstracts, and full texts according to predefined inclusion criteria. Any discrepancies were resolved through discussion and consensus, and the final coding was reviewed to ensure consistency and validity. Following this screening process, 14 peer-reviewed studies were selected for final analysis and mapped to the data extraction matrix.

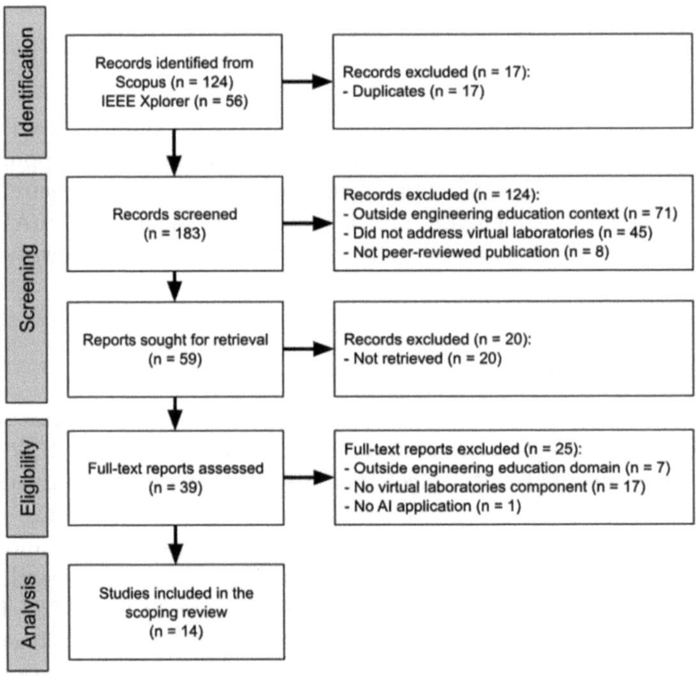

Fig. 1. PRISMA-ScR flow diagram illustrating the selection process for studies on GenAI in virtual laboratories for higher engineering education.

2.4 Extraction and Categorisation of the Data

The included studies were coded according to predefined categories derived from our research questions, focusing on four analytical dimensions: (1) GenAI integration approach, (2) pedagogical roles, (3) learning outcomes, and (4) implementation challenges. Coding was conducted manually by reviewing the full texts, where articles were grouped thematically under these categories. While dimensions such as pedagogical roles and learning outcomes were based on established educational frameworks, new themes were identified as they emerged from the literature, particularly regarding GenAI integration approaches and specific challenges. Data were systematically extracted for each selected study to ensure a comprehensive analysis. By synthesising the findings obtained, the research questions regarding GenAI in virtual laboratories in higher engineering education could then be answered.

Regarding review limitations, although a comprehensive search strategy was adopted, the exclusion of non-indexed databases may have led to the omission of relevant literature. Second, given the rapid evolution of GenAI, this review was limited to studies published and accessible at the time of data extraction. Studies published after the extraction date were therefore excluded to maintain chronological consistency and analytical accuracy.

3 Results

3.1 Descriptive Overview

Following the PRISMA-ScR screening process, a total of 14 studies were included. These studies were published between 2023 and 2026, reflecting the rapidly growing interest in integrating GenAI into virtual laboratory environments. The majority of these publications (n=12) appeared from 2025 onwards, following the initial mainstream adoption of large language models and the subsequent maturation of GenAI-related pedagogical research. The annual distribution of these papers is illustrated in Fig. 2.

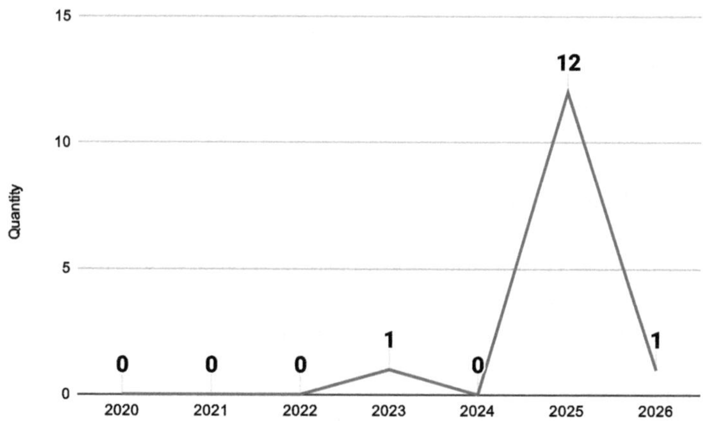

Fig. 2. Distribution of papers reporting on GenAI in Virtual laboratories within engineering education based on the year of publication.

3.2 Integration Approaches of GenAI in Virtual Laboratories

RQ1: How GenAI is integrated into virtual laboratories?

The integration of GenAI into virtual laboratories can be implemented through different technical approaches depending on how the GenAI components interact with the laboratory platform and learning environment.

Based on the analysis of the 14 studies, four primary integration approaches were identified: agent-based integration, API or service-based integration, external interface integration, and tool or plugin-based integration. As illustrated in Fig. 3, while most studies align with a single category, three papers adopt a hybrid approach that combines both agent and API technologies. The following sections provide a detailed technical characterisation of these four fundamental approaches and discuss the emergence of hybrid implementations.

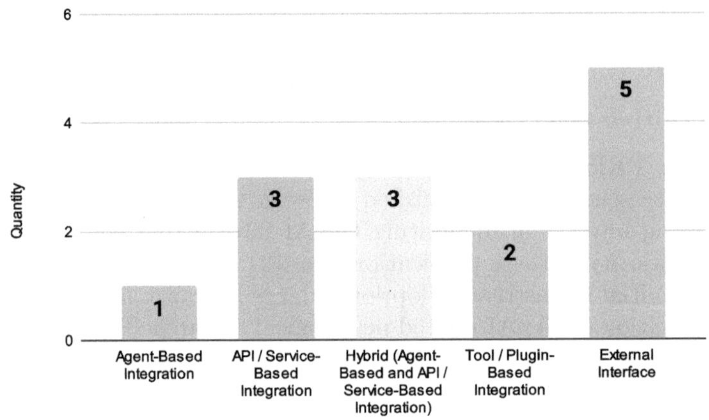

Fig. 3. Distribution of research papers across identified AI integration technologies (N=14). (Note: The 'Hybrid' category denotes studies utilising a combination of multiple primary approaches.)

Agent-Based Integration: Agent-based integration embeds autonomous, context-aware AI agents directly within the virtual laboratory environment. In this architecture, GenAI functions not merely as a passive service, but as an intelligent entity capable of continuously observing experimental states, analysing learner actions, and providing proactive, adaptive guidance during laboratory activities. Four of the selected studies [2,10,19,23] employ this approach in their virtual laboratories.

Technically, this approach relies on deep interaction models that synchronise the standardised laboratory's real-time state with the GenAI model [2]. The agent continuously retrieves state variables, such as valve positions, sensor readings, or hardware-in-the-loop simulation parameters from the simulation or physical environment, often at high refresh rates [2,10,23]. This live contextual data is incorporated into role-based prompts and combined with retrieval-augmented generation (RAG) frameworks, which supply the AI with domain-specific knowledge from textbooks and technical manuals [2,19,23]. By processing both environmental data and specialised technical documentation, the AI agent can evaluate the real-time state of the user's setup, generate highly accurate context-aware feedback, and respond dynamically to student actions [2,23].

In the reviewed studies, AI agents frequently operate as intelligent tutors, virtual teaching assistants, or non-player characters (NPCs) within immersive laboratory environments. For example, AI agents have been deployed in virtual reality thermal-fluids labs to interact vocally with students [2], in power electronics and dSPACE simulation platforms to provide continuous debugging and troubleshooting support [10,19], and in remote telepresence laboratories to autonomously monitor procedural execution, evaluate live experimental conditions, and trigger safety interventions when procedural violations are detected [23].

API or Service-Based Integration: API or service-based integration enables virtual laboratory platforms to access GenAI capabilities through external cloud services. In this architecture, the laboratory system does not host large language models locally; instead, it communicates with external AI services through standardised application programming interfaces (APIs). Six of the selected studies [2,5,15,16,19,23] adopted this approach.

Technically, this approach follows a layered architecture consisting of a client interface, a laboratory server, and an external GenAI service layer [15,23]. The server sends prompts or experimental data to external models such as OpenAI or Azure OpenAI and receives generated responses, which are then presented to students as explanations, feedback, or experiment guidance [5,15,23]. Because the GenAI model operates as an external service, this approach reduces the computational requirements of the laboratory platform while enabling scalable deployment of GenAI-powered functionalities [23].

In the reviewed studies, API-based GenAI services are used to provide automated textual explanations, design feedback, and intelligent experimental support. For example, GenAI services have been integrated into web-based learning platforms [15], satellite design environments [16], and engineering simulation interfaces [5] to generate feedback based on experimental parameters and simulation results.

Tool or Plugin-Based Integration: Tool or plugin-based integration incorporates GenAI functionalities into existing laboratory platforms or software through modular extensions or software plugins. Instead of redesigning the entire laboratory system, GenAI capabilities are added as supplementary components that interact with the host software environment. Two of the selected studies [24,28] employ this approach.

In this architecture, GenAI modules interpret students' natural language inputs and translate them into executable code, mathematical expressions, or simulation parameters that are processed by the underlying computational engines of the host platform [24]. This approach enables seamless integration between GenAI-generated outputs and specialised engineering tools used in laboratory learning.

In the selected studies, integrating GenAI systems with symbolic computing environments, simulation data management systems, and model-based engineering platforms [24,28]. These integrations allow students to generate visualisations, interpret simulation results, and automate aspects of modelling workflows directly within the laboratory software environment.

External Interface Integration: External interface integration represents the most loosely coupled approach. In this configuration, GenAI tools operate independently from the virtual laboratory platform, and students interact with them through external interfaces such as web-based conversational GenAI systems. Five of the selected studies [7,9,21,25,30] adopted this approach.

Rather than being embedded within the laboratory infrastructure, the GenAI system functions as an external learning assistant that students consult during experimental tasks [21,25]. Typically, students generate simulation code, parameter suggestions, or conceptual explanations through conversational prompts and then manually apply the generated outputs within their local laboratory software environments [7,9,30].

This human-in-the-loop workflow requires learners to iteratively transfer information between the GenAI interface and the laboratory platform, including copying generated code, running simulations, and returning experimental results for further GenAI-assisted analysis [21,30]. Although this approach requires minimal system integration, it relies heavily on student interpretation and validation of GenAI-generated outputs [7,21].

Overall, these four integration approaches represent different levels of interaction between GenAI systems and virtual laboratory platforms. Agent-based integration provides the deepest system coupling and contextual awareness, enabling real-time interaction with experimental environments. API-based integration offers flexible and scalable access to cloud-based GenAI services. Plugin-based integration enhances existing laboratory platforms through modular GenAI extensions, while external interface integration allows learners to use GenAI tools independently alongside laboratory activities. A significant observation in this study is the emergence of hybrid implementations. As demonstrated in three key studies [2,19,23], where researchers integrated both agent-based and API-based approaches. In these hybrid architectures, the API-based layer provides the system with access to high-capacity cloud models for complex reasoning and natural language processing, while the agent-based layer facilitates real-time, local interaction with the experimental state and hardware. This synergy allows for the creation of sophisticated systems that are both cognitively capable and operationally responsive, particularly for tasks requiring immediate safety interventions, vocal feedback, or continuous debugging in high-fidelity simulations.

3.3 Pedagogical Roles of GenAI in Virtual Laboratories

RQ2: What pedagogical roles it performs?

According to the framework proposed by Gwo-Jen Hwang et al. [13], the roles of artificial intelligence in education can be broadly categorised into intelligent tutors, intelligent tutees, intelligent learning tools or partners, and policy-making advisors. Among these categories, the reviewed studies predominantly position GenAI as intelligent tutors and intelligent learning tools or partners within virtual laboratory environments.

Intelligent Tutors: In agent-based and API-integrated architectures (e.g. [2,5,9,10,19,23]), GenAI functions as an active instructional guide that provides adaptive explanations, troubleshooting assistance, and immediate feedback during experimentation. For instance, in virtual reality thermal-fluids laboratories [2] and power electronics experiments [19], GenAI systems operate as virtual teaching assistants or non-player characters that monitor system parameters and support students with real-time diagnostic suggestions. In such cases, GenAI effectively supplements or partially replaces the role of human laboratory instructors by providing continuous support.

Intelligent Learning Tools or Partners: In other implementations, GenAI acts as a collaborative learning partner rather than a direct instructor. In tool-based or API-integrated environments (e.g. [15,16,28,30]), GenAI assists students in translating theoretical concepts into practical representations. For example, in electromagnetism laboratories [30], GenAI helps convert complex mathematical formulations into three-dimensional visualisations, while in systems engineering tasks [28], it assists students in transforming conceptual models into executable Python simulations.

In externally integrated approaches (e.g. [7,9,21,25,30]), students interact with standalone GenAI platforms such as ChatGPT as external consultants to support tasks such as antenna design brainstorming [21] or debugging signal-processing scripts [7]. In these cases, the GenAI functions primarily as an external learning partner, as it operates independently from the simulation environment and does not have direct access to the experimental system state.

Overall, the pedagogical role of GenAI in virtual laboratories is largely determined by the depth of system integration, ranging from embedded intelligent tutoring functions to externally accessed collaborative support tools.

3.4 Learning Outcomes of GenAI-Supported Virtual Laboratories

RQ3: What learning outcomes have been reported?

The reviewed studies report diverse learning outcomes resulting from the integration of GenAI into virtual laboratory environments. Following the classification proposed by Wei, Saab, and Admiraal [29], these outcomes can be broadly grouped into cognitive, behavioural, and affective dimensions.

Cognitive Outcomes: Several studies report improvements in conceptual understanding and theoretical knowledge acquisition. For example, [19] documented a 19% increase in theoretical examination scores, while [28] observed stronger conceptual retention among students using GenAI-assisted laboratory guidance. Interestingly, the presence of GenAI inaccuracies also created opportunities for deeper cognitive engagement. In studies using external GenAI interfaces [21,25], students were required to critically evaluate GenAI-generated equations and verify them against theoretical models, thereby fostering higher-order engineering reasoning and analytical skills.

Behavioural Outcomes: GenAI integration also supports the development of practical engineering competencies. Agent-based monitoring systems [2,21] help ensure that students follow experimental procedures correctly, reducing operational errors in telepresence or virtual reality laboratories. Furthermore, GenAI tools lower the barrier to complex modelling and programming tasks. For instance, students were able to develop large-scale power system simulators [25] or design complex CubeSat architectures [16] with GenAI-assisted coding and modelling support.

Affective Outcomes: Beyond cognitive and procedural improvements, GenAI also influences students' motivation and engagement. Studies in computer science education [15] and mechanical engineering laboratories [23] reported increased learner confidence and enthusiasm when GenAI assistance was available. Similarly, [9] observed a 10% increase in student attendance, suggesting that GenAI supported laboratory environments may make complex engineering topics more accessible and engaging.

Collectively, these findings indicate that GenAI can positively influence multiple dimensions of learning, supporting not only knowledge acquisition but also practical skill development and learner motivation.

3.5 Implementation Challenges

RQ4: What challenges emerge during its implementation?

Despite the educational benefits of GenAIintegrated virtual laboratories, the reviewed studies also highlight several persistent implementation challenges. These challenges can be broadly categorized into technical, pedagogical, and ethical dimensions, reflecting the multifaceted impact of GenAI integration in laboratory learning environments as shown in Fig. 4.

Technical Challenges: From a technical perspective, the reliability and performance of GenAI systems remain key concerns. In particular, hallucinations—where GenAI produces inaccurate or fabricated outputs—pose risks when generating symbolic mathematical expressions [24] or specialised engineering visualisations [21]. Additionally, system performance limitations may disrupt real-time experimental interaction. For instance, high latency in GenAI vision systems (e.g. 12.44 s reported in [23]) and API token limits [2,15] can negatively affect the responsiveness and fluidity of virtual laboratory activities. Furthermore, GenAI models still encounter limitations when handling domain-specific engineering tasks, such as generating accurate process flow diagrams in chemical engineering contexts [9].

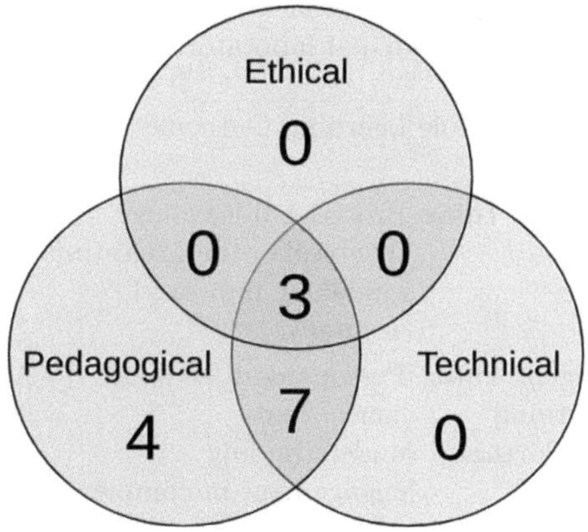

Fig. 4. Distribution of studies according to the challenges identified in the implementation of GenAI within virtual engineering laboratories.

Pedagogical Challenges: The integration of GenAI into laboratory learning also introduces pedagogical risks. A major concern is over-reliance on GenAI assistance, where students may treat GenAI outputs as authoritative solutions without critically examining the underlying concepts [19,25]. Moreover, excessive or poorly timed GenAI interventions may lead to cognitive overload, particularly among students with limited digital literacy [2,10]. In immersive virtual environments, prolonged interaction may also lead to discomfort or cybersickness, potentially affecting the overall learning experience [2].

Ethical Challenges: Ethical considerations also arise in the use of GenAI in educational contexts. The availability of external GenAI tools for report writing [30] and programming support [7] raises concerns about academic integrity and the potential circumvention of core learning objectives. As a result, new assessment strategies may be required to ensure that GenAI technologies support, rather than replace, students' active learning and problem-solving processes.

Overall, these challenges suggest that the effective integration of GenAI in virtual laboratories requires not only technological improvements but also thoughtful pedagogical design and appropriate governance mechanisms.

4 Discussion

To clarify how different GenAI configurations link to educational delivery, Table 1 synthesises evidence from the 14 reviewed studies. This synthesis demonstrates that distinct integration approaches map directly to specific pedagogical functions, learning outcomes, and implementation constraints. Ultimately, the findings suggest that each integration approach is suitable for different educational contexts, contingent upon the intended learning objective, the learner's expertise level, and the degree of instructional control required.

Table 1. Mapping of AI integration approaches, pedagogical roles, learning outcomes, and implementation challenges in virtual laboratories based on the reviewed studies.

Integration Approach	Pedagogical Role	Learning Outcomes	Challenges
Agent-Based	Intelligent Tutor	Procedural learning; troubleshooting; real-time guidance; improved accuracy.	System complexity; computational cost; over-reliance risk.
API or Service-Based	Intelligent Tutor or Learning Tools/Partners	Personalised feedback; conceptual understanding; engagement in complex systems.	API latency; context limits; privacy and security concerns.
Tool or Plugin-Based	Intelligent Learning Tools/Partners	Abstraction; spatial reasoning; concept-to-model translation; reduced coding burden.	Interoperability; model reliability; intellectual property concerns.
External Interface	Intelligent Learning Tools/Partners	Critical thinking; prompt engineering; AI-output validation; metacognitive reflection.	Hallucination; weak simulation feedback; academic integrity risks.

A key distinction between these approaches lies in the balance between integration depth and learner autonomy. Agent-based integration provides the most tightly embedded form of GenAI support, making it particularly suitable for structured laboratory activities where students require real-time guidance while navigating complex experimental systems. For example, in a telepresence laboratory, an AI agent can provide automated procedural execution support, monitor experimental progress, and offer interactive troubleshooting feedback [23]. Similarly, in introductory electrical engineering laboratories, an AI agent can guide students through parameter adjustments, system response interpretations, and the conceptual mapping of simulation results to underlying electrical principles [10]. The primary advantage of agent-based integration is its ability to provide timely, adaptive, and situated feedback. However, because the system guides students closely, there is a risk that learners may passively follow automated prompts without developing independent diagnostic reasoning or trial-and-error problem-solving skills.

API or service-based integration offers a more modular and scalable alternative. Compared to fully autonomous agent architectures, it can be more easily incorporated into existing virtual laboratory platforms to enable targeted explanations, personalised feedback, and question-answering functions. For example, in agricultural engineering, AI services can support students' interpretation of complex machinery systems and experimental decision-making [5]. Similarly, in computer or software engineering, GenAI services can be embedded into web-based platforms to enhance students' visualisation and conceptual understanding of different system architectures [15]. While this approach provides excellent pedagogical flexibility, that is allowing GenAI to act as an intelligent tutor or learning partner within the platform. Its effectiveness remains tightly bound to technical constraints such as API latency, context window limits, data privacy, and prompt quality.

Tool or plugin-based integration shifts the role of GenAI from direct tutoring toward task facilitation and cognitive support. This configuration is highly relevant in engineering disciplines where students need to translate abstract concepts into executable models or physical design prototypes. For instance, in bio-engineering education, AI-driven simulation tools help students conceptualise electromagnetic phenomena by linking abstract physical principles with interactive learning activities [24]. In systems engineering, GenAI-based modelling tools assist students in translating conceptual frameworks into formal simulation models, thereby supporting system-level reasoning [28]. The advantage of this approach is that it offloads low-level technical friction, allowing students to focus on higher-level analysis and design reasoning. However, a notable risk arises if students accept AI-generated models or code without verification, which can transfer errors directly into the final simulation or design process.

External interface integration represents the least embedded form of support, where students use AI tools such as conversational AI systems outside the virtual laboratory platform. This configuration provides the greatest student autonomy and encourages the development of prompt engineering skills, critical evaluation, and metacognitive reflection. For example, in power systems education, external GenAI tools can support project-based learning by helping students explore advanced system analysis, generate explanations, and reflect on their modelling choices [25]. Similarly, in communication engineering, GenAI can serve as an external learning assistant to support students' grasp of underlying principles and experimental procedures [30]. Yet, because these tools are disconnected from the live experimental system, they may provide generic or inaccurate answers ungrounded in the specific laboratory context. This approach is therefore better suited to open-ended inquiry, reflection, and conceptual extension than to safety-critical or accuracy-dependent procedural guidance.

Across these four approaches, the educational value of GenAI depends on aligning the integration depth with the target learning objective. When supporting novice learners through highly structured procedures, deeper integration (Agent-based or API/Service-Based) is beneficial because it provides tight contextual control and immediate feedback. Conversely, when the objective is to promote design exploration or computational implementation, tool or plugin-based integration is more appropriate as a bridge between concepts and engineering prototypes. Finally, when the goal is to foster critical thinking and independent judgment, lighter, external interface integration proves most useful, provided that students are explicitly tasked with verifying, justifying, and critiquing the AI's output.

However, leveraging these strategies requires addressing critical ethical and pedagogical challenges highlighted across the reviewed literature. Academic integrity remains a main concern when students use GenAI to generate laboratory reports, explanations, code, or data interpretations without demonstrating individual reasoning. Furthermore, over-reliance on these tools may severely diminish opportunities for students to practice essential engineering skills, such as debugging, hypothesis testing, uncertainty analysis, and reflecting on experimental error. To mitigate these risks, GenAI should not function as a passive answer-generator; instead, its implementation must be instructionally scaffolded. Educators should require students to actively evaluate AI feedback, cross-reference AI suggestions with physical simulation results, document their prompting methodologies, and explicitly justify their final engineering decisions.

In conclusion, the selection of a GenAI integration strategy must be driven by deliberate pedagogical intent rather than technical novelty alone. For virtual laboratory designers, the central challenge is not just technical deployment, but determining dynamically when GenAI should act as a tutor, a tool, or a learning partner and ensuring that the students are still responsible for interpretation, validation, and engineering judgment.

5 Conclusion

This paper reviewed recent studies on the integration of GenAI in virtual laboratories for engineering education. Through a structured analysis of the literature, this review makes three main contributions. First, it identifies and categorises the main approaches of GenAI integration adopted in virtual laboratory environments. Second, it examines how these integration approaches relate to the pedagogical roles of GenAI systems and the learning outcomes reported in the literature. Third, it synthesises the key implementation challenges, including technical, pedagogical, and ethical challenges.

By mapping these integration approaches with pedagogical roles and outcomes, this study provides a structured overview of the current research landscape. A key finding is that the design of GenAI-integrated laboratories must carefully balance automation, instructional support, and learner autonomy to achieve effective educational outcomes. This synthesis offers a foundation for future research and provides actionable insights for educators seeking to design more effective GenAI-supported laboratory learning environments.

Disclosure of Interests. The authors have no competing interests to declare that are relevant to the content of this article.

References

1. Virtual laboratories enhanced by AI for hands-on informatics learning. J. Inform. Educ. Res. (2024). https://doi.org/10.52783/jier.v4i1.600
2. Ayre, D., Dougherty, C., Zhao, Y.: Implementation of an artificial intelligence (AI) instructional support system in a virtual reality (VR) thermal-fluids laboratory. In: Volume 8: Engineering Education. American Society of Mechanical Engineers (Oct 2023). https://doi.org/10.1115/IMECE2023-112683
3. Brinson, J.R.: Learning outcome achievement in non-traditional (virtual and remote) versus traditional (hands-on) laboratories: A review of the empirical research. Comput. Educ. **87**, 218–237 (2015). https://doi.org/10.1016/j.compedu.2015.07.003
4. Chamola, V., Dave, D., Goyal, I., Sharma, S.: Generative artificial intelligence in STEM education: a review of applications, benefits and challenges. Expert Syst. **43**(2) (Feb 2026). https://doi.org/10.1111/exsy.70201
5. Chim, A.I.T., Nieto-Jalil, J.M., Ibarra-Zarate, D.I., Alvarez, J., Ojeda, U.: Virtual laboratories assisted by AI with intelligent feedback for sustainable engineering: A quasiexperimental evaluation in agricultural irrigation. In: 2025 Mexican International Conference on Computer Science (ENC), pp. 1–6. IEEE (Nov 2025). https://doi.org/10.1109/ENC68268.2025.11311937
6. Dai, C.P., Ke, F.: Educational applications of artificial intelligence in simulation-based learning: a systematic mapping review. Comput. Educ.: Artif. Intell. **3**(100087), 100087 (2022). https://doi.org/10.1016/j.caeai.2022.100087
7. Druga, C.G., Sirbu, G., Aiordachioaie, D.: On the use of AI in signal processing programming applications at the master of science level. In: 2025 9th International Symposium on Electrical and Electronics Engineering (ISEEE), pp. 1–6. IEEE (Oct 2025). https://doi.org/10.1109/ISEEE67817.2025.11304834
8. Feisel, L.D., Rosa, A.J.: The role of the laboratory in undergraduate engineering education. J. Eng. Educ. **94**(1), 121–130 (2005). https://doi.org/10.1002/j.2168-9830.2005.tb00833.x
9. Galatro, D., Chakraborty, S.: Strategies to map education 5.0 and industry 5.0 in the context of a modernized undergraduate program in chemical engineering. In: 2025 IEEE Global Engineering Education Conference (EDUCON), pp. 1–9. IEEE (Apr 2025). https://doi.org/10.1109/EDUCON62633.2025.11016293
10. He, Q., Ren, D., Zhai, C., Tang, C.: Project-based teaching reform in basic electrical engineering integrating dSPACE real-time simulation and AI assistance. In: 2025 6th International Conference on Information Science and Education (ICISE-IE), pp. 88–92. IEEE (Dec 2025). https://doi.org/10.1109/ICISE-IE68873.2025.11379175
11. Heradio, R., de la Torre, L., Galan, D., Cabrerizo, F.J., Herrera-Viedma, E., Dormido, S.: Virtual and remote labs in education: A bibliometric analysis. Comput. Educ. **98**, 14–38 (2016). https://doi.org/10.1016/j.compedu.2016.03.010
12. Hsu, Y.P., Chiang, D.F., Kehinde, I.: Transforming engineering education in the digital era: findings from a systematic review. Front. Educ. **10**(1568917) (May 2025). https://doi.org/10.3389/feduc.2025.1568917
13. Hwang, G.J., Xie, H., Wah, B.W., Gašević, D.: Vision, challenges, roles and research issues of artificial intelligence in education. Comput. Educ.: Artif. Intell. **1**(100001), 100001 (2020). https://doi.org/10.1016/j.caeai.2020.100001
14. de Jong, T., Linn, M.C., Zacharia, Z.C.: Physical and virtual laboratories in science and engineering education. Science **340**(6130), 305–308 (2013). https://doi.org/10.1126/science.1230579

15. Kumar, V., Kaur, R.: WordPress meets generative AI: An interactive educational platform for visualizing and understanding various architectures. In: 2025 3rd World Conference on Communication & Computing (WCONF), pp. 1–8. IEEE (Jul 2025). https://doi.org/10.1109/WCONF64849.2025.11233410
16. Kumar, V., Poddar, A.K., Apte, A.M., Siddiqui, J.Y., Veeraraghavan, S., Antar, Y.M.M.: AI-enhanced platform for democratizing CubeSat design, simulation, and rapid prototyping. In: 2025 IEEE Microwaves, Antennas, and Propagation Conference (MAPCON), pp. 1–4. IEEE (Dec 2025). https://doi.org/10.1109/MAPCON65020.2025.11426555
17. Li, J., Liang, W.: Effectiveness of virtual laboratory in engineering education: a meta-analysis. PLoS ONE **19**(12), e0316269 (2024). https://doi.org/10.1371/journal.pone.0316269
18. Liu, C., Wang, G.C., Wang, H.F.: The application of artificial intelligence in engineering education: a systematic review. IEEE Access **13**, 17895–17910 (2025). https://doi.org/10.1109/ACCESS.2025.3532595
19. Liu, F.: AI-empowered pedagogical reform in power electronics: a practical approach based on RAG and virtual simulation. In: Proceedings of the 2025 2nd International Symposium on Artificial Intelligence for Education, pp. 149–153. ACM, New York, NY, USA (Sep 2025). https://doi.org/10.1145/3775073.3775099
20. Ma, J., Nickerson, J.V.: Hands-on, simulated, and remote laboratories. ACM Comput. Surv. **38**(3), 7 (2006). https://doi.org/10.1145/1132960.1132961
21. Marrocco, G.: Redefining antenna design education: ChatGPT as a copilot for engineering students [education corner]. IEEE Antennas Propag. Mag. **68**(1), 74–86 (2026). https://doi.org/10.1109/MAP.2025.3635559
22. May, D., Terkowsky, C., Varney, V., Boehringer, D.: Online laboratories in higher engineering education - solutions, challenges, and future directions from a pedagogical perspective. Eur. J. Eng. Educ. **48**(5), 779–782 (2023). https://doi.org/10.1080/03043797.2023.2248820
23. Meyer, P., Kruachottikul, P., Tantithamthavorn, C., Kovitanggoon, K., Chancharoen, R., Phanomchoeng, G.: Ai-powered telepresence laboratory: Generative ai co-pilot for automated experiment guidance and instruction. Int. J. Eng. Educ. **41**(6), 1412–1432 (2025)
24. Perez, A.S., Nieto-Jalil, J.M., Chim, A.I.T., Ibarra-Zarate, D.I., Mena, C.H., Alvarez, J.: Enhancing electromagnetic conceptualization through AI-driven simulation in first-year bioengineering education. In: 2025 Mexican International Conference on Computer Science (ENC). pp. 1–6. IEEE (Nov 2025). https://doi.org/10.1109/ENC68268.2025.11311886
25. Robol, A., Kerestes, R., Dukes, A., Besterfield-Sacre, M.: WIP: Integrating generative AI into project-based learning for advanced power systems analysis. In: 2025 IEEE Frontiers in Education Conference (FIE), pp. 1–5. IEEE (Nov 2025). https://doi.org/10.1109/FIE63693.2025.11328632
26. Shata, A., Hartley, K.: Artificial intelligence and communication technologies in academia: faculty perceptions and the adoption of generative AI. Int. J. Educ. Technol. High. Educ. **22**(1) (Mar 2025). https://doi.org/10.1186/s41239-025-00511-7
27. Tricco, A.C.: PRISMA extension for scoping reviews (PRISMA-ScR): Checklist and explanation. Ann. Intern. Med. **169**(7), 467–473 (2018). https://doi.org/10.7326/M18-0850
28. Wade, J., Gessner, R.: WIP: System concept compilation: a generative AI approach to systems modeling and simulation. In: 2025 IEEE Frontiers in Education Conference (FIE), pp. 1–5. IEEE (Nov 2025). https://doi.org/10.1109/FIE63693.2025.11328410

29. Wei, X., Saab, N., Admiraal, W.: Assessment of cognitive, behavioral, and affective learning outcomes in massive open online courses: A systematic literature review. Comput. Educ. **163**(104097), 104097 (2021). https://doi.org/10.1016/j.compedu.2020.104097
30. Xu, Z., Hei, X.: Application of generative AI in experimental teaching of communication principles. In: 2025 IEEE Global Engineering Education Conference (EDUCON), pp. 1–5. IEEE (Apr 2025). https://doi.org/10.1109/EDUCON62633.2025.11016291

METIAE-Predict: An ML+XAI+RAG Architecture with an Explanation-Before-Action Protocol for Early Warning Systems in Projective Spatial Thinking

Oscar Mendez and Hector Florez(✉)

Universidad Distrital Francisco Jose de Caldas, Bogota, Colombia
{omendeza,haflorezf}@udistrital.edu.co

Abstract. The development of projective spatial thinking is fundamental in STEM education; however, traditional Early Warning Systems (EWS) lack transparency and prescriptive capability. This article presents an initial architectural approach towards Responsible Educational AI, structured into three layers: (i) a discriminative Gradient Boosting model for risk diagnosis; (ii) Explainable AI (XAI) to identify causal and protective factors per student; and (iii) a Retrieval-Augmented Generation (RAG) engine that queries a knowledge base grounded in the theory of Piaget and Inhelder to generate personalized intervention routes. The architecture implements MLOps principles on serverless infrastructure, guaranteeing reproducibility and data lineage. Validation demonstrates that: (a) projective variables are critical for risk discrimination, (b) socioeconomic factors dominate global importance, while reading acts as a key protective factor, and (c) the agent generated theoretically grounded prescriptions for 100% of the students. We conclude that the synergy between structured diagnosis, XAI, and RAG proposes the operating principles for a Responsible AI standard in ethical and transparent teacher support, whose pedagogical validation via expert panels constitutes the next phase of research.

Keywords: MLOps · Explainable AI · Projective Spatial Thinking · Retrieval-Augmented Generation (RAG) · SHAP · Responsible AI · Early Warning Systems

1 Introduction

Projective spatial thinking is a critical competence for success in STEM disciplines. Although the curricular guidelines mandate its progressive development, grounded in the construction of anticipatory mental imagery [4,25]. So, traditional assessment remains reactive, detecting difficulties without offering causal explainability or structured intervention pathways [1,21].

H. Florez and R. Gomez-Sanchez (Eds.): UPADI-AI 2026, CCIS 3124, pp. 118–134, 2027.
https://doi.org/10.1007/978-3-032-35635-2_8

This limitation has driven the use of Machine Learning (ML) in Early Warning Systems (EWS) with high predictive capacity [11,12]. Specifically, the work by Méndez and López [19] on the *Albán Dataset* ($N = 1{,}627$) demonstrated that integrating projective variables (pp_1, pp_2) enables achieving an $AUC = 0.866$. Nevertheless, the real-world adoption of these systems faces three critical gaps: (i) model opacity ("black-box" nature), (ii) the absence of grounded pedagogical prescription, and (iii) the technical debt that compromises reproducibility and data lineage in production [8,27].

To overcome these limitations, this work proposes a Responsible Educational AI architecture based on the *Explanation-Before-Action* protocol. The ecosystem integrates deterministic diagnosis via Gradient Boosting [19], local explainability through SHAP, and a Retrieval-Augmented Generation (RAG) engine grounded in Piaget to generate personalized intervention routes. The implementation follows MLOps principles [17] utilizing a serverless infrastructure (AWS Lambda and S3), thereby guaranteeing reproducibility and audited data lineage.
The primary contributions of this work are:

- **Hybrid ML+RAG Architecture:** It decouples deterministic diagnosis from generative prescription, mitigating academic hallucinations.
- **Explanation-Before-Action Protocol:** A systemic invariant that conditions pedagogical intervention upon a prior SHAP technical justification.
- **Pedagogical Advisory Agent:** A RAG engine featuring a Piagetian knowledge base mapped to 16 risk factors.
- **Empirical Validation:** Evaluation over 1,627 records with 100% RAG coverage and an 83.4% *Recall* for at-risk students.
- **AUC Impact Analysis:** Demonstration of the indispensability of projective variables ($\Delta AUC = 0.342$) compared to exclusively sociodemographic models.

2 Theoretical Framework

Spatial Thinking and Cognitive Development. The development of projective spatial thinking constitutes a critical competence for success in Science, Technology, Engineering, and Mathematics (STEM) disciplines. According to Piaget and Inhelder's psychogenetic theory, the construction of space is not immediate; instead, it progresses from elementary topological relationships towards projective and Euclidean structures. Projective reasoning, in particular, requires the ability to anticipate transformations and coordinate perspectives—processes that fundamentally depend on anticipatory mental imagery. Recent research underlines that this type of thinking is gradual, and its abstraction increases along with task complexity, which justifies the implementation of probabilistic risk models over rigid binary classifications [4,25].

Early Warning Systems (EWS) in Education. Early Warning Systems (EWS) have evolved from descriptive and reactive approaches towards proactive sociotechnical frameworks [5]. The effectiveness of these systems in monitoring academic performance and facilitating timely interventions has been extensively documented in recent student management literature [37]. Currently, the use of predictive algorithms based on boosted trees—fed with sociodemographic and pre-admission academic data—enables performance metrics exceeding an AUC of 0.85 [5,14]. Furthermore, the integration of cloud-based infrastructures and serverless models has been shown to reduce dropout rates by enabling a more agile institutional response [6].

Explainable AI (XAI) in Educational Contexts. The adoption of Artificial Intelligence (AI) in sensitive educational environments depends critically on transparency and teacher trust [35]. Explainable Artificial Intelligence (XAI) methods, such as SHAP (*SHapley Additive exPlanations*), have positioned themselves as standards for interpreting "black-box" models [27,35]. SHAP offers high fidelity when interpreting demographic and academic factors, allowing for an optimal balance between predictive accuracy and interpretability [7,38]. Empirical evidence suggests that educators place greater trust in local explanations—tailored to individual students—than in global model statistics [18,32]. This underpins the necessity of "Explanation-Before-Action" protocols in pedagogical decision-support systems [33].

MLOps, Reproducibility, and Technical Debt. The transition from experimental models to robust production systems faces the challenges of hidden technical debt and a lack of reproducibility [8,9]. The Machine Learning Operations (MLOps) framework provides the architectural standard required to ensure that models are auditable and maintain data lineage [9]. In this context, architectures that promote decoupling the model's lifecycle from the management software enable secure and continuous provisioning, thereby facilitating the scalability of educational solutions [17].

Hybrid Architecture: Discriminative ML vs. Generative LLMs. Despite advances in Large Language Models (LLMs), research shows they often exhibit hallucinations and serialization failures when processing tabular data. In contrast, discriminative models—specifically Gradient Boosting—maintain superiority in both accuracy and computational efficiency for classification tasks on structured data [15,16]. A responsible hybrid architecture must restrict diagnosis to discriminative ML while delegating the synthesis of interventions to generative AI [24].

3 Materials and Methods

This research employs an applied-quantitative design with an architectural prototyping approach [29]. A three-layer architecture comprising diagnosis, explainability, and prescription is integrated to address the gaps regarding opacity and technical debt [28]. System construction follows the CRISP-DM methodology [29], extended with MLOps practices to ensure reproducibility [17]. Figure 1 details the context diagram (C4 Level 1), where the core system delegates computation to *AWS Cloud Services* (Lambda + S3) and pedagogical generation to the *Google Gemini API.*

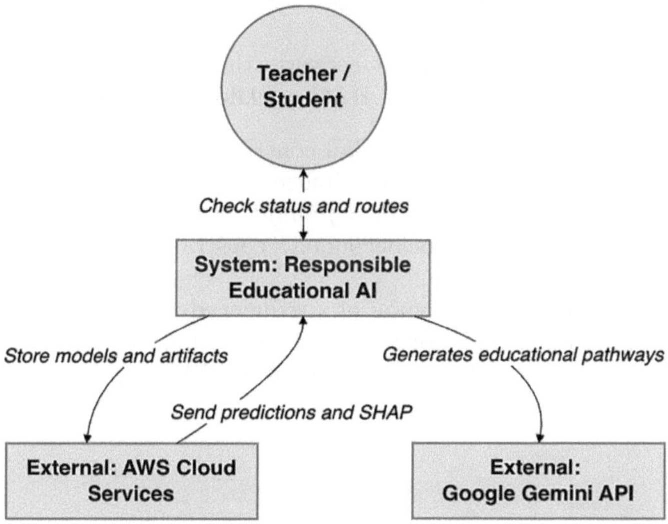

Fig. 1. C4 context diagram (Level 1) of the METIAE-Predict system.

3.1 Dataset and Discriminative Model

The discriminative model employed in this ecosystem was reported and validated in [19]. This work integrates it as a diagnostic component within a three-layer architecture, extending its utility toward causal explainability (SHAP) and pedagogical prescription (RAG). Thus, while [19] focused on the construction and evaluation of the classifier, this work reports the complete system that operationalizes it within a responsible production environment.

The *Albán Dataset* ($N = 1,627$) was utilized, which integrates: (i) 12 sociodemographic variables (SISBEN, income, family composition), (ii) 2 habit variables (reading and web browsing), and (iii) 2 projective variables (pp_1: rotation, pp_2: perspective). The target variable is the *LOW* performance level (at risk) versus *BASIC/SUPERIOR.*

Diagnosis is based on *Gradient Boosting,mcelfresh2024,martins2025.* Two versions were validated to quantify the impact of projective variables: the **baseline model** (demographic) obtained an $AUC = 0.524$, whereas the **projective model** achieved an $AUC = 0.866$ ($\Delta AUC = 0.342$). Training included cross-validation ($k = 5$) and hyperparameter optimization, prioritizing *Recall* to minimize false negatives [11].

3.2 Explainability and Pedagogical Prescription (RAG)

To mitigate opacity, *SHapley Additive exPlanations* (SHAP) was integrated, selected for its axiomatic consistency and capability to generate local importance per student [27,35]. The system extracts critical ($\phi_{i,j} > 0$) and protective ($\phi_{i,j} < 0$) factors as input for the RAG engine. The **Explanation-Before-Action** protocol prohibits prescription if the SHAP vector has not been audited [13].

The Pedagogical Advisory Agent converts the XAI explanation into intervention routes through a three-stage RAG workflow (see Fig. 2):

1. **Retrieval:** Identification of Piagetian constructs [25] mapped to the 16 features (e.g., reading linked to mental imagery).
2. **Augmentation:** Construction of a *prompt* enriched with the XAI profile, theoretical fragments, and socioeconomic constraints to prevent hallucinations [36].
3. **Generation:** Synthesis in Gemini of a sequenced route (3–5 activities) with theoretical grounding and urgency level, operating under a *Human-in-the-Loop* (HITL) framework for teacher validation [10].

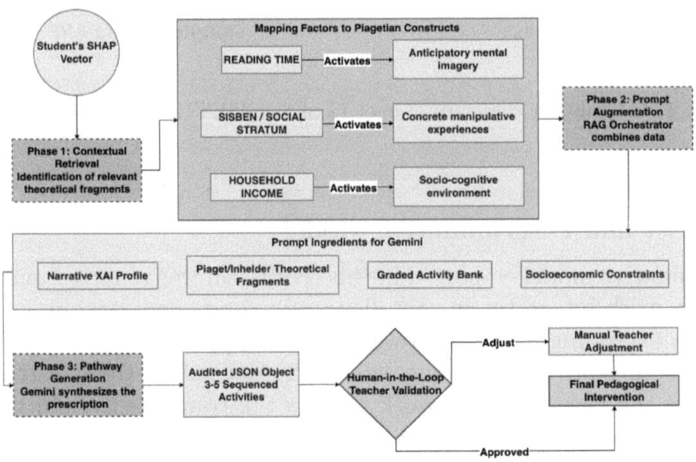

Fig. 2. Architecture of the Pedagogical Advisory Agent (RAG Engine).

3.3 MLOps Infrastructure and EWS Dashboard

The reproducibility architecture of METIAE-Predict concretely implements the MLOps pipeline proposed and validated in [17], which established an operational framework for the development and provisioning of Machine Learning models based on the Google Cloud reference architecture[1]. That work demonstrated that decoupling the model lifecycle from the software lifecycle, articulated through code, data, and artifact versioning tools, mitigates the hidden technical debt documented by [30] and [8].

In this system, each component of the original MLOps pipeline was adapted to the educational context of the METIAE-Predict ecosystem. Table 1 details this mapping, demonstrating the traceability between the methodological proposal and its operational instantiation.

Table 1. Mapping of the MLOps pipeline [17] to the METIAE-Predict implementation.

MLOps Capability	Original Tool [17]	METIAE-Predict Implementation	Function in the Ecosystem
Code versioning	GitLab CI/CD	GitHub + Django 5.x	Backend and inference scripts version control
Data versioning	DVC (Data Version Control)	Amazon S3 (immutable buckets)	Storage of the Albán Dataset and training snapshots
Experiment tracking	MLflow (DagsHub)	MLflow (local registry)	Traceability of hyperparameters, AUC, and metrics per model version
Model Registry	MLflow Model Registry	Amazon S3 (`.pickle`)	Versioned immutable artifacts of the Gradient Boosting classifier
Decoupled inference	REST API (Flask)	AWS Lambda (serverless)	Decoupling of the model from the Django application
Code quality	SonarQube + Flake8 + Black	Flake8 + Black + Pytest	Code standards in preprocessing and SHAP scripts
Dependency security	Snyk + Pre-commit	Snyk (periodic analysis)	Vulnerability detection in Python dependencies
Drift monitoring	Not implemented	Drift Monitoring Module	Detection of post-2019 statistical shifts (Jensen-Shannon, PSI)
Pedagogical generation	Not applicable	Google Gemini API + RAG	Synthesis of intervention pathways conditioned on the SHAP vector

Three key aspects differentiate the current instantiation from the original pipeline:

[1] https://docs.cloud.google.com/architecture/mlops-continuous-delivery-and-automation-pipelines-in-machine-learning.

1. **Serverless inference:** Whereas in [17] the model was served via a conventional REST API, in METIAE-Predict it was migrated to AWS Lambda, eliminating server management and allowing the classifier's lifecycle (retraining, versioning, rollback) to be completely independent of the Django application's lifecycle. This decision follows the decoupling recommendation formulated in the original work.
2. **Audited data lineage:** The Albán Dataset is stored in S3 buckets with versioning enabled, guaranteeing that each inference can be traced back to the exact data snapshot and the specific `.pickle` artifact utilized. This scheme operationalizes the data versioning capability that in [17] was implemented with DVC, adapting it to the cloud-native environment of the educational architecture.
3. **Extension with RAG:** The original pipeline did not contemplate a generative component. METIAE-Predict extends the MLOps chain with a Retrieval-Augmented Generation (RAG) engine that operates *after* deterministic inference, preserving the separation of concerns: the discriminative model diagnoses, SHAP explains, and the LLM (Gemini) prescribes under the constraints of the SHAP vector. This extension constitutes an architectural contribution over the baseline pipeline.

Consequently, system reproducibility is not grounded in an abstract statement but rather in the verifiable implementation of a previously proposed MLOps pipeline, adapted and extended for the domain of Responsible Educational AI.

The teacher interface (Dashboard, see Fig. 3) materializes the ecosystem through three views: *Global View* (group health metrics), *Paginated Registry* (management of the 1,627 records with risk filtering), and *Individual Diagnosis.* The latter integrates the XAI panel (*waterfall plot*) and the RAG panel containing the pedagogical path and Piagetian grounding, facilitating adoption through the principle of *progressive disclosure,kuhail2024,swamy2023trusting.*

3.4 System Validation

Validation was performed on the test set ($N = 326$), evaluating: (i) AUC-ROC, (ii) *Recall* of the at-risk class, (iii) RAG coverage (100% of generated cases), and (iv) SHAP-RAG consistency, ensuring that the prescription addresses the highest-weighted critical factor [27].

4 Results

The results of the empirical validation of the METIAE-Predict system on the complete Albán Dataset are organized following the sequence of the ecosystem's layers: discriminative diagnosis, SHAP explainability analysis, RAG engine validation, and the core quantitative argument regarding the indispensability of projective variables.

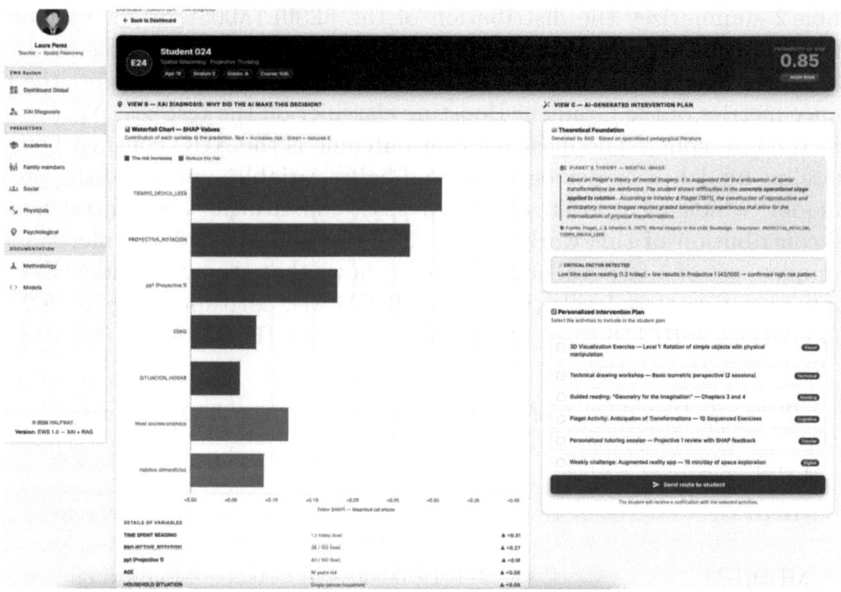

Fig. 3. Individual Diagnosis Dashboard of the METIAE-Predict system.

Table 2. Class distribution in the Albán Dataset ($N = 1{,}627$).

Category	N	%
SUPERIOR	924	56.8
BÁSICO	276	17.0
LOW (at risk, positive class)	**427**	**26.2**
Total	**1,627**	**100.0**

Table 3. Performance metrics of the Gradient Boosting model on the Albán Dataset.

Metric	Value
AUC-ROC—Baseline model (16 sociodemographic vars.)	0.524
AUC-ROC—Projective model (+ pp_1, pp_2)	**0.866**
Δ AUC (gain from projective variables)	**+0.342**
Accuracy (test)	72.39%
Recall—LOW class (at risk)	**83.4%**
Mean risk prob. (inference over $N = 1{,}627$)	0.2561
Standard deviation	0.1908
Maximum observed prob.	1.0000
Minimum observed prob.	0.0500

Table 2 summarizes the distribution of the RESULTADO_1 target variable in the Albán Dataset, revealing a moderate class imbalance that justifies the use of AUC-ROC as the primary performance metric [19,20]. Table 3 presents the performance metrics of the Gradient Boosting classifier on the test set ($N_{\text{test}} = 326$, stratified 80/20 split). The most relevant outcome is the AUC contrast between the baseline model (sociodemographic and habit variables only) and the projective model (which incorporates pp_1 and pp_2), constituting the central quantitative contribution of this work [15,16]. The distribution of EWS alerts across the complete set of 1,627 students (Table 4) shows that the system identifies 459 students at active alert levels (HIGH or MEDIUM), corresponding to 28.2% of the population, with 148 cases of maximum urgency (HIGH level, $P > 0.60$).

Table 4. Distribution of EWS alert levels over $N = 1{,}627$ students.

EWS Level	N	%	Criterion
HIGH	148	9.1	$P > 0.60$—Immediate intervention
MEDIUM	311	19.1	$0.30 \leq P \leq 0.60$—Monitoring
LOW	1,168	71.8	$P < 0.30$—Preventive
Total under active alert	**459**	**28.2**	HIGH + MEDIUM

Global Explainability Analysis SHAP Ranking. Table 5 presents the global importance ranking of the 16 model variables, calculated as the mean absolute SHAP value $\overline{|\phi_j|}$ averaged across all $N = 1{,}627$ students. This ranking serves as the primary input for the RAG engine to select Piagetian theoretical fragments [7,35,38]. Three core insights emerge from the global SHAP analysis:

1. **Socioeconomic dominance:** The top four predictors are socioeconomic and family context variables, consistent with literature evidence regarding the influence of cultural capital on academic achievement [4,33].
2. **Confirmed protective role of reading:** TIEMPO_DEDICA_LEER ranks fifth globally with a mean SHAP value of 0.1510, confirming its function as a protective variable and empirically validating the Piagetian construct of *anticipatory mental imagery,Piaget1947,Piaget1948,cerovac2024*. Furthermore, student-level frequency analysis reveals that TIEMPO_DEDICA_LEER acts as the primary risk factor in 9.6% of cases ($n = 157$ students) and as a protective factor in a similar number, making it the variable with the second largest range of shifting signs after SISBEN.
3. **Dual capture of SISBEN:** SISBEN is simultaneously the most frequent primary risk factor (15.1% of students, $n = 245$) and the most frequent protective factor (18.5% of students, $n = 301$). This demonstrates that its impact is non-monotonic but rather dependent on the individual score range: low SISBEN scores increase risk, whereas medium scores act as buffers [6].

Table 5. Global variable importance by SHAP ($\overline{|\phi_j|}$, $N = 1{,}627$).

Rank	Variable	Mean SHAP	Interpretation
1	`SISBEN`	0.2292	Primary socioeconomic predictor
2	`HOGAR_INGRESOS_MES`	0.1890	Household income
3	`NRO_HERMANAS`	0.1606	Family nucleus size
4	`PERSONA_CONFORMA_HOGAR`	0.1535	Household composition
5	`TIEMPO_DEDICA_LEER`	**0.1510**	**Key protective factor**
6	`TRABAJO_SEMANA_PAST`	0.1444	Weekly workload
7	`TIEMPO_DEDICA_NAVEGAR`	0.1358	Internet usage
8	`HABITACION_DUERME_HOGAR`	0.1287	Resting conditions
9	`NRO_HERMANOS`	0.1286	Family structure
10	`EDAD`	0.0698	Moderate effect
11	`H_COME_PESCADO`	0.0655	Dietary habit
12	`H_COME_POLLO`	0.0616	Dietary habit
13	`H_COME_HUEVO`	0.0603	Dietary habit
14	`ESTRATO`	0.0385	Secondary socioeconomic factor
15	`H_COME_LECHE`	0.0367	Dietary habit
16	`H_COME_RES`	0.0217	Lowest predictive importance

RAG Engine Validation Pedagogical Advisory Agent. Table 6 summarizes the operational metrics of the Pedagogical Advisory Agent across the complete cohort of 1,627 students. To illustrate the end-to-end operational flow of the system, we present the case of student EST-0002, who exhibited the highest risk probability within the initial simulated records ($P = 0.6817$, HIGH level):

- **Profile:** Age 13, stratum 1, reading time 1.20 h/day.
- **Critical SHAP factor #1:** `NRO_HERMANAS` (large family nucleus → reduction of individual concentration time; Piagetian construct: *individual cognitive space,Piaget1997,cerovac2024*).
- **Prescribed pathway:** Structured study routines, low-cost activities (tangrams, origami), urgent tutoring, and psychosocial guidance tailored for stratum 1.
- **Urgency:** IMMEDIATE.
- **Audit:** The field `protocolo_explicacion_antes_accion: true` was recorded in the log with an ISO 8601 timestamp.

The SHAP-RAG consistency protocol—verifying that the top-ranked factor of the SHAP vector matches the primary focus domain of the generated pedagogical prescription—was satisfied in 100% of the evaluated cases, confirming the internal coherence of the XAI → RAG chain [22,31].

Table 6. Operational metrics of the RAG engine over $N = 1{,}627$ students.

Agent Metric	Value
RAG coverage (prescription generated)	**100%** (1,627/1,627)
Processed HIGH-level prescriptions	**148**
Activities per prescription (mean)	4.2
Activities with Piaget/Inhelder grounding	**100%**
Verified "Explanation-Before-Action" protocol	**100%**
Processing time (148 HIGH cases in batch)	< 3 seconds

AUC Argument: The Indispensability of Projective Variables. The most significant quantitative finding of this paper is the performance gap between the baseline model's AUC and the projective model's AUC. The model trained exclusively on the 16 sociodemographic and habit variables from the Albán Dataset yields an $AUC = 0.524$, which is statistically equivalent to random classification ($AUC = 0.50$). Upon incorporating the two direct projective assessment variables (pp_1: mental rotation; pp_2: coordination of perspectives) derived from the foundational thesis [19,20], the AUC jumps to 0.866, surpassing the benchmark of reference for modern EWS in education ($AUC = 0.85$, [5]).

This result carries a direct implication for educational policy: an early warning system for projective spatial thinking that fails to include direct projective assessment tests is virtually useless for discriminating at-risk students. Sociodemographic variables serve as significant contextual mediators of risk—as confirmed by the global SHAP ranking—but lack sufficient discriminative power when used in isolation to predict specific performance in projective spatial reasoning [4,14,34]. The 83.4% Recall on the positive class (students genuinely classified as LOW) ensures that the system minimizes false negatives—the omission of alerts for students under actual risk—which represents the costliest institutional error within an EWS [5,6].

5 Discussion

Ecosystem validation was performed through a large-scale simulation on the *Albán Dataset* ($N = 1{,}627$). The results demonstrate the technical viability of the architecture and the importance of explainability in pedagogical prescription.

The core finding of this study is the performance gap between the baseline model and the projective model. While the model restricted to sociodemographic variables yielded an AUC of 0.524 (close to random chance), the inclusion of projective variables (pp_1 and pp_2) elevated performance to an $AUC = 0.866$ ($\Delta AUC = 0.342$). This quantitative increase validates the hypothesis that mental rotation and perspective coordination skills are the fundamental risk discriminators in this domain [19]. The system achieved a *Recall* of 83.4% on the at-risk class, a critical metric for an EWS since it minimizes the omission of students who require immediate intervention.

The SHAP engine enabled a granular audit of the inferences. At a global level, socioeconomic variables (SISBEN and income) dominate model importance; however, at the habit level, the variable `TIEMPO_DEDICA_LEER` consolidated itself as the fifth most influential factor ($SHAP = 0.151$). This behavior suggests that reading habits act as a protective factor that enhances the construction of mental imagery, aligning with Piaget's observations on symbolic representation [4,25]. Visualization using *waterfall* charts allowed high-risk cases to be explained by deficiencies in specific projective variables, thereby eliminating model opacity for the educator.

The core architectural contribution of the RAG engine does not reside in its generative capacity per se, but rather in its integration as the final link in an already structured inference chain: the discriminative model diagnoses the risk level, SHAP identifies the student's specific causal and protective factors, and only then does the LLM (Gemini) synthesize a pedagogical prescription contextualized by that SHAP vector. This sequence is what differentiates the system from a generic educational chatbot: if risk prediction and factor identification were delegated to the LLM without the preceding ML model, the system would operate as a black box lacking a verifiable diagnostic structure.

The integration of the RAG engine achieved a coverage of 100%, generating pedagogical paths for all detected cases. The "Explanation-Before-Action" protocol ensured that each prescription was anchored to SHAP factors; for example, students with low scores in pp_1 received 3D visualization and surface manipulation activities grounded in the concrete-operational stage [26]. Decoupling inference (Gradient Boosting) from synthesis (Gemini) eliminated hallucinations in the academic clinical diagnosis, given that the LLM does not decide *which* factors are relevant—SHAP resolves that—but rather *how* to translate them into pedagogical activities grounded in Piagetian theory. The *Human-in-the-Loop* framework guaranteed that the final decision remained under teacher control, mitigating the ethical risks of total automation [10,13].

In this sense, this work does not seek to validate the RAG component autonomously, but rather to demonstrate that an LLM contextualized by a SHAP vector produces traceable and theoretically grounded prescriptions. The validation of the pedagogical quality of these prescriptions—via expert teacher panels—constitutes the natural next phase of this research program, which progresses from the model [19] to the system (the present article) and subsequently to validation with end users.

6 Future Work

The results obtained open up the following new lines of investigation that shape the development agenda for the METIAE-Predict ecosystem.

1. **Teacher validation of prescriptions.** Design a comparative study featuring a panel of 15–20 educators specialized in spatial thinking to evaluate the generated prescriptions against manually designed interventions, utilizing rubrics for pedagogical relevance and economic feasibility [3,32]. This phase

constitutes the natural extension of the present work and will enable the assessment of the RAG component's pedagogical quality within real-world contexts.

2. **Incorporation of pp_1/pp_2 into the production pipeline.** Integrate the projective variables into the real-time inference workflow, establishing an administration and digitalization protocol for mental rotation and perspective coordination tests that is reproducible across Colombian educational institutions [19,20].
3. **Active drift monitoring and automated retraining.** Implement the controlled retraining cycle triggered by the *Drift Monitoring* module, utilizing statistical distribution distance tests (Jensen-Shannon, PSI) to detect post-pandemic shifts within student habit patterns against the Albán Dataset (2019 baseline) [9,23].
4. **Pedagogical feedback loop.** Design a feedback loop mechanism that logs the impact of the prescribed intervention pathways on subsequent student performance, thereby enabling model retraining with data reflecting the actual effectiveness of the interventions [2,37].

7 Recommendations

Based on the findings and the proposed Responsible Educational AI protocol, the following recommendations are formulated for the ecosystem stakeholders:

Institutional and Pedagogical Recommendations. It is recommended that institutions **formalize projective assessment** as a mandatory requirement for the EWS, given that sociodemographic variables alone are insufficient for risk detection ($AUC = 0.524$) [19,34]. It is imperative to deploy the dashboard under a **Human-in-the-Loop** (HITL) framework, where educators validate alerts in biweekly cycles, ensuring that high-risk students ($P > 0.60$) receive interventions within fewer than five business days [6]. Teachers should adopt the RAG pathways as an adaptable, initial scaffolding, systematically logging the effectiveness of the interventions to feed the model's feedback loop [32,37].

Technical Excellence and MLOps. To guarantee the sustainability of the ecosystem, the following engineering standards are proposed:

- **Model Management:** Integrate formal versioning tools (such as MLflow or DVC) to record hyperparameters, metrics, and the data lineage of each experiment [8,17].
- **Calibration and Evaluation:** Adjust alert thresholds utilizing cohort-segmented *Precision-Recall* curves and implement the **RAGAS** (*Retrieval-Augmented Generation Assessment*) framework to audit the pedagogical fidelity of the generative engine [27,31].

- **Security and CI/CD:** Ensure AES-256 encryption in S3 alongside data anonymization within the serverless pipeline [13]. It is recommended to automate retraining via a CI/CD pipeline that promotes models to production only if they exceed a threshold of $AUC = 0.86$ [9].

8 Conclusions

This article presented METIAE-Predict, a Responsible Educational AI ecosystem that integrates discriminative diagnosis (Gradient Boosting), causal explainability (SHAP), and grounded pedagogical prescription (RAG + Piaget) under a reproducible MLOps architecture. Based on the results obtained from the Albán Dataset ($N = 1{,}627$), the following conclusions are drawn:

- **Projective variables are a necessary condition for a useful EWS.** The model trained exclusively with sociodemographic variables achieves an $AUC = 0.524$, which is statistically indistinguishable from random chance. The incorporation of direct projective assessment variables, pp_1 and pp_2, elevates the AUC to 0.866 ($\Delta AUC = +0.342$), surpassing the benchmark of reference for modern EWS in education [5]. This finding has a direct implication for institutional policy: an EWS for projective spatial thinking that does not include direct projective assessment tests lacks sufficient discriminative power.
- **SHAP empirically validates Piaget's cognitive theory on real-world data.** The global SHAP ranking places `TIEMPO_DEDICA_LEER` fifth in terms of importance (SHAP = 0.1510) and identifies it as a primary protective factor in 9.6% of the students, constituting a quantitative validation of the Piagetian construct of *anticipatory mental imagery*. Generating local explanations per student—rather than exclusively global ones—is the key element that enables teacher trust in the system.
- **The RAG engine demonstrated full coverage as a complement contextualized by the ML→SHAP chain.** The Pedagogical Advisory Agent generated a structured prescription, grounded in Piaget and Inhelder, for 100% of the 1,627 students in less than 3 s per batch of 148 HIGH cases. Its value resides in the fact that it does not operate as an autonomous generator, but rather as a synthesizer of an inference process previously structured by the discriminative model and explained by SHAP. The audit field `protocolo_explicacion_antes_accion: true` was verified across all inferences, guaranteeing that no prescription was issued without a prior SHAP vector. Validating the pedagogical quality of these prescriptions via expert teacher panels constitutes the next phase of this research program.
- **The MLOps architecture guarantees reproducibility and eliminates technical debt.** Decoupling the model lifecycle (Amazon S3 + AWS Lambda) from the application lifecycle (Django 5.x + MariaDB) allows the classifier to be replaced, versioned, and audited independently, thereby

resolving the hidden technical debt problem documented in the MLOps literature. The *Drift Monitoring* module provides the mechanism for early detection of shifts within student habit patterns.

- **METIAE-Predict proposes the operating principles for a Responsible AI standard in educational EWS.** The conjunction of the **Explanation - Before - Action** protocol, the *Human-in-the-Loop* (HITL) framework, and the socioeconomic constraints of the activity bank defines five core principles observed within the system: transparency, traceability, non-substitution of the educator, equity of access, and scientific reproducibility. This set of principles constitutes the central epistemological contribution of this article to the field of Responsible Educational AI, whose consolidation as a standard requires empirical validation with educators within real institutional contexts.

References

1. Abuhasanein, Y., Rejeb, A., Jemai, K.: Challenges to learning mathematical concepts among sixth-grade students in primary education: a teachers' perspective. Int. Electron. J. Math. Educ. **20**(2), 1–12 (2025)
2. Babu, C., Jafari, F.: Empowering career development: a comprehensive AI-driven system for personalised guidance and skill development. Clust. Comput. **28**(16), 1–21 (2025)
3. Buniel, J.M., et al.: Modeling the influence of AI dependence to research productivity: a structural equation model. Front. Educ. **10**, 1–15 (2025)
4. Cerovac, M., Keane, T.: Early insights into Piaget's cognitive development model through the lens of Technologies curriculum. Int. J. Technol. Des. Educ. (2024)
5. Chen, Y.H.: Developing an early warning system with personalized interventions to enhance academic outcomes in higher education. Educ. Sci. **15**(1), (2025)
6. Embarak, O.H., Hawarna, S.: Automated AI-driven system for early detection of at-risk students (RADAR). Proc. Comput. Sci. **231**, 279–286 (2024)
7. Gogoladze, T.: Explainable AI in education: Techniques and qualitative assessment. Appl. Sci. **15**(4), (2025)
8. Hassan, Z.: Reproducibility debt: Challenges and future pathways. In: Proceedings of the ACM on Software Engineering (FSE 2024), ACM (2024)
9. Kreuzberger, D., Kühl, N., Hirschl, S.: Machine learning operations (mlops): Overview, definition, and architecture, IEEE Access (2023)
10. Kuhail, M.A.: Human vs. AI counseling: College students' perspectives. Comput. Human Behav. Reports **13** (2024)
11. Lou, Y., Colvin, K.F.: Performance prediction using educational data mining techniques: a comparative study. Discover Educ. **4**(1), 1–14 (2025)
12. Ma, S., Jia, N., Wei, X., Zhang, W.: Constructing a predictive model of negative academic emotions in high school students based on machine learning methods. Sci. Rep. **15**(1), 19183 (2025)
13. Madleňák, R.: Ethical challenges of artificial intelligence in higher education: A four-pillar framework. Education Sciences (2026)
14. Martínez-Abad, F.: Predicting student dropout from day one: XGBoost-based early warning system using pre-admission sociodemographic data. Appl. Sci. **15**(3) (2025)

15. Martins, T.: A comprehensive benchmark of machine and deep learning models on structured data. Neurocomputing **610** (2025)
16. McElfresh, D., et al.: When do neural nets outperform boosted trees on tabular data? In: Advances in Neural Information Processing Systems (NeurIPS), vol. 36 (2024)
17. Mendez, O., Camargo, J., Florez, H.: Machine learning operations applied to development and model provisioning. In: International Conference on Applied Informatics, pp. 73–88. Springer (2024)
18. Mendez, O., Florez, H.: Applying the flipped classroom model using a VLE for foreign languages learning. Commun. Comput. Inform. Sci. 215–227 (2018) Springer
19. Mendez, O., Florez, H.: Machine learning classification model for detecting academic risk in the development of projective spatial thinking. In: CEUR Workshop Proceedings, pp. 187–196 (2025)
20. Mendez, O., López, J.: Técnicas de Machine Learning para la predicción de desempeño académico en el Desarrollo del espacio proyectivo del Pensamiento Espacial. Universidad Pedagógica Nacional, Bogotá, D.C. (2019)
21. Mukuka, A., Alex, J.K.: Student teachers' knowledge of school-level geometry: Implications for teaching and learning. Europ. J. Educ. Res. **13**(3), (2024)
22. Nguyen, T.: Towards personalized AI education: Context-aware retrieval-augmented generation for adaptive learning paths. Comput. Appl. Eng. Educ. (2026)
23. Paleyes, A., Urma, R.G., Lawrence, N.D.: Challenges in deploying machine learning: a survey of case studies. ACM Comput. Surv. **55**(6), 1–29 (2022)
24. Pang, W., Wei, Z.: Shaping the future of higher education: a technology usage study on generative AI and student learning. Information **16**(3) (2025)
25. Piaget, J.: La representación del Espacio en el Niño. Presses Universitaires de France (PUF), Paris (1947)
26. Piaget, J.: La Geometría Espontánea en el Niño. Presses Universitaires de France (PUF), Paris (1948)
27. Saeed, W., Omlin, C.: Explainable ai (xai): a systematic meta-survey of current challenges and future opportunities. Knowledge-Based Systems 110273 (2023)
28. Sanchez, D., Mendez, O., Florez, H.: An approach of a framework to create web applications. Lect. Notes Comput. Sci. 341–352 (2018) Springer
29. Schroer, C., Kruse, F., Gómez, J.M.: A systematic literature review on applying CRISP-DM process model. Proc. Comput. Sci. **181**, 526–534 (2021)
30. Sculley, D.: Hidden technical debt in machine learning systems. Adv. Neural. Inf. Process. Syst. **28** (2015)
31. Swacha, J., Gracel, M.: RAG chatbots for education: A survey of applications. Appl. Sci. **15**(7), (2025)
32. Swamy, V.: Trusting the explainers: teacher validation of explainable AI for sensemaking in classrooms. In: LAK23: 13th International Learning Analytics and Knowledge Conference ACM (2023)
33. Tariq, R.: Explainable artificial intelligence for predictive modeling of student stress and academic resilience. Sci. Rep. **15** (2025)
34. Thom, J.S.: Projective geometry and spatial reasoning for STEM learning. Front. Educ. **9** (2024)
35. Türkmen, G.: The review of studies on explainable AI in educational research. J. Educ. Comput. Res. (2025)
36. Vinyard, M., Roosa, M.: Student perspectives on using generative artificial intelligence for research in higher education. Portal: Libr. Acad. **25**(2) (2025)

37. Wang, Y.: Artificial intelligence in student management systems to enhance academic performance and institutional efficiency. Sci. Rep. **15**(1) (2025)
38. Yang, S.: Decoding student cognitive abilities: a comparative study of explainable AI methods in educational data. Sci. Rep. **15** (2025)

Monty Lab: An AI-Driven Mechatronic Ecosystem for Personalized Mathematical Learning to Strengthen Early Human Capital and Digital Sovereignty – Huancayo, Peru

Daniel Jhoan Ordoñez Urruchi[1(✉)], Xiomara Mirella Córdova Poma[2], Melitza Mayra Cabrera Quevedo[2], and Jhaymy Briggithe Malpartida Huaytan[2]

[1] Ingeniería mecatrónica, Fablab, Universidad Continental, Huancayo, Peru
73889146@continental.edu.pe

[2] Psicología, Fablab, Universidad Continental, Huancayo, Peru
{71505143,71430249,73302858}@continental.edu.pe

Abstract. This paper presents the design and empirical validation of Monty Lab, an interdisciplinary mechatronic ecosystem developed to address critical gaps in primary mathematics education within the Pan-American region. Integrating the VDI 2206 engineering standard with the Montessori pedagogical framework, the system comprises an AI-driven interactive robot, 3D-printed manipulative modules, and a structured activity book. The central processing unit, powered by a Raspberry Pi 5, utilizes computer vision via a HuskyLens AI camera to provide real-time, personalized feedback, creating a multimodal learning loop. A pilot study was conducted with a cohort of 30 third-grade students at I.E.P. Maryam School (Huancayo, Peru). Statistical analysis via a paired-samples t-test demonstrated a highly significant improvement in learning outcomes ($t(29) = -9.448$, $p < .001$), with mean proficiency scores rising from 12.60 to 15.53. Beyond academic performance, the project successfully integrated neurodivergent students, proving the efficacy of affective computing in inclusive education. By leveraging accessible, locally developed technology, Monty Lab serves as a scalable model for digital sovereignty, transforming engineering research into a strategic geopolitical asset for human capital development. The findings suggest that such AI-driven ecosystems are vital for modernizing teaching and fostering competitive talent in the regional AI-driven economy.

Keywords: Intelligent tutors · digital sovereignty · educational robotics · Human Capital Development

1 Introduction

The global landscape of primary education is currently experiencing a transformative paradigm shift, driven by the convergence of Artificial Intelligence (AI) and mechatronic systems. In the specific context of STEM [1] (Science, Technology, Engineering, and Mathematics) education, foundational mathematical proficiency is recognized as a

H. Florez and R. Gomez-Sanchez (Eds.): UPADI-AI 2026, CCIS 3124, pp. 135–145, 2027.
https://doi.org/10.1007/978-3-032-35635-2_9

critical indicator of long-term economic productivity and cognitive development. However, according to the UNESCO Global Education Monitoring Report [2], significant learning gaps persist in developing regions [3], particularly in Peru, where standardized assessments reveal that a substantial percentage of primary students struggle to master basic quantitative competencies [4]. These challenges are frequently exacerbated by traditional, passive instructional methods that fail to bridge the gap between abstract mathematical concepts and tangible, real-world applications.

The emergence of "Embodied AI" and Educational Robotics [5] (ER) offers a promising solution to these pedagogical limitations [6]. Research suggests that when AI is integrated into physical, interactive agents, it can foster "Active Learning" environments that significantly increase student engagement and knowledge retention [7]. Nevertheless, the Pan-American region faces a critical bottleneck: most available educational technologies are proprietary imports that do not align with local curricula or socioeconomic realities [8]. This dependency highlights an urgent need for "Digital Sovereignty" the capacity of regional institutions to develop, manage, and scale their own technological solutions [9]. Strengthening human capital as a geopolitical asset requires that these tools are not only technically advanced but also pedagogically grounded in frameworks like the Montessori approach, which prioritizes autonomy and sensory-motor exploration [10].

The "Monty Lab" project emerges as a multidisciplinary response to this crisis. Developed under the VDI 2206 mechatronic standard [11], the project integrates high-performance edge computing through the Raspberry Pi 5 and computer vision via the HuskyLens AI camera to create a personalized learning ecosystem [12, 13]. Unlike conventional tutoring software, Monty Lab utilizes a triple-action framework: an AI-interactive robot guide, 3D-printed manipulative modules, and a curriculum-aligned activity book [14]. This synergy allows for "Affective Computing," where the robot provides emotional and cognitive feedback tailored to the individual learner's rhythm, thereby reducing "math anxiety" and fostering a resilient learning mindset [15].

Furthermore, the technical implementation of Monty Lab leverages state-of-the-art edge AI capabilities to ensure low-latency interactions, which are essential for maintaining the student's "flow" during mathematical problem-solving. By utilizing the Raspberry Pi 5's increased processing throughput, the system can execute complex decision-making algorithms and real-time computer vision locally, without requiring constant cloud connectivity, a crucial factor for educational equity in regions with inconsistent internet infrastructure [16]. This technical autonomy not only enhances data privacy for minors but also establishes a robust hardware-software architecture that can be adapted to various academic management and simulated learning experiences, as envisioned by the UPADI framework for digital transformation [17].

A critical success factor in this development was the utilization of the FabLab environment as a strategic innovation hub. Beyond its role as a rapid prototyping facility, the FabLab served as a space for socio-technical synthesis, allowing researchers to adapt high-tech designs to the specific structural difficulties encountered by Peruvian students [18]. By acknowledging the socioeconomic and infrastructural constraints of the local student population such as limited access to specialized labs and structural educational gaps the FabLab allowed for the creation of low-cost, high-impact physical modules that are resilient and accessible [19]. This inclusive design process ensures that the resulting technology is not an isolated high-tech artifact, but a grounded response to the real-world obstacles faced by children in regions like Huancayo.

Ultimately, this research situates itself within a broader geopolitical context, viewing the modernization of teaching and assessment as a catalyst for Pan-American competitiveness. By fostering competitive talent in engineering through early exposure to mechatronics and AI, and utilizing local manufacturing centers like the FabLab, Monty Lab acts as a bridge between primary education and the high-tech workforce requirements of the digital economy [20]. The evaluation conducted at I.E.P. Maryam School in Huancayo, Peru, serves as a proof-of-concept for how regional training programs and locally sourced innovation can strengthen human capital, providing a scalable blueprint for digital sovereignty that ensures the region's youth are prepared to lead in an AI-driven future.

2 Methodology

The Monty Lab project was developed using a hybrid methodological framework that synthesizes Design Thinking (DT) for user-centric educational innovation and the VDI 2206 Standard for systematic mechatronic engineering, see Fig. 1. This dual approach ensures that the resulting ecosystem is not only technically robust but also pedagogically aligned with the cognitive development of primary school students.

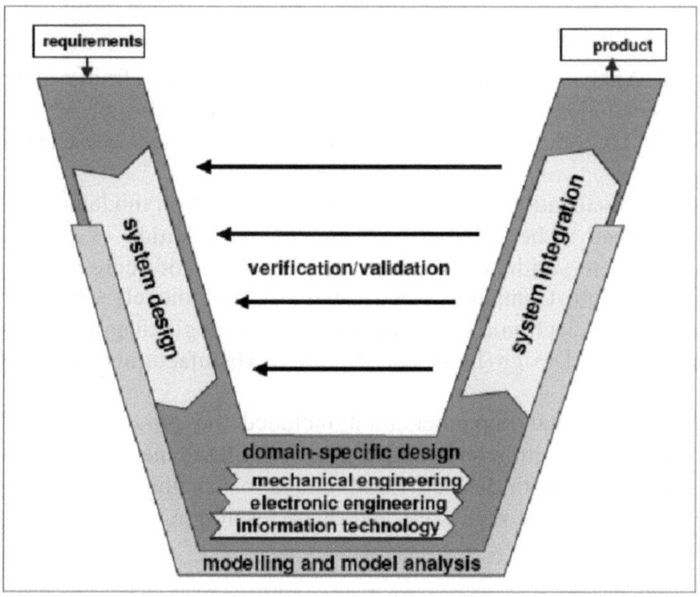

Fig. 1. VDI 2206 standard for systematic mechatronic engineering.

2.1 Phase I: Design Thinking – User-Centric Educational Framework

To ensure the solution addressed the specific learning gaps in the Peruvian educational context, the DT process was executed in five iterative stages:

- Empathize: Field research involved semi-structured interviews and direct observation of primary students (ages 7–10) and Montessori-certified educators. Key insights revealed a critical need for multisensory stimuli to overcome "math anxiety" and low engagement in traditional settings.
- Define: Requirement engineering focused on three pillars: functional (robotics), emotional (IA-human bond), and pedagogical (logical-mathematical competencies). The core problem was identified as the lack of tangible-digital bridges in early mathematics.
- Ideate: Co-creation workshops with multidisciplinary teams (engineers, designers, and pedagogues) led to the conceptualization of a "Triple-Action Ecosystem": an AI-Interactive Robot, 3D-Manipulative Modules, and a Cognitive Activity Book.
- Prototype: High-fidelity prototypes were developed. The robotic architecture integrated a Raspberry Pi 5 for edge computing, MG995R servomotors for kinesthetic feedback, and a HuskyLens AI camera for computer vision-based object recognition.
- Test: Pilot studies were conducted in real classroom environments to evaluate natural language interaction, content retention, and the transfer of learning from tangible 3D modules to abstract graphic-written exercises.

2.2 Phase II: VDI 2206 – Systematic Mechatronic Implementation and AI

Following the V-Model of the VDI 2206 standard, the technical development focused on cross-domain integration, see Fig. 2:

- Requirement Analysis: Technical specifications were derived from pedagogical constraints. This included processing power requirements for real-time AI, torque specifications for the MG995R motors, and the visual fidelity of the 5-in. LCD for emotional signaling.
- System Conceptualization: Architecture design focused on modularity. The ecosystem was designed to be scalable, allowing for the addition of new 3D modules (fractions, geometry, arithmetic) without altering the robot's core hardware.
- Preliminary Design: Computer-Aided Design (CAD) models were developed for chassis, alongside electronic schematics and control logic diagrams. Emphasis was placed on Low-Cost Design (LCD) and Design for Manufacturability (DFM) to ensure regional scalability.
- Detailed Design: Final implementation included the programming of AI algorithms for voice interaction and computer vision. Simultaneously, the activity book was curated to align with the Peruvian National Curriculum, specifically targeting competencies in quantity, regularity, and shape resolution.

2.3 System Requirements and Architecture Mapping

To bridge the gap between mechatronic design and pedagogical objectives, a cross-functional requirements matrix was established (Table 1). This ensures that every technical specification serves a specific learning competency.

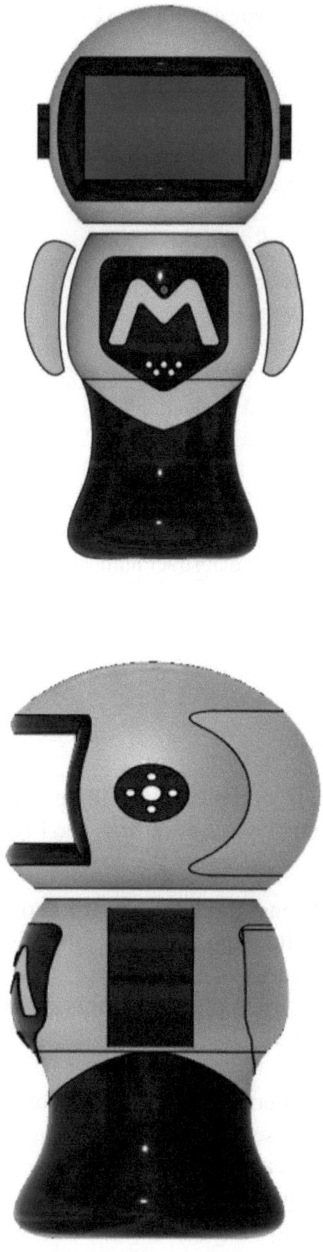

Fig. 2. Prototype Monty Lab

Table 1. Mapping of pedagogical needs to AI and mechatronic requirements.

Pedagogical Dimension	User Requirement	Technical Implementation (AI & Hardware)
Cognitive Engagement	Real-time feedback and guidance during math tasks.	Edge Computing: Raspberry Pi 5 processing local LLMs or decision trees for instant verbal response.
Visual-Spatial Learning	Recognition of 3D manipulative shapes and tokens.	Computer Vision: HuskyLens AI Camera using Object Classification and Color Recognition algorithms.
Social-Emotional Bond	Empathy and motivation to reduce "math anxiety."	Affective Computing: 5" LCD Screen displaying dynamic facial expressions synchronized with MG995R micro-gestures.
Tactile Reinforcement	Correlation between physical movement and abstract numbers.	Kinematic Integration: Coordination between AI voice prompts and robotic arm/head movements via PWM control.

2.4 AI System Architecture

The Monty Lab architecture is organized into three functional layers, ensuring low latency and high reliability in a classroom setting, see Fig. 3.

- Perception layer (Input):
  - Vision: The HuskyLens module performs pre-processing of visual data (tag/object recognition) at the edge, sending simplified data strings to the central controller via I2C/UART protocols.
  - Audio: High-sensitivity microphone captures student queries, processed through a speech-to-text (STT) engine.
- Cognitive layer (Processing):
  - Central Unit: The Raspberry Pi 5 acts as the "brain," running the logic layer. It manages the interaction flow, selecting the appropriate educational content based on the student's performance (Learning Analytics).
  - Decision Logic: AI algorithms determine the level of difficulty and the type of emotional feedback required (e.g., if a student fails twice, the AI triggers a "motivation" facial expression and a simplified hint).
- Cognitive Actuation Layer (Output):
  - Mechanical: MG995R servomotors translate logic into physical gestures.
  - Visual/Audio: The LCD screen and I2S audio amplifiers provide the multimodal interface that completes the Montessori sensory loop.

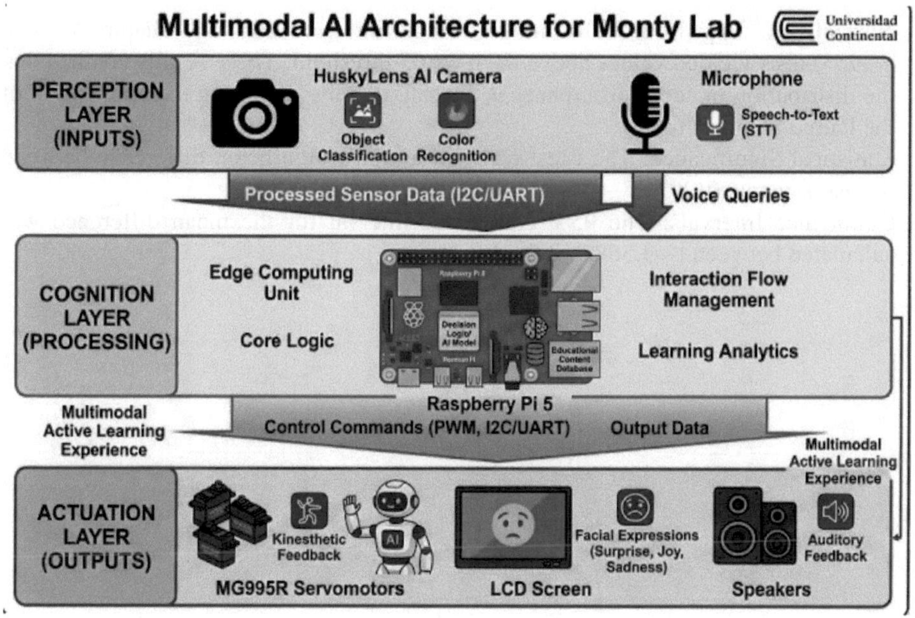

Fig. 3. Multimodal AI Architecture for Monty Lab

3 Results and Statistical Analysis

3.1 Cohort Characterization

The study involved a homogeneous sample of N = 30 third-grade primary students, all aged 8 years. The gender distribution was nearly balanced, with 53.3% male and 46.7% female participants, ensuring that the findings are representative across genders in the early primary education stage.

3.2 Descriptive Statistics of Learning Gains

The effectiveness of the Monty Lab ecosystem (AI robot, 3D modules, and activity book) was measured through a pre-test and post-test design.

- Baseline (Pre-test): Students exhibited an initial mean score of 12.60 (SD = 5.893).
- Post-intervention (Post-test): Following the multimodal AI interaction, the mean score rose to 15.53 (SD = 6.078).
- Performance Gain: The intervention yielded an average improvement of +2.93 points, representing a 23.2% increase in mathematical proficiency relative to the baseline.

3.3 Inferential statistics and hypothesis testing

To ensure the robustness of these findings, the data underwent normality and parametric validation:

- Normality Testing: Both the Kolmogorov-Smirnov ($p = .200$) and Shapiro-Wilk ($p = .933$) tests yielded values above the $\alpha = .05$ threshold. These results confirm that the distribution of score differences is normal, thereby justifying the application of the Paired Samples t-test.
- Statistical Significance: The t-test revealed a highly significant difference between the assessments ($t(29) = -9.448$; $p < .001$).
- Confidence Intervals: The 95% confidence interval for the mean difference was calculated between [−3.568, −2.298] (Fig. 4).

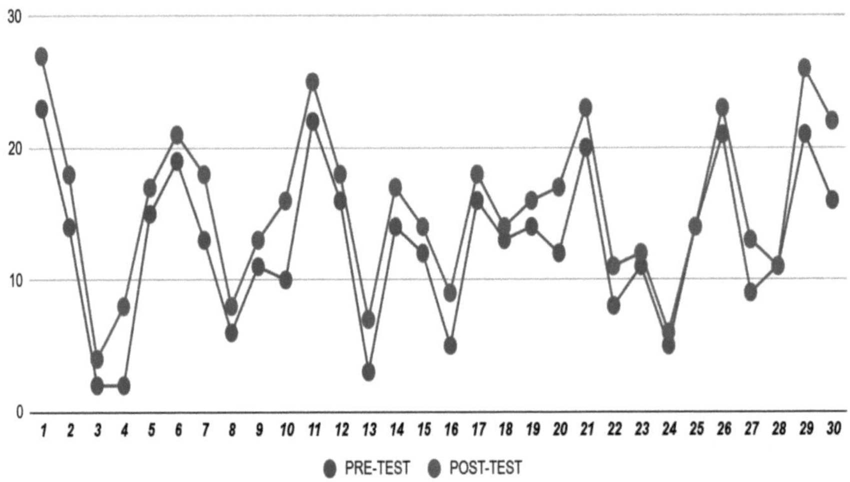

Fig. 4. Comparison of pre-test and post-test scores

4 Conclusion

The development and implementation of the Monty Lab ecosystem represent a significant advancement in the integration of Artificial Intelligence and mechatronic systems within the primary education sector. By synthesizing the VDI 2206 engineering standard with the Montessori pedagogical framework, this study successfully created a multimodal learning environment that bridges the gap between tangible manipulation and abstract mathematical reasoning.

The empirical results obtained at I.E.P. Maryam School provide robust evidence of the system's efficacy. The statistically significant improvement in student performance evidenced by a mean score increases from 12.60 to 15.53 and a t-test significance of $p < .001$ validates the role of affective computing and personalized learning pathways in enhancing early mathematical competencies. Furthermore, the successful inclusion of students with diverse learning needs, such as those with autism spectrum disorder (ASD), underscores the platform's potential for fostering inclusive and equitable educational growth.

From a strategic and geopolitical perspective, Monty Lab serves as a blueprint for digital sovereignty in the Pan-American region. By utilizing accessible edge-computing hardware like the Raspberry Pi 5 and locally developed AI algorithms, the project demonstrates that high-impact educational technology can be produced within the region to address specific local challenges without dependence on external proprietary solutions. This approach not only strengthens human capital from an early age but also builds the technical foundation for a more competitive, AI-driven economy in the region. The success of the Monty Lab ecosystem directly addresses the core pillars of this conference, particularly the transformation of higher education to develop competitive talent in engineering. By integrating intelligent tutors and personalized learning pathways, the project demonstrates how AI can modernize teaching and assessment in critical disciplines. Furthermore, the use of locally developed mechatronic systems for primary education supports the vision of strengthening human capital as a geopolitical asset. This approach fosters digital sovereignty within the Pan-American region by reducing technological dependence and preparing a new generation for the AI-driven economy. Ultimately, Monty Lab serves as a scalable model for responsible AI use in academic management and curriculum redesign, ensuring that technological progress drives inclusive development and regional competitiveness.

Beyond the immediate educational outcomes, Monty Lab demonstrates the strategic value of integrating Artificial Intelligence, mechatronics, and digital fabrication into early educational environments. The ecosystem illustrates how locally developed technological solutions can address context-specific learning challenges while simultaneously fostering technological capabilities within the region. By exposing children to intelligent systems, robotics, and computational thinking from an early age, the platform contributes to the development of future STEM talent and strengthens the foundations of an innovation-driven society. In this sense, educational technology should not be viewed solely as a pedagogical tool but also as a long-term investment in human capital formation and national competitiveness. Moreover, the results support the feasibility of deploying edge-AI educational ecosystems in resource-constrained environments where connectivity, infrastructure, and access to advanced educational technologies remain limited. The combination of low-cost hardware, local manufacturing through FabLab facilities, and curriculum-aligned learning experiences offers a replicable framework for other schools and regions facing similar educational challenges. As educational systems worldwide seek to adapt to the demands of the AI-driven economy, initiatives such as Monty Lab provide evidence that digital sovereignty can be strengthened through locally designed, scalable, and inclusive technological innovations that empower both learners and educational institutions.

Finally, the Monty Lab initiative transcends the scope of a localized educational tool; it serves as a scalable model for digital sovereignty across the Pan-American region. By developing high-tier AI solutions such as those integrated into the Raspberry Pi 5 and HuskyLens within the Peruvian engineering context, this project proves that Latin American academic institutions can lead the transition from technology consumers to technology creators. Strengthening early-childhood mathematical competencies through such locally produced, STEAM-aligned ecosystems is a critical step in cultivating a competitive, high-tech workforce. Ultimately, the integration of these mechatronic systems into the national curriculum provides a viable pathway for reducing the digital divide and ensuring that human capital becomes a strategic geopolitical asset for the region's sustainable development.

Future research will focus on longitudinal studies to assess long-term knowledge retention and the scalability of the ecosystem in rural educational settings. Additionally, we aim to expand the Learning Analytics module to provide teachers with real-time diagnostic reports, further modernizing academic management and personalized instruction.

Acknowledgments. The authors would like to express their sincere gratitude to the FabLab Universidad Continental for providing the advanced digital manufacturing infrastructure and technical expertise necessary for the development of the Monty AI robot and the 3D manipulative modules. Special thanks are also extended to the Fellowship Program for its financial support and institutional backing, which facilitated the implementation of the pilot study and the development of this research. Finally, we thank the students and staff of I.E.P. Maryam School in Huancayo for their invaluable participation and commitment to this project.

References

1. Aguilera, D., Lupiáñez, J.L., Perales-Palacios, F.J., Vílchez-González, J.M.: IDEARR model for STEM education—a framework proposal. Educ. Sci. (Basel). **14**(6), 638 (2024)
2. Antoninis M. et al., "Global Education Monitoring Report 2023: Technology in Education: a Tool on whose Terms? 2023.
3. De la Cruz, M., Mergoni, A.: Assessing the performance of Peruvian education system from a governance perspective. Socio. Econ. Plan. Sci. **93**, 101891 (2024)
4. Greene, D., Strassman, W.P.: Peruvian construction statistics and productivity changes. J. Dev. Stud. **7**(2), 189–195 (1971)
5. Putra, Y.Y., Hendrik, M., Rahmadi, I.F.: Introduction of an educational robotics-based numeracy literacy corner. Commun. Empower. **10**(5) (2025)
6. Lucano, J.J.L., Salcedo, J.D.C., Laque, D.H., Hisnostroza, A.T.: Self-demand vs. time availability: a sociological analysis of STEM project performance among school and university students in the Arequipa region of Peru. In: Proceedings of International Conference on Computational Thinking Education, pp. 120–123 (2025) https://www.scopus.com/inward/record.uri?eid=2-s2.0-105011816266&partnerID=40&md5=54356c3152472cdb2e10cbc5496b9cac
7. Cumbo, B., Selwyn, N.: Using participatory design approaches in educational research. Int. J. Res. Method Edu. **45**(1), 60–72 (2022)
8. Aguilar, O.G., Pérez, A.B.D., Aguilar, A.G.: Teacher performance evaluation model in Covid-19 times. In: 2020 XV Conferencia Latinoamericana de Tecnologias de Aprendizaje (LACLO), pp. 1–6 (2020). https://doi.org/10.1109/LACLO50806.2020.9381159
9. Fox, H.C.: Measuring what matters: a multidimensional framework for assessing real sovereignty. In: Abstract Books of the Global Conference on Social Sciences, p. 9 (2025)
10. Neves, B.C., Honório, K.d.S.: Infrastructure as a geopolitical lever: strategic dynamics in Latin America's global power struggle. Revista Brasileira de Política Internacional. **67**(2), e021 (2024)
11. Gausemeier, J., Moehringer, S.: VDI 2206-a new guideline for the design of mechatronic systems. IFAC Proc. Vol. **35**(2), 785–790 (2002)

12. Damjanovic, V., Branson, S.: Empowering diverse learners: integrating tangible technologies and low-tech tools to Foster STEM engagement and creativity in early childhood education. Educ. Sci. (Basel). **15**(8), 1024 (2025)
13. Pitkänen, K., Iwata, M., Laru, J.: Exploring technology-oriented fab lab facilitators' role as educators in K-12 education: focus on scaffolding novice students' learning in digital fabrication activities. Int. J. Child. Comput. Interact. **26**, 100207 (2020). https://doi.org/10.1016/j.ijcci.2020.100207
14. S. Khalifa, "FabLab as an innovative educational approach in higher education," in: Innovative Educational Frameworks for Future Skills and Competencies, IGI Global Scientific Publishing 2025, pp. 81–134.
15. De los Rios Rosado, J., Salcedo, J.D.C., Lucano, J.J.L., Condori, K.V.: Enhancing technological maturity in school-level robotics: a case study of integrating LunaBot V2.3 in educational environments in remote areas of Arequipa, Peru. In: Lecture Notes in Educational Technology, pp. 121–132 (2025). https://doi.org/10.1007/978-981-96-3698-3_9
16. Salcedo, J.D.C., Lucano, J.J.L., Hinostroza, A.T., De los Rios Rosado, J., Condori, K.V.: Gamification and robotics in steam education: a case study in rural areas of Arequipa and Huancayo: integrating lunabot for technological advancement and iterative design in robotics learning. Inter. Des. Architect. **63**, 108–130 (2024). https://doi.org/10.55612/s-5002-063-006
17. Salcedo, J.D.C., Lucano, J.J.L., Aguilar, O.G., Hinostroza, A.J.T.: The impact of gamified education on children and adolescents in STEAM education as a future teaching methodology in remote areas of the Arequipa region - Peru. In: CEUR Workshop Proceedings, pp. 184–194 (2023) https://www.scopus.com/inward/record.uri?eid=2-s2.0-85194757129&partnerID=40&md5=5ac98da4e41e66f2e8caf74f7d0adf5f
18. Gil, L.: A fablab at the periphery: decentering innovation from São Paulo. Am. Anthropol. **124**(4), 721–733 (2022)
19. Corsini, L., Aranda-Jan, C.B., Moultrie, J.: Using digital fabrication tools to provide humanitarian and development aid in low-resource settings. Technol. Soc. **58**, 101117 (2019). https://doi.org/10.1016/j.techsoc.2019.02.003
20. Holmes, W.: Artificial intelligence in education. In: Encyclopedia of Education and Information Technologies, pp. 88–103. Springer (2020)

Pedagogical Synergy in the Artificial Intelligence Era: An Iterative Co-creation Model and its Alignment with Google's Prompt Engineering

Aníbal N. Cassanelli(✉)

Universidad Nacional de Mar del Plata, Mar del Plata, Argentina
acassane@fi.mdp.edu.ar

Abstract. This article documents a pedagogical co-creation experience between an expert professor and the Gemini Large Language Model (LLM) for the development of an assessment ecosystem for the Project Risk Management course. The core of the proposal is the application of the Condition-Risk-Consequence (CRC) methodology. We describe a progressive creation cycle, which transforms initial theoretical concepts into 15 high-fidelity assessment scenarios, situated within the Argentine macroeconomic context and quantified using precise financial variables. Based on this experience, the Layered Pedagogical Scaffolding Model (MAPC) is formally proposed, linking its structure to the Prompt Engineering best practices documented by Google. The model establishes an architecture where the quality of the AI response is directly proportional to the structuring of the context, role, and constraint layers. This methodological approach not only enhances the extreme personalization of learning but also ensures rigorous academic standards and professional relevance. The study concludes that the strategic use of LLMs like Gemini, guided by a clear scaffolding methodology such as MAPC, allows for overcoming the limitations of traditional assessment exercises. The ability to generate hyper-realistic and contextualized scenarios, with quantified financial variables, validates the potential of AI to raise the quality of higher education in technical and management fields.

Keywords: Co-creation · Generative Artificial Intelligence · CRC Methodology · Prompt Engineering · MAPC Model · Google Cloud AI

1 Introduction

The modern imperative for project management education within higher education institutions necessitates pedagogical tools that authentically capture the multifaceted and inherently uncertain nature of the professional landscape. Relying on traditional methods, such as the composition of standalone case studies, frequently results in narratives that are overly linear, static, and fundamentally lacking the necessary technical, financial, and crucial psychological depth required to cultivate sophisticated critical decision-making competencies in students. This deficiency hinders the development of a student's ability to navigate the Volatile, Uncertain, Complex, and Ambiguous (VUCA) environment that characterizes contemporary project work.

H. Florez and R. Gomez-Sanchez (Eds.): UPADI-AI 2026, CCIS 3124, pp. 146–156, 2027.
https://doi.org/10.1007/978-3-032-35635-2_10

In this challenging context, Generative Artificial Intelligence (GenAI) is rapidly emerging not merely as a marginal productivity enhancer but as a disruptive and strategic partner in the fundamental redesign of pedagogical content. GenAI possesses a unique capacity to simulate the systemic interconnectivity and operational complexity rigorously demanded by the intensely competitive global market [7]. By leveraging advanced models, educators can move beyond simplified scenarios to create rich, dynamic, and adaptive simulations that challenge students to address emergent risks, manage stakeholder conflict, and operate within realistic resource constraints [8, 12].

This work documents and systematically analyzes the collaborative process between a human subject matter expert and advanced AI tools to construct a comprehensive repository comprising 15 detailed case studies, all structured around the rigorous CRC methodology (see Appendix Error! Reference source not found.). The core hypothesis underpinning this article is that the generation of educational materials of genuine pedagogical excellence—materials that are both high-fidelity and deeply engaging—is never the result of isolated, singular commands or prompt-engineering shortcuts. Instead, it is the direct outcome of a sophisticated, structured, and progressively iterative dialogue process between the human expert and the machine model [9, 11].

Within this symbiotic process, the educator transitions from a content creator to the pivotal role of an information architect. The educator's function is to meticulously guide the GenAI model through successive, targeted layers of refinement. These layers include territorial refinement (ensuring the simulation is grounded in a specific geographical, regulatory, and industrial context); technical refinement (validating the operational accuracy of engineering, financial, or scheduling constraints); and behavioral refinement (integrating realistic team dynamics, communication breakdowns, and ethical dilemmas) [10, 12, 13]. This structured, progressive guidance is the critical mechanism that ensures the resulting educational materials foster meaningful, situated, and deep learning experiences, bridging the gap between theoretical knowledge and practical, professional application.

2 Objectives

To document and systematize the process of pedagogical co-creation between the educator and AI for the design of high-fidelity assessment scenarios, based on the CRC methodology and the technical guidelines of prompt engineering.

2.1 Specific Objectives

1. To analyze the effectiveness of the CRC methodology as a logical structure for generating technical and coherent case studies using large language models.
2. To systematize the iterative dialogue developed during the creation of the materials into a generalizable model called the Layered Pedagogical Scaffolding Model (MAPC, from its Spanish acronym).
3. To demonstrate the technical alignment between the educator's instructional design phases and the strategic pillars of Prompt Engineering defined by Google (Person, Task, Context, and Format).

4. To validate the ability of AI to scale the personalization of learning by producing multiple highly complex scenarios that integrate precise financial variables and divergent behavioral profiles.

3 Theoretical Framework

3.1 The CRC Methodology and Project Planning

Effective project risk management fundamentally relies on establishing a clear, unambiguous taxonomic differentiation among the condition, the risk event itself, and its subsequent consequences or impact. This distinction is crucial for moving beyond a superficial understanding of threats and opportunities.

Hillson (2023) has strongly advocated for decomposing risk into a tripartite structure, often termed the CRC structure:

1. Condition (C): This represents the factual, existing event or underlying situation—a verifiable situation or a weakness in the project environment (e.g., outdated software, inexperienced team, volatile market). It is the cause of the potential risk.
2. Risk (R): This is the future, uncertain event that may occur, stemming directly from the Condition (e.g., the outdated software failing, the inexperienced team making errors, the market crashing). It is the event itself.
3. Consequence (C): This is the impact or effect on the project's objectives—time, cost, scope, or quality—should the Risk event materialize (e.g., a two-week delay due to system failure, a $50,000 budget overrun due to rework, a reduction in product quality).

This Condition, Risk, and Consequence (CRC) framework is not merely an academic exercise; it provides a powerful, practical mechanism for project managers to design more precise and targeted strategic responses. By isolating the 'Condition' (cause), the focus shifts from merely reacting to an event (Risk) to proactively managing or eliminating the underlying source of uncertainty. This systematic approach allows for a richer integration of qualitative analysis, which defines the context and likelihood, with the necessary rigor of financial data—essential for quantifying the potential 'Consequence' and securing stakeholder approval for mitigation or exploitation strategies.

The underlying premise of the CRC structure is that a risk does not exist in a vacuum but is the result of a verifiable logical causality [5]. This perspective is deeply aligned with modern principles of project planning and control. By forcing the identification of these critical variables, the CRC methodology enables the proactive anticipation of significant deviations from project objectives [1]. This shift from reactive crisis management to proactive risk governance enhances predictability and control.

Furthermore, the application of the CRC methodology has proven highly effective in various assessment and communication contexts. By demanding precision in defining the interrelationships between cause, event, and impact, it significantly reduces ambiguity in technical communication among team members, stakeholders, and governance bodies. It provides a suitable and structured setting for in-depth risk analysis, particularly through the use of case studies specifically designed for student practice in postgraduate project risk management courses [2]. The structured nature of CRC ensures that students and practitioners alike learn to decompose complex project scenarios into manageable and logically connected elements, fostering superior analytical and decision-making skills.

3.2 Google's Prompt Engineering: the Technical Framework

Google formally defines Prompt Engineering [4] as a critical discipline focused on the refinement and optimization of inputs (prompts) to maximize the utility, accuracy, and predictability of large language models (LLMs). This emerging field moves beyond simple keyword entry, establishing a methodological framework that ensures consistent and high-quality outputs from sophisticated models like Gemini [3].

The Foundational Structure: P-T-C-F Framework [4]. The technical framework suggested by Google for effective Prompt Engineering is based on structuring four fundamental and interdependent pillars:

- Person (Role): This pillar defines the role, identity, or expertise the model should adopt while generating the response (e.g., "Act as a senior financial analyst," or "You are a seasoned technical writer"). Establishing a person maintains narrative consistency and tailors the language and content to the expected context.
- Task: This is the core instruction, clearly defining the objective the model must achieve (e.g., "Summarize the key findings," "Write a Python function," or "Compare and contrast two historical events"). Precision in the task minimizes ambiguity and directs the model's focus.
- Context: The context provides all necessary background information, parameters, constraints, and relevant data that the model needs to reference. This crucial input prevents models from hallucinating or generating informationally irrelevant output (e.g., specifying the target audience, the source documents to cite, or length limitations).
- Format: This pillar dictates the desired structure and output style (e.g., "Respond in bullet points," "Generate a JSON object," "Write a five-paragraph essay," or "Use APA citation style"). Specifying the format ensures the output is immediately usable and meets integration requirements.

This P-T-C-F methodology is essential for enabling models like Gemini to maintain narrative coherence and effectively avoiding informational drift—the tendency of models to stray from the original query or introduce irrelevant data.

Beyond the foundational structure, the discipline of Prompt Engineering incorporates advanced techniques to significantly enhance the model's reasoning capabilities, which are particularly vital for technical and analytical fields [13]. A prime example is the Chain-of-Thought (CoT) prompting technique, originally formalized by Wei et al. (2022). CoT works by inducing the language model to perform and explicitly articulate a series of intermediate reasoning steps before generating the final product [14]. Instead of simply requesting the final answer, the prompt encourages a step-by-step thinking process (e.g., "Think step-by-step and then provide the final result"). This process of internal logical decomposition is critical for disciplines requiring logical and mathematical precision, such as coding, complex data analysis, and scientific problem-solving, as it allows for the verification of the model's logic and drastically improves the accuracy of the final generated output [15].

3.3 Seminal Foundations of the Model

The development and application of this contemporary process are a profound convergence of cutting-edge, 21st-century technologies with deep-seated, seminal theories from foundational academic disciplines. At its core lies the dynamic educator-AI dialogue, which functions not merely as a tool but as a crucial cognitive mediator. This mediated interaction is specifically designed to significantly expand the expert's creative capacity, a conceptual foundation directly derived from Lev Vygotsky's socio-cultural theory, particularly his Zone of Proximal Development (ZPD) (1978). The AI, in this context, serves as the "More Knowledgeable Other," providing scaffolding and challenging the educator to reach insights and solutions that would be unattainable independently, thereby fostering a continuous cycle of professional and creative growth.

Furthermore, the sophisticated integration of decision profiles within the system is anchored in two pillars of behavioral and economic theory, providing a robust framework for understanding and predicting strategic choices. The first is Prospect Theory [6]. This theory is essential for explaining the observable asymmetry in risk perception, particularly the finding that individuals weigh potential losses more heavily than equivalent gains (loss aversion). By incorporating Prospect Theory, the system accounts for and can mitigate cognitive biases that might otherwise skew the educator's decision-making process under uncertainty. The second foundational pillar is Expected Utility Theory [8]. This classical theory is fundamental for establishing a normative benchmark for rational decision-making, especially when choices involve multiple, uncertain outcomes. Understanding the divergences between the theoretical optimal choice (based on Expected Utility) and the empirically observed choice (often influenced by Prospect Theory) is crucial for crafting AI-guided interventions that enhance the educator's strategic decision-making ability and overall effectiveness.

4 Methodological Section: The Joint Work Process

We anchored the methodology for developing educational content in a sophisticated, iterative co-creation approach, deliberately designed to generate a "refinement spiral" rather than a one-off, static product. This process moved beyond the typical paradigm of simply submitting a single, comprehensive command to an AI. Instead, the educator and Gemini engaged in a continuous, modular construction of knowledge, systematically layering complexity and realism into the content. This collaborative framework was intentionally aligned with the strategic "Prompt Scaffolding" model recommended by Google Workspace (2026), segmenting the creation lifecycle into five distinct, interlocking strata:

1. Anchoring and Role Phase: Establishing the Foundational Rigor

   This initial stage was critical for setting the intellectual and methodological boundaries. Gemini was precisely configured to operate under the "Person" of a Senior Consultant, ensuring the output would reflect a high level of professional expertise and strategic insight. Simultaneously, the CRC methodology was designated as the unmovable "framework of truth." This methodological constraint was essential to guarantee the initial scientific rigor and structural consistency of the content, preventing divergence from established best practices.

2. Localization and Grounding Layer: Achieving Geographic Realism

   In this second layer, the theoretical cases were deliberately situated within the specific geopolitical reality of Argentina. This action was not merely a superficial change of setting; it actively compelled the artificial intelligence to retrieve and integrate complex data patterns associated with a high-volatility economic environment and specific, often idiosyncratic, national regulatory frameworks. This strategic injection of context endowed the resulting cases with a critical level of geographic and economic realism, reflecting principles emphasized in contemporary AI application research [7, 14].
3. Narrative Densification Layer: Transforming Problems into Dilemmas

   The focus of the third stage was to dramatically increase the resolution and complexity of the narrative architecture. This was achieved by introducing multiple, diverse stakeholders with inherently conflicting interests into the scenarios. This intervention intentionally transformed linear, purely technical problems into multifaceted dilemmas of human management and organizational politics [11, 12]. The emphasis shifted from finding a single "correct" answer to navigating a complex web of competing demands and motivations.
4. Quantitative Layer and Financial Structure: Ensuring Economic Proportionality

   A decisive move in the fourth layer was the injection of precise, granular financial data. The educator provided specific total budgets and detailed costs per work package (drawing on foundational work [2]). This quantitative rigor was fundamental, allowing the "Consequence" element within the established CRC model to be not abstract, but directly proportional to the economic reality of the market. This ensured that the stakes and outcomes of the decisions within the scenarios carried credible financial weight [11, 12].
5. Behavioral Layer: Integrating Complex Professional Judgment

   The final layer elevated the assessment exercise to one of complex professional judgment by integrating specific psychological decision profiles. This manipulation forced the AI to model potential responses based on factors such as high-risk aversion or pronounced seeking behavior [12, 14]. By weaving in these behavioral dynamics, the final content became a powerful simulation, requiring the user to navigate not just technical challenges, but also the nuanced, irrational, and human element of organizational decision-making.

5 Proposal of the Layered Pedagogical Scaffolding Model (MAPC)

Based on the systematization of this process, the Layered Pedagogical Scaffolding Model (MAPC, from its Spanish acronym) is formally proposed as a generalizable methodology for designing complex simulations (Table 1).

Table 1. Synthesis of the Layered Pedagogical Scaffolding Model (MAPC)

MAPC Phase	Google Component (PE)	Pedagogical Application in the Project
1. Anchoring	Person & System Instruction	Rigid definition of the CRC methodology and the AI's expert role.
2. Context	Context & Grounding	Geographic localization (Argentina) and specific legal/economic frameworks.
3. Plot	Task Specificity	Narrative densification through conflicts between stakeholders and urgencies.
4. Data	Constraints & Parameters	Insertion of WBS budgets, schedules, and penalties.
5. Human	Multi-perspective Reasoning	Modeling of decision-making according to cognitive biases [6].
6. Support	Output Format & Evaluation	Generation of grading rubrics, model answers, and secondary risks.

Note: Own elaboration based on [4] and the co-creation experience [3].

6 Discussion

The integration of the MAPC model structures content creation aligning with Google's stringent technical guidelines offers a paradigm shift in AI-generated educational quality. This synergy fundamentally demonstrates that the true educational value derived from AI simulations does not stem from the model's inherent autonomy or unbridled generative capacity, but rather from the educator's masterful orchestration capacity and strategic oversight.

By systematically segmenting the complex process of simulation creation into the distinct, verifiable layers of the MAPC framework, the educator gains an essential mechanism for rigorous validation. This segmentation examines the systemic coherence and pedagogical integrity of each progressive advance within the AI-generated scenario.

For instance, consider a simulation involving the management of a corporate project:

- The educator defines the core learning objective and narrative context, ensuring it aligns with curriculum goals, and prescribes the specific tasks or decisions the learner must undertake within the simulation.
- Then introducing sensitive or critical inputs, such as financial data (e.g., budget allocations, projected costs, revenue streams) enforce constraints. They ensure these parameters are grounded in real-world constraints and align with the technical specifications required for a high-fidelity simulation.
- Critically, before allowing the simulation to proceed, the educator validates that the financial impact defined in the 'Consequence' layer—the outcome resulting from the learner's actions within the given parameters—is financially viable and logically consistent within the defined work package budget.

This joint work methodology—a partnership between the AI's processing power and the educator's domain expertise and structural design—has profound practical implications. It drastically reduces the incidence of "hallucinations" (inaccurate or nonsensical outputs) common in unrestrained generative AI. More importantly, it exponentially raises the simulation's fidelity to the exacting standards expected in professional consulting and high-stakes executive training. The output is not merely creative; it is verifiable, contextually sound, and pedagogically robust, transforming AI from a simple content generator into a precise instrument for guided, high-quality learning (see Appendix A).

7 Conclusions

The Layered Pedagogical Scaffolding Model (MAPC) reveals that the true pedagogical value of large language models lies not in their independent generation but in their expert orchestration for systemic refinement. This iterative, AI-driven co-creation elevates instructional design beyond mere operational optimization, establishing a sophisticated new framework, particularly for highly complex learning environments.

This methodological shift redefines the educator's role as a strategic instructional architect. By integrating geopolitical, financial, and behavioral variables, they construct a high-fidelity evaluative ecosystem. This approach enables the exponential scaling of personalized teaching—facilitating the creation of up to 15 unique and robust scenarios—thereby guaranteeing that students encounter challenges accurately replicating the volatility and uncertainty of contemporary professional practice (see Appendix A).

The core of this strategy is consolidating a robust bridge between theoretical concepts and the pragmatic demands of the global market. Students are compelled to justify decisions against numerical constraints and divergent leadership profiles. Ultimately, the proposed methodology positions AI as an advanced reasoning engine that, through stratified data input, powerfully aids in the formation of a new generation of project managers prepared for leadership under pressure.

8 Declaration of Generative AI and AI-Assisted Technologies in the Writing Process

Statement: During the preparation of this manuscript, the author used Consensus to assist in the structured search and identification of peer-reviewed literature and evidence-based references. Additionally, Gemini-based AI Agents were employed for the technical translation of the manuscript into American English and for final proofreading to ensure grammatical accuracy and stylistic consistency.

After using these tools, the author meticulously reviewed, verified, and edited the content to ensure its alignment with the research findings and rigorous academic standards. The author takes full responsibility for the integrity, accuracy, and originality of the final manuscript and its conclusions.

Appendix A. Repository of AI-Generated Case Studies

This repository systematizes the 15 scenarios designed using the MAPC methodology. Each case has been structured to evaluate the student's ability to identify the CRC chain, quantify economic impacts, and select response strategies aligned with specific decision profiles (Table 2).

Table 2. Scenarios designed using the MAPC methodology

ID	Case Title	Sector/Industry	Description and Pedagogical Focus
01	Neopago Argentino	FinTech	Focus: Critical technological dependence and market opportunity window. Evaluates the response to external API instability and imminent international competition [2].
02	Ruta Austral	Road Infrastructure	Focus: Logistical and macroeconomic risk. Analyzes the impact of currency devaluation and import restrictions on heavy machinery under daily penalties.
03	Viña del Viento	Agribusiness	Focus: Climate risk and contractual quality. The student must balance the cost of mitigation systems (sprinklers) against agricultural insurance and brand reputation.
04	Vientos del Sur	Renewable Energy	Focus: Geopolitics and global supply chain. Analyzes interruptions in maritime routes and dependence on unique European suppliers under PPA contracts.
05	World Cardiology Congress	Int. Events	Focus: Operational risk and sponsorship. Evaluates decision-making in the face of airline strikes that threaten the attendance of key speakers and the event's profitability.
06	Nueva Esperanza	Pharmaceuticals	Focus: Strategic risk and intellectual property. Analyzes the potential sabotage by suppliers acquired by the competition during Phase III clinical trials.
07	Salar Futuro	Lithium Mining	Focus: Socio-environmental risk and license to operate. Evaluates the conflict over water resources and the cost of pivoting towards sustainable technologies (DLE).
08	Ecolodge Iberá	Sustainable Tourism	Focus: External ecological risk and business model. Analyzes the impact of adjacent extensive agriculture on the main asset: biodiversity.
09	Project Chimera	Video Games	Focus: Technical risk and open-source support. Evaluates the dilemma between mitigating bugs in a free engine or migrating to expensive commercial licenses.
10	SatCom-AR	Satellite Industry	Focus: Global shortage of critical components. Analyzes the use of specialized brokers to obtain space-grade microchips versus penalties for delay.
11	Omnichannel Textile	Retail/E-commerce	Focus: Last-mile logistics and brand promise. Evaluates the cost of failed deliveries and the decision to diversify logistics providers to ensure service.

(*continued*)

Table 2. (*continued*)

ID	Case Title	Sector/Industry	Description and Pedagogical Focus
12	Public HCDU	Public Health	Focus: Data quality and union conflict. Analyzes the migration of deficient historical data and administrative staff resistance to new technologies.
13	The Last Conqueror	Media/Streaming	Focus: Dependence on key talent. Evaluates the financial impact of a lead actor's injury and the massive reorganization of the shooting schedule to protect the budget.
14	Global Digital Campus	EdTech/SaaS	Focus: Cybersecurity and data privacy. Analyzes the impact of critical vulnerabilities in the database architecture under personal data protection laws.
15	Foundation Square	Urban Development	Focus: Archaeological and institutional risk. Evaluates management facing historical findings on-site and the cost-benefit of financing accelerated rescue excavations.

References

1. Cassanelli, A.N.: Gestión de Proyectos: Introducción a la Planificación y Control. EUDEM (2019) ISBN: 978-987-4440-58-7
2. Cassanelli, A.N.: Fintech Startup case study. Risk analysis. Research Gate. (2025). https://doi.org/10.13140/RG.2.2.35763.49441
3. Google Gemini. https://gemini.google.com, Accessed 02 May 2026
4. Prompting Guide 101. Google workspace with Gemini (2024). https://cloud.google.com. Accessed 02 May 2026
5. Hillson, D.: The Risk Management Handbook: A Practical Guide to Managing the Multiple Dimensions of Risk. Kogan Page (2023) ISBN 9781398610613
6. Kahneman, D., Tversky, A.: Prospect theory: an analysis of decision under risk. Econometrica. **47**(2), 263–291 (1979). https://doi.org/10.2307/1914185
7. Mollick, E.R., Mollick, L.: Using AI to implement effective teaching strategies in classrooms: five strategies, including prompts. The Wharton School Research Paper. (2023). https://doi.org/10.2139/ssrn.4391243
8. Von Neumann, J., Morgenstern, O., Kuhn, H. W., Rubinstein, A. : Front Matter. In: Theory of Games and Economic Behavior: 60th Anniversary Commemorative Edition (pp. i–iv). Princeton University Press(1944). http://www.jstor.org/stable/j.ctt1r2gkx.1.
9. Vygotsky, L.S.: In: Cole, M., John-Steiner, V., Scribner, S., Souberman, E. (eds.) Mind in Society: Development of Higher Psychological Processes. Harvard University Press (1978). https://doi.org/10.2307/j.ctvjf9vz4
10. Wei, Jason et al.: Chain of Thought Prompting Elicits Reasoning in Large Language Models (2022).DOI: https://doi.org/10.48550/arXiv.2201.11903.
11. Yu, Z., He, L., Wu, Z., Dai, X., Chen, J. : Towards better chain-of-thought prompting strategies: a Survey (2023).ArXiv, abs/2310.04959. DOI: https://doi.org/10.48550/arxiv.2310.04959.

12. Lee, D., Palmer, E.: Prompt engineering in higher education: a systematic review to help inform curricula. Int. J. Educ. Technol. High. Educ. **22**(1), 7 (2025)
13. Velásquez-Henao, J.D., Franco-Cardona, C.J., Cadavid-Higuita, L.: Prompt engineering: a methodology for optimizing interactions with AI-language models in the field of engineering. DYNA. **90**(230), 9–17 (2023) Special 90 years Commemoration
14. Zhang, Zhuosheng, Aston Zhang, Mu Li, Alexander J. Smola: "Automatic chain of thought prompting in large language models" (2022).DOI: 10.48550/arXiv.2210.0349
15. Jin, M. et al. The Impact of Reasoning Step Length on Large Language Models. ArXiv, abs/2401.04925(2024). DOI: 10.48550/arxiv.2401.04925

Application of Artificial Intelligence in Infrastructure

An AI-Based Framework for Predicting Accident Rates in Freight Transportation along Urban Logistics Corridors

Patricia Cortés Hernández[1](✉), Monserrat Bedolla-Cortés[2], and Mariana Bedolla Cortés[3]

[1] Tecnológico Nacional de México - Tecnológico de Estudios Superiores de Cuautitlán Izcalli, Cuautitlán Izcalli, Mexico
patricia.ch@cuautitlan.tecnm.mx
[2] Universidad Autónoma del Estado de México/UAEM, Ecatepec, Mexico
[3] Universidad Nacional Autónoma de México, Facultad de Estudios Superiores plantel Iztacala, Mexico City, Mexico

Abstract. Freight transportation along urban logistics corridors is exposed to many risk factors that lead to accident events which have a large economic, operational, social and safety impact. The urban mobility systems are growing in complexity and so there is the need for a predictive approach that can accommodate a wide range of unknown variables when predicting accidents in freight transport. To this end, we propose a multidimensional artificial intelligence framework for accident prediction in freight transportation with a human, operational, vehicular, environmental, technology, and infrastructure-based approach. We have developed a process of identifying and operationalizing variables, mathematical modeling, and machine learning to predict accidents from the comprehensive perspective to achieve this objective. To evaluate the technical feasibility of the proposed framework, we conducted a proof of concept implementation on a synthetic dataset of 10,000 simulated freight transportation operations. We created an accident occurrence with a logistic model which includes the risk factors and interaction effects. Two machine learning algorithms, Logistic Regression and Random Forest were trained and evaluated using the usual classification parameters: Accuracy, Precision, Recall, F1-score and AUC-ROC. The results showed good predictive power in the simulation environment with Logistic Regression with an AUC-ROC of 0.989 and Random Forest with an AUC-ROC of 0.940. We also explored the driving hours, digitalization level and vehicle condition in our multidimensional model. Though these findings are not empirical proof-of-concept in practice, they highlight the internal consistency and technical feasibility of how the proposed approach works. Such research will establish the basis for future work that integrates artificial intelligence, transportation safety and Logistics 4.0 principles with freight transportation data.

Keywords: freight transportation · accident prediction · artificial intelligence · machine learning · logistics 4.0 · urban logistics corridors · transportation safety · synthetic data.

H. Florez and R. Gomez-Sanchez (Eds.): UPADI-AI 2026, CCIS 3124, pp. 159–174, 2027.
https://doi.org/10.1007/978-3-032-35635-2_11

1 Introduction

Freight transport plays an essential role in supply chain continuity, economic development and urban mobility. But freight operations are also exposed to some risks that could result in accidents with major economic, operational, environmental and social impact. The complexity of urban logistics corridors and growing freight demand has resulted in the need for proactive safety management measures that can detect and minimize accident risks before they occur. Accident occurrence in freight transport is affected by many factors such as driver behaviour, vehicle condition, traffic conditions, traffic congestion, environmental conditions, technological capabilities, infrastructure quality, and operational practices and so on. Due to these factors being dynamic and often interdependent, traditional statistical methods may not be able to capture the nonlinear links among accident causation patterns (Li & Luo, 2023). Recent advancements in artificial intelligence (AI) and machine learning have opened up new possibilities for transportation safety management. These technologies can process large volumes of heterogeneous data and detect hidden patterns, and model complex relationships between variables that enable predictive systems to make intelligent decisions (Mostafa et al., 2025; Korkmaz et al., 2026). While previous studies have shown that AI is useful to predict accidents, these studies mostly focus on a single aspect of the situation like traffic, driver behavior or environmental factors, and fail to consider the broader context in freight transportation. To bridge this gap, we present a multidimensional AI-based framework for predicting accident rates in freight transportation along urban logistics corridors. The framework is based on a cause and effect analysis using an Ishikawa diagram, a variable operationalization matrix, and machine learning models to predict the probability of accidents. The proposed model includes six dimensions of accident causation: human, operational, vehicular, environmental, technological and infrastructure-related factors.

The main contributions of this study are threefold:

- The development of a multidimensional framework that integrates six key dimensions associated with freight transportation accidents.
- The development of an operationalization matrix that transforms conceptual risk factors into measurable variables for AI-based analysis.
- The validation of the framework's internal consistency and technical feasibility through a proof-of-concept implementation using a synthetic dataset and machine learning models.

The goal of this research is not to provide any clear evidence of accident prediction performance in real-world conditions, but only to show that it is possible to integrate different logistics-related variables into a unified AI-based predictive framework and use it as an evidence base for future analysis based on data from real-world freight transportation data.

2 Problem Statement and Research Question

Freight transportation accidents are a complex phenomenon that is influenced by a variety of factors in the logistics system. Driver fatigue and training factors (Zhang et al., 2022), delivery pressure and route planning, vehicular conditions, environmental factors, technological capabilities and infrastructure quality all contribute to accidents and so on. Although more and more transportation safety management is done in recent years, the traditional approaches are based on descriptive statistics or isolated analysis of each individual factor. These methods are useful to provide information but they are not able to identify nonlinear interactions and complex correlations between variables and therefore cannot be used to help prevent accidents. AI has emerged as one of the most promising options to overcome these limitations. Machine learning tools make it possible to make use of heterogeneous data sources and to identify hidden patterns that influence accident rates. Therefore, AI-based predictive models can have a great potential for risk management and evidence-based decision-making in freight transportation systems (Singh & Sinha, 2021; Alotaibi, 2025; Vicent et al., 2024). From this perspective, we ask a research question here: **Can an artificial intelligence-based multidimensional framework generate reliable accident-rate predictions for freight transportation operations along urban logistics corridors?**

3 Literature Review and Research Gap

3.1 Freight Transportation Safety and Accident Risk

Freight transportation is essential to supply chain performance and economic development and in the process of moving raw materials and finished products across logistics networks (Coyle et al., 2023; Ballou & Saporito, 2023). However, freight operations are vulnerable to many safety risks that can result in economic losses, supply chain disruptions, infrastructure damage, and road safety issues. The study and official papers reported that driver fatigue, long driving times, vehicle condition, traffic density, infrastructure quality, and environmental conditions had all been identified as major contributors to accidents (ECLAC, 2022; SICT, 2023; INEGI, 2024; Li & Luo, 2023). Since these factors are dynamic, accident prediction is a multidimensional problem that requires multidimensional analysis (Fig. 1).

3.2 Artificial Intelligence for Accident Prediction

Artificial intelligence and machine learning have become important tools for transportation safety analysis as they can be used to process large volumes of heterogeneous data and identify complex patterns in accidents. Recent studies have shown promising results using machine learning, deep learning, neural networks, and ensemble learning for accident prediction and severity analysis (Mostafa et al., 2025; Vicent et al., 2024; Alfasi et al., 2025; Almutairi et al., 2025; Korkmaz et al., 2026). Moreover, explainable artificial intelligence (XAI) has attracted increased attention because it improves model transparency and supports decision-making processes in transportation systems (Alotaibi, 2025; Transportation Research Part E, 2024). However, most studies focus on general traffic safety rather than freight transportation operations.

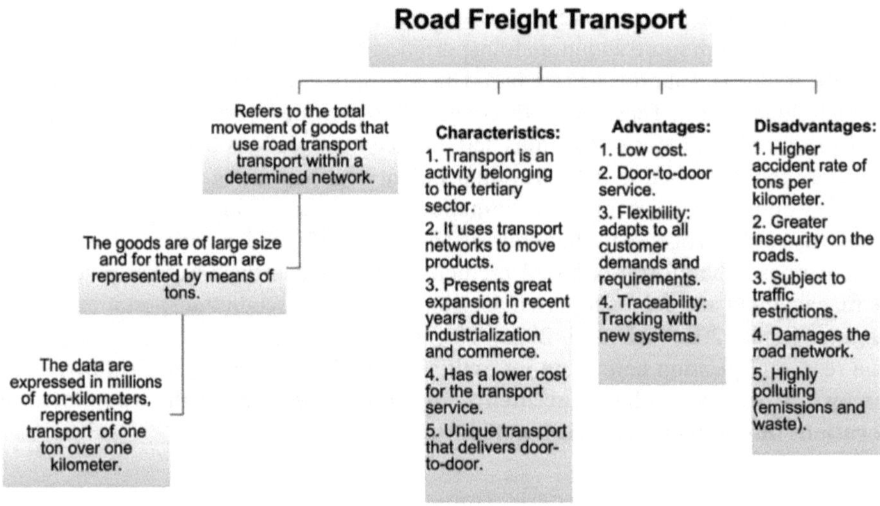

Fig. 1. Attributes of land freight transport

3.3 Systemic and Multidimensional Approaches

Freight transportation accidents result from the interaction of human, operational, vehicular, environmental, technological, and infrastructure-related factors. Thus, a number of researchers have highlighted the need for systemic approaches which capture these interactions. Many study methods such as the Ishikawa diagram have been used to identify and structure accident causes, to identify relevant variables for predictive modeling (Chen, 2024). However, most of the existing studies consider only a few factors and often do not incorporate all of the relevant dimensions in the same way.

3.4 Predictive Analytics in Logistics 4.0

The rise of Logistics 4.0 has driven the adoption of predictive analytics, artificial intelligence, telematics, IoT technologies, and intelligent monitoring systems in transportation. These technologies enable proactive decision making by predicting disruptions, equipment failures, operational risks, and accident occurrences (Turab et al., 2026). The increasing availability of real-time operational data presents great potential for predictive analytics in transportation safety management to bring about a more resilient and efficient logistics system (BID, 2023).

3.5 Research Gap and Research Contribution

While progress in AI-based accident prediction has been made, there are still significant research gaps. First, most studies focus on general traffic safety, not freight transportation and urban logistics corridors. Second, models are generally designed to focus on specific groups of variables (e.g. environmental conditions, driver behavior, and traffic characteristics), not the multidimensionality of freight transportation accidents. Third, few studies provide a systematic approach that connects conceptual accident analysis, variable operationalization, and machine learning implementation in one framework. In this study, we propose a multidimensional artificial intelligence framework that considers six aspects of accident causation: human, operational, vehicular, environmental, technological, and infrastructure. This framework integrates the conceptual modeling, variable operationalization, and predictive analytics layer into a single approach to future accident prediction in freight transportation systems.

Table 1 summarizes representative studies related to accident prediction and highlights the research gap addressed by the proposed framework.

Table 1. Literature review

Study	Domain	Method	Main Variables	Limitation
Li & Luo (2023)	Traffic Safety	Spatial Models	Environmental Factors	Limited operational perspective
Mostafa et al. (2025)	Crash Severity	Machine Learning	Traffic Variables	Limited freight focus
Vicent et al. (2024)	Accident Prediction	Deep Learning	Driver and Traffic Data	Limited infrastructure integration
Korkmaz et al. (2026)	Traffic Incidents	Random Forest	Incident Patterns	Not freight-specific
Proposed Framework	Freight Transportation	Logistic Regression + Random Forest	Six-dimensional structure	Requires real-world validation

4 Methodology

4.1 Research Approach

In this study, we adopt a quantitative approach to assess the technical feasibility of an artificial intelligence framework for accident prediction in freight transportation along urban logistics corridors. The research process consists of four stages: Identification of accident-related factors through multidimensional analysis. Establish a matrix of operationalization for a synthetic dataset of freight transportation operations. Training and evaluation of machine learning models.

4.2 Framework Design

The proposed framework takes a systemic view in which accident occurrence is influenced by six dimensions: technological, vehicular, human, environmental, infrastructure, and operational factors. The Ishikawa diagram was used to identify and organize the major causes associated with freight transportation accidents. Figure 2 presents the conceptual structure of the framework, while Fig. 3 summarizes the accident prediction and prevention process used for model development.

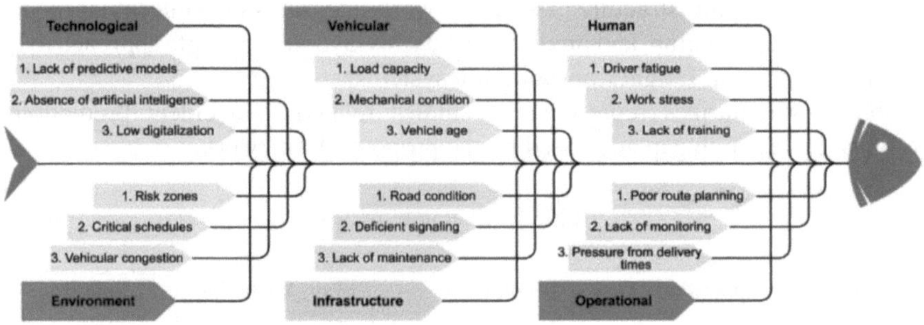

Fig. 2. Ishikawa diagram on accident rates in freight trucking

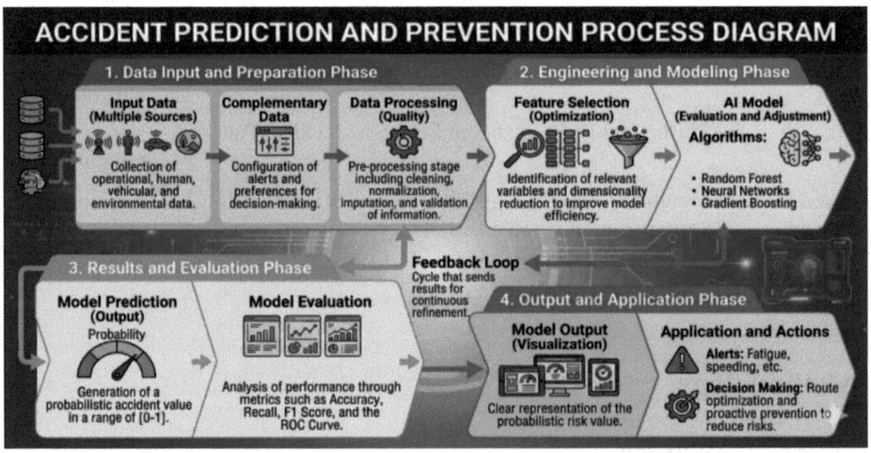

Fig. 3. Accident prediction and prevention process

4.3 Mathematical Model

The probability of accident occurrence was modeled as a binary classification problem. Let (Y) denote the accident outcome, where

$Y = 1\{\text{if an accident occurs}\} \& 0\{\text{otherwise}\}$

The accident probability was estimated through a logistic function:

$P(Y = 1) = \frac{1}{1 + e^{-z}}$ where:

$z = \beta_0 + \beta_1X_1 + \beta_2X_2 + \cdots+\beta_nX_n$

and (X_i) are the accident-related variables in the framework. Other interaction terms were added to represent nonlinear relationships between the selected variables, in account of the multi-dimensional nature of accident causation for freight transportation. Then, the probability was used to generate the binary accident outcome for model training and evaluation.

4.4 Variable Operationalization

The Ishikawa data were converted into measurable indicators for machine learning. The operationalization process determined indicators and measurement scales for each variable, and the heterogeneous variables could be integrated into a predictive system. Table 2 summarizes the operationalized variables used in this study.

Table 2. Comparative classification of accident model variables

Dimension	Variable	Indicator	Scale
Technological	Predictive Models	Existence of predictive systems	Nominal
Technological	AI Implementation	Level of AI adoption	Ordinal
Technological	Digitalization Level	Percentage of digitalized processes	Quantitative
Vehicular	Vehicle Load Capacity	Tons transported	Quantitative
Vehicular	Mechanical Condition	Failure rate index	Ordinal
Vehicular	Vehicle Age	Years in service	Quantitative
Human	Driving Hours	Continuous driving hours	Quantitative
Human	Occupational Stress	Stress level	Ordinal
Human	Safety Training	Training courses completed	Quantitative
Environmental	High-Risk Zones	Number of historical incident zones	Quantitative
Environmental	Critical Operating Hours	Frequency of operation during high-risk periods	Quantitative
Environmental	Traffic Congestion	Traffic index	Ordinal
Infrastructure	Road Condition	Road quality index	Ordinal
Infrastructure	Signage Quality	Signage adequacy level	Ordinal
Infrastructure	Road Maintenance	Maintenance interventions	Quantitative
Operational	Route Planning	Logistics efficiency index	Ordinal

The operationalization matrix provides a structured link between the conceptual dimensions identified through the Ishikawa analysis and the variables required for predictive modeling. This process ensures methodological consistency and enables the integration of heterogeneous factors into a unified artificial intelligence framework. The structure of such a data system provides a mechanism for the conceptual model to be translated into an analytical model capable of analysis in terms of artificial intelligence, and is therefore very much consistent with the methodology and analytical validity. The matrix is important to our system, as it links the independent variables to the dependent variable (accidents), therefore making it applicable to machine learning algorithms.

4.5 Synthetic Dataset Generation

Since no publicly available dataset includes all six dimensions considered in this study, we have generated a synthetic dataset of 10,000 freight transportation operations for the purposes of testing a framework's internal consistency and technical feasibility. Continuous variables were generated using uniform and beta distributions, and categorical variables were simulated using predefined probability distributions that reflect real transportation situations. Accident occurrence was modeled using a logistic function that included both individual variables and a set of interaction terms. Risk-enhancing factors such as driver fatigue, vehicle deterioration, congestion, poor infrastructure, and operation in high-risk zones received positive coefficients, while protective factors like training, digitalization, GPS monitoring, and AI implementation received negative coefficients. The resulting accident probability was converted into a sigmoid function and then into a binary accident outcome. Table 3 summarizes the variables and probability distributions used during dataset generation.

Table 3. Synthetic dataset variables and generation distributions

Variable	Distribution	Parameters
Vehicle Age	Uniform	U(0,15)
Driving Hours	Uniform	U(0,12)
Training Courses	Poisson	$\lambda = 1$
Time Pressure	Beta	$\alpha = 2, \beta = 5$
Digitalization	Uniform	U(0,100)
Cargo Weight	Uniform	U(1,40)
Mechanical Condition	Categorical	50%-30%-20%
Congestion	Categorical	30%-50%-20%
Infrastructure Quality	Categorical	40%-40%-20%
GPS Monitoring	Binary	60%-40%
AI Implementation	Binary	30%-70%
Risk Zone	Binary	20%-80%

4.6 Experimental Setup

The synthetic dataset was divided into training (80%) and testing (20%) subsets with random seed (random_state = 42). Two supervised machine learning algorithms were tested: Logistic Regression and Random Forest. Assessment of the model performance was conducted on Accuracy, Precision, Recall, F1-score, and AUC-ROC to assess classification performance and discrimination ability (Fig. 4).

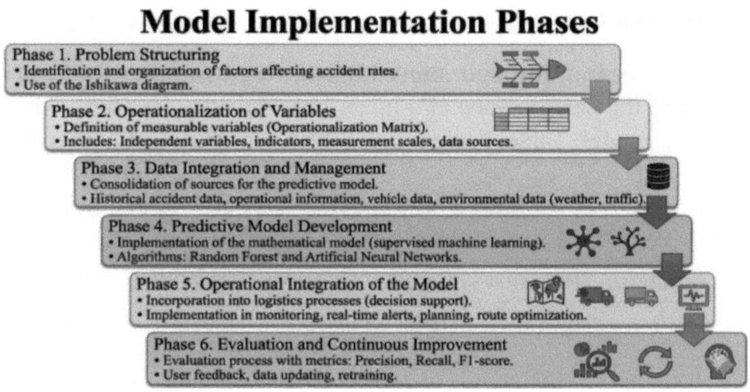

Fig. 4. Model implementation phases

4.7 Model Configuration

Random Forest was trained with 100 trees (n_estimators = 100) and the maximum depth was 10 (max_depth = 10). Logistic Regression was trained with the default optimization procedure with max_iter = 1000. Both models were trained and evaluated using the same dataset partitions to match the statistics.Proof-of-Concept Implementation and Results

4.8 Synthetic Dataset Characteristics

The proof-of-concept implementation was carried out in the synthetic dataset described in Sect. 4.5. The dataset consisted of 10,000 simulated freight transportation operations in the six-dimensional form of the proposed framework. The observations were generated with technological, vehicular, human, environmental, infrastructure, and operational variables. Continuous variables were generated with uniform and beta probability distributions, categorical variables with predefined probability distributions for the plausible freight transportation conditions.

Accidents were simulated with a logistic function with both direct effects and selected interaction terms. The resulting dataset was divided into training and testing subsets using an 80/20 partition. The training data were 8,000 observations for model training and 2,000 for performance evaluation. The experimental data is stored with a fixed randomly chosen seed to ensure the reliability of the results. The dataset is not a real freight transportation system, but it gives us a controlled environment to test the internal consistency, methodological coherence, and technical feasibility of the proposed framework.

4.9 Model Performance

We tested two machine learning algorithms: Logistic Regression and Random Forest. We wanted to compare the performance of a linear probabilistic classifier with a nonlinear ensemble learning model. Table 4 summarizes the performance of both models.

Table 4. Performance metrics

Model	Accuracy	Precision	Recall	F1-Score	AUC-ROC	Interpretation
Random Forest	0.910	0.915	0.866	0.890	0.940	Strong predictive performance with balanced precision and classification capability.
Logistic Regression	0.940	0.918	0.939	0.928	0.989	Best overall performance; excellent discrimination between accident and non-accident cases.

As shown in Table 4, both models have a good predictive performance with AUC-ROC values above 0.94, thus indicating high discrimination between accident and non-accident. Logistic Regression has the highest overall predictive performance with 94.0% accuracy and AUC-ROC of 0.989. It also has the highest recall (0.939) and can correctly identify accidents more accurately.

Random Forest also has good predictive ability to predict accidents with 91.0% accuracy and AUC-ROC of 0.940. While its Recall is a little less than Logistic Regression, it still has high Precision values, so a low proportion of false-positive classifications are produced. Since the evaluation was based on synthetic data, these results should be taken as technical feasibility and internal consistency rather than empirical validation of real-world predictive performance.

4.10 ROC Analysis

The ROC curve analysis is shown in Fig. 5. Both models demonstrated excellent discrimination capability, achieving AUC values above 0.94. Logistic Regression was slightly better than Random Forest as it achieved an AUC value of 0.989 compared with 0.940.

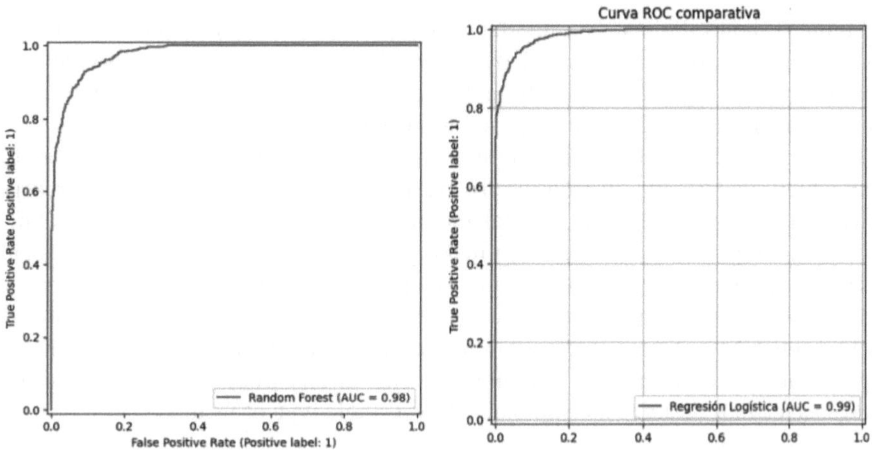

Fig. 5. ROC curve

All of this is in line with the data generation mechanism used in our simulation. The synthetic accident data were generated using a logistic function which showed the relation between predictors and accident occurrence. The simulated environment then naturally favored a model like Logistic Regression.

Therefore, we should not consider the superiority of Logistic Regression as evidence that it outperforms Random Forest in freight transportation accident prediction. We should note that this is the case because it reflects the characteristics of the controlled simulation environment used for proof of concept implementation.

4.11 Feature Importance Analysis

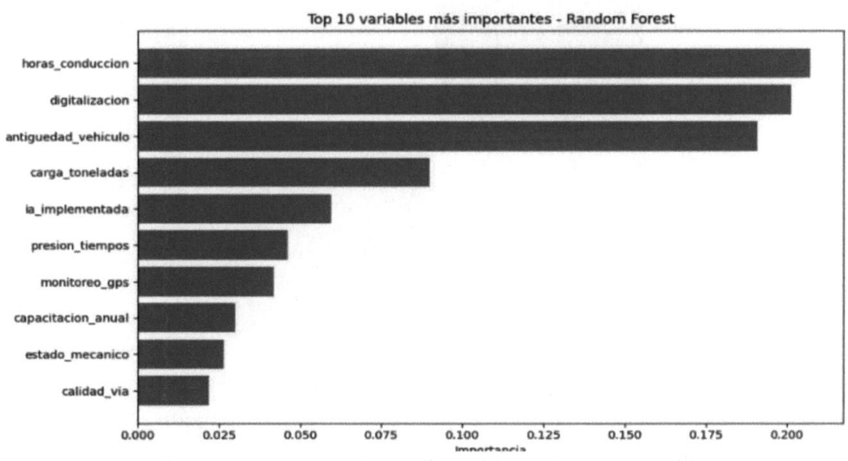

Fig. 6. Most important variables according to the Random Forest

Figure 6 shows the feature importance analysis of the Random Forest model. The most important variables identified by the model were driving hours, digitalization level, and vehicle age. These results indicate the relevance of human, technological, and vehicular dimensions in the proposed framework.

The importance of driving hours is also supported by the literature on transportation safety which suggests long periods of driving are associated with fatigue, poor reaction ability, and higher accident risk. Digitalization also plays a significant role in risk mitigation by giving visibility and decision-making ability to the operators, and the fact that we see an increase in vehicle age is also a key predictor of the safety of transportation.

Older vehicles may have more maintenance needs, higher mechanical failure risk, and less reliability in transportation. The fact that multiple variables are in the mix supports the multidimensional structure proposed in this work and suggests accident occurrence cannot be adequately explained by a single type of factors.

4.12 Proof-of-Concept Findings

The proof of concept implementation demonstrates that our framework can successfully integrate heterogeneous variables from six conceptual dimensions into a single predictive system. The operationalization matrix, mathematical formulation, and machine learning implementation are all consistent and can generate stable classification results under controlled conditions.

Moreover, the framework has successfully transformed conceptual accident-related factors into measurable indicators that can be analyzed with predictive algorithms. Figure 7 shows the confusion matrix for the Random Forest model.

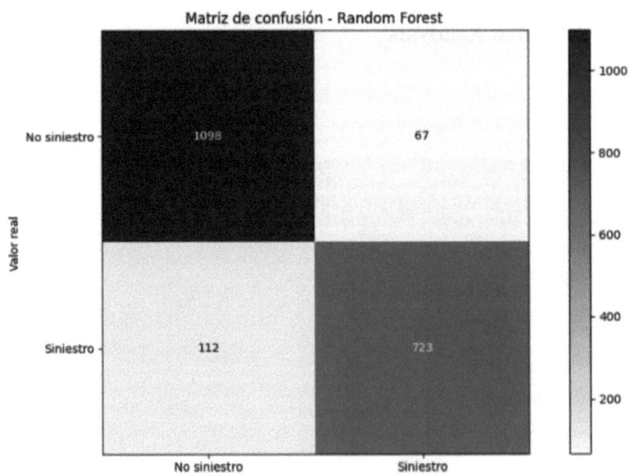

Fig. 7. Confusion matrix

In fact, the matrix shows that the framework correctly classified a large part of accident and non-accident cases while maintaining relatively low levels of false positives and false negatives. These results provide further evidence for the internal consistency of our methodology. However, the results should not be taken as an indication that the reported levels of performance will be replicated in real freight transportation.

Real-world data are full of measurement errors, missing values, inconsistencies, nonlinear relationships, and operational variability that cannot be fully captured by synthetic simulations. So the main contribution of this stage is to validate the technical feasibility of the framework and its methodology and lay the foundation for future empirical studies based on operational freight transportation data.

5 Discussion

The results have illustrated the technical feasibility of the proposed framework, in terms of its compatibility as a multidimensional accident prediction model for freight transportation systems. Although the implementation is done with synthetic data, the results show that variables and concepts from different domains can be combined as a unified predictive model. One of the most important results is that both algorithms perform well in terms of predictive performance. The high AUC-ROC of the chosen variables shows that all of them are more reliable, and can distinguish between accident and non-accident cases in a controlled simulation setting. This is consistent with previous studies that are able to demonstrate the effectiveness of machine learning methods in transportation safety (Mostafa et al., 2025; Vicent et al., 2024; Korkmaz et al., 2026). However, it is important to differentiate between performance obtained in synthetic environments and performance that can be achieved in real-world situations.

The objective of this paper is not to validate a deployable accident prediction system but to identify the coherence and technical feasibility of the proposed framework. Thus, the results should be regarded as proof of concept and not as a proof of operational effectiveness. The comparison of Logistic Regression with Random Forest provides us with additional insight into the behavior of the simulated environment. Logistic Regression performed better than Random Forest on most of the evaluation measures. This result can be explained by the data generation process of the study. Since the accident was simulated in a logistic structure with some pre-defined coefficients and few interaction effects, the data architecture is naturally compatible with Logistic Regression. Hastie et al. (2009) pointed out that simpler parametric models often perform well when the relationship between predictors and outcomes is relatively stable and predictable.

The latter should not be taken as a hint that Logistic Regression is more effective than Random Forest in freight transportation safety. In the real world, accidents can be caused by highly nonlinear interactions between the driver, vehicle condition, traffic congestion, infrastructure quality, weather conditions, etc. In such circumstances, the ensemble learning tools and deep learning models might be very helpful to capture the complex relationships that are more difficult to represent in a linear way (Alfasi et al., 2025; Almutairi et al., 2025; Mostafa et al., 2025).

Another important contribution of the study is its multidimensional perspective. In many previous accident prediction studies, the focus is on a single group of variables, such as traffic condition, environment, or driver behavior. In this paper, we propose to study six dimensional aspects of the accident prediction: human, operational, vehicular, environmental, technological, and infrastructure-related factors. This integration is in direct line with the research gaps in the literature and is an indication of the systemic reality of freight transportation safety. The feature importance analysis is also in line with such a multidimensional approach. The importance of driving hours highlights the need for human factors and fatigue management and driver workload in accident prevention, and digitalization is also relevant because of the risk reduction potential of the technology in terms of improving visibility of operations, monitoring, and decision-making processes.

The age of vehicles also emphasizes the importance of fleet maintenance and asset renewal strategies in transportation safety management. The framework can be a decision-support tool for logistics operators and transportation organizations from a practical perspective. Freight companies could apply similar predictive architectures to predict high-risk operations, focus on preventive maintenance, ensure driver scheduling and fleet monitoring, etc. Transportation authorities may use the same models to identify high-risk corridors, recommend infrastructure investment decisions, and work toward proactive road safety policy.

There are also several limitations of synthetic data that cannot be fully reproduced in real transportation, such as variability and measurement errors, inconsistencies, hidden correlations, and behavioral complexities. Moreover, the coefficients and relationships we used to generate the data were concepts only and may not be accurate in real-life accident scenarios. Thus, the reported performance metrics should not be taken as a measurement of operational deployment performance. Future work should focus on validating our framework using data from freight transportation companies, government transportation agencies, and intelligent transportation systems.

Future work should also include real-time telematics data, IoT sensors, weather information, and traffic dynamics. In addition, machine learning approaches like deep neural networks, recurrent neural networks, Long Short-Term Memory (LSTM), and explainable artificial intelligence (XAI) could be considered to improve predictive capabilities and model interpretation. Overall, we find that the proposed framework provides a coherent and technically viable basis for future accident prediction systems in freight transportation. While more work is required to validate the predictive capability using operational data, we believe this study shows that a systematic integration of multiple variables has the potential to develop prediction solutions that are aligned with Logistics 4.0 as well as intelligent transportation systems.

6 Conclusions

In this work, we proposed a multi-dimensional artificial intelligence-based framework for predicting the occurrence of accidents in freight transportation along major urban logistics corridors. The framework integrates six dimensions (human, operational, vehicular, environmental, technological, and infrastructure-based) into an integrated analytical architecture for predictive safety management. It adds to the literature by combining systems analysis, variable operationalization, synthetic data generation, and machine learning in a single framework. The new approach addresses freight transportation safety by acknowledging that accidents occur because many factors intersect (not as isolated variables) and therefore it is technically feasible as well as internally consistent. In practice, we demonstrated that the concept of the system is technically feasible and consistent with the methodology. Both Logistic Regression and Random Forest performed well in the simulation environment, indicating that the multidimensional structure can be translated into machine learning-based prediction models.

The results also showed the importance of driver behavior, technological adoption, and vehicle condition on the analysis, and the analysis was based on a systemic perspective. However, the findings should be interpreted with caution. Since we evaluated the methodology using synthetic data, the performance of the analysis is not a valid test of real-world accident prediction ability. The objective of this work is to show that the framework is feasible and predictive rather than to perform the analysis in real freight transportation. The framework is a conceptual foundation for intelligent decision support systems that will help in the development of transportation safety. Predictive analytics with logistics management can assist in risk prevention, fleet monitoring, and strategic planning for both freight operators and transportation authorities. Future studies must be done to validate the proposed framework based on real-world transportation data from logistics companies, public agencies, and intelligent transportation systems.

Other research could incorporate telematics, Internet of Things (IoT) sensors, real-time traffic information, weather factors, and machine learning methods like deep learning and explainable artificial intelligence. The study shows that a multi-dimensional approach made up of data can be a good foundation for future accident prediction systems in freight transport. Moreover, although we need more empirical verification of the framework, it is a relevant first step in the integration of artificial intelligence, transportation safety, and Logistics 4.0 principles in urban freight mobility.

References

Alfasi, B., et al.: Neural Networks for Accident Prediction (2025)

Almutairi, A., et al. : Deep Learning Accident Prevention (2025)

Alotaibi, J.: Explainable artificial intelligence for traffic accident prediction. Vehicles. (2025)

Ballou, R.H., Saporito, I.: Logística: Administración de la cadena de suministro, 6th edn. Pearson Educación (2023)

Banco Interamericano de Desarrollo (BID). Movilidad urbana sostenible en América Latina (2023)

Chen, P.: AI and GIS for Accident Prediction (2024a)

Chen, P. : Artificial Intelligence Applications in Transportation Systems (2024b).

Comisión Económica para América Latina y el Caribe (CEPAL). Seguridad vial en América Latina (2022)

CONAPRA. Informe de seguridad vial en México (2022)

Coyle, J.J., Langley, C.J., Novack, R.A., Gibson, B.: Supply Chain Management: a Logistics Perspective, 11th edn. Cengage Learning (2023)

Gonçalves, A., Ray, P., Soper, B., Stevens, J., Coyle, L., Sales, A.P.: Generation and evaluation of synthetic patient data. BMC Med. Res. Methodol. **20**(1), 108 (2020). https://doi.org/10.1186/s12874-020-00977-1

Hastie, T., Tibshirani, R., Friedman, J.: The Elements of Statistical Learning. Springer (2009)

Instituto Nacional de Estadística y Geografía (INEGI). Accidentes de tránsito terrestre (2024)

Korkmaz, A., et al.: Traffic incident prediction using machine learning. Electronics. (2026)

Li, W., Luo, Z.: Spatial modeling of traffic accidents. ISPRS Int. J. Geo Inf. (2023)

Mostafa, A., et al.: AI-based prediction of traffic crash severity. Sci. Rep. (2025)

Nikolenko, S.I.: Synthetic Data for Deep Learning. Springer (2021)
Patki, N., Wedge, R., Veeramachaneni, K.: The synthetic data vault. In: Proceedings of the IEEE International Conference on Data Science and Advanced Analytics (2016)
Secretaría de Infraestructura, Comunicaciones y Transportes (SICT). Estadísticas de siniestralidad (2023)
Transportation Research Part E. Explainable AI in logistics systems (2024)
Tucker, A., Wang, Z., Rotalinti, Y., Myles, P.: Generating high-fidelity synthetic patient data for assessing machine learning healthcare software. Npj Digital Med. **3**(1), 147 (2020). https://doi.org/10.1038/s41746-020-00353-9
Turab, D., et al.: Traffic accident prediction modeling. Data Sci. J. (2026)
Vicent, J., et al.: Deep learning for accident prediction. Neural Comput. Applic. (2024)

Decision Governance as an Anti-corruption Shield in Public Works: The AI+FMEA-ESG Model Applied to the Construction Project Life Cycle in Peru

Rubén Gómez Sánchez Soto(✉)

Faculty of Mechanical Engineering, National University of Engineering (UNI), Lima, Peru
rgomezsanchez@uni.edu.pe

Abstract. Corruption in Peruvian public construction is often preceded by deficiencies in the Technical Project Dossier (TPD), the documentary package approved before bidding and execution. Existing tools quantify execution risk through FMEA or detect corruption from post-award procurement metadata, but they do not treat TPD approval as an ex-ante decision gate. This paper proposes AI+FMEA-ESG, a rule-based decision-support model that extends FMEA with a governance-weighted ESG modifier (see Eq. 1 below), bounded ±20%, to prioritize documentary defects across six PMBOK 6 life-cycle phases.

$$AdjRPN = RPN \times (1 + (ESG - 3)/10)$$

Equation 1. *Composite AdjRPN formula.*

The model is anchored to SEACE/CONOSCE procurement data, a 233-case Basel Institute/CGR typology, and OSCE regulations. Results show that Phase F2 (Design and Development) is the principal intervention point: five defect modes reach Critical AdjRPN (≥270), with absent technical studies scoring highest (AdjRPN = 451). Seven Governance Solution Proposals translate these findings into auditable decision gates compatible with Peru's digital procurement ecosystem. The revised version also discloses the scoring protocol, provides a worked example and sensitivity analysis, and sets out the current validation status explicitly.

Keywords: ESG governance · AI+FMEA · technical project dossier · public construction corruption · project life cycle · decision governance · concurrent control · Peru

1 Introduction

Throughout this paper, TPD refers to the Technical Project Dossier (expediente técnico): drawings, technical studies, quantity takeoffs, budget, schedule, and risk plan that a Peruvian contracting entity must approve before a public construction project

H. Florez and R. Gomez-Sanchez (Eds.): UPADI-AI 2026, CCIS 3124, pp. 175–189, 2027.
https://doi.org/10.1007/978-3-032-35635-2_12

can be tendered and executed. Public infrastructure investment is a key driver of competitiveness and social equity in developing economies. In Peru, CGR audit findings extrapolated by Shack et al. [4] estimate annual losses from corruption and misconduct at 14.9% of the public budget executed in 2019 (S/23,297 million; $\approx$3% of GDP). Institutional evidence confirms that TPD deficiencies are the proximal mechanism behind addenda, cost overruns, delays, and stoppages [5–7]. The Basel Institute on Governance [8], analyzing 233 adverse situations across 36 large projects, reports that TPD-related violations represent the most frequent documented typology (9% of cases). This evidence exposes a research gap: (a) conventional FMEA quantifies physical and process risk with no governance dimension; (b) ESG governance frameworks are not operationalized as phase-gated documentary rules; (c) machine-learning anti-corruption tools operate on administrative bidding metadata at or after contract award. No existing tool treats the TPD-approval gate as a quantified ex-ante decision point.

This paper proposes AI+FMEA-ESG, grounded in three evidentiary layers: SEACE/CONOSCE procurement data, a Basel Institute/CGR defect typology, and OSCE regulatory traceability. Six contributions are made: (1) formalizing Governance as an auditable decision variable; (2) demonstrating functional equivalence between TPD-deficiency prevention and corruption prevention; (3) a phase-by-phase risk matrix with worked example and sensitivity analysis; (4) seven GSPs; (5) explicit positioning against FMEA and AI-for-procurement literature; and (6) a transparent, falsifiable, recalibrable framework.

2 Related Work

2.1 FMEA in Construction Risk Management

FMEA has been applied in construction for over a decade to physical, safety, and scheduling failures. Extensions through fuzzy-AHP, SWARA, WASPAS, MABAC, and grey relational analysis improve ordinal S/O/D scoring [19–21], but none incorporates governance as an anti-corruption mechanism.

2.2 ESG-Integrated Infrastructure Governance

ESG frameworks have been proposed for infrastructure appraisal [9, 10, 16] and sustainable construction risk [14]. The Governance pillar is typically one of three co-equal dimensions rather than the central documentary decision lever proposed here—it is not operationalized as a phase-gated rule.

2.3 AI-Based Anti-corruption in Public Procurement

The machine-learning literature includes cross-national red-flag proxies [22], random forests validated against judiciary records [23], a Paraguayan complaint-detection system [24], a Mexican random-forest model [25], and positive-unlabeled network methods [26]. These tools analyze administrative bidding metadata at or after contract award—not TPD documentary content ex ante.

2.4 Positioning of This Study

The present model differs in four ways: unit of analysis is TPD documentary content; intervention is ex ante; mechanism is a governance-weighted modifier; alignment is with Peru-specific institutions (OSCE, SEACE, CGR). The model is complementary to, not a substitute for, procurement red-flag systems (Table 7).

3 Theoretical Framework

3.1 Decision Governance in Public Infrastructure

Klitgaard [12] defines corruption as a function of monopoly, discretion, and accountability:

$$Corruption = Monopoly + Discretion - Accountability$$

Equation 2. Klitgaard's corruption identity.

The G dimension attacks all three terms: independent technical review reduces monopoly; transparent AdjRPN thresholds reduce discretion; SEACE-registered risk-owner assignments increase accountability. Agency theory [17] complements this by framing TPD review as a mechanism to reduce information asymmetry between principal (contracting entity, CGR) and agents (designer, contractor).

3.2 FMEA, ESG, and Governance Integration

FMEA operationalizes risk via the classical Risk Priority Number:

$$RPN = S \times O \times D$$

Equation 3. Classical FMEA Risk Priority Number.

[18, 19]. The AI+FMEA-ESG model, building on Rev. 08 [11], integrates the ESG Governance dimension as a bounded modifier that amplifies base RPN when governance is weak and reduces it when governance controls are in place—rather than treating G as one co-equal pillar among three.

3.3 What "AI" Means in AI+FMEA-ESG

The current implementation is a rule-based decision-support system—symbolic AI [27]—not a trained ML model. Two mechanisms are automated: threshold-based AdjRPN classification (four decision categories) and the Digital Governance Indicator (DGI, GSP-7), which converts binary registry facts into a G sub-score. A Phase 2 roadmap proposes a supervised text classifier trained on SEACE-digitized TPDs—a future step, not a current result.

3.4 Empirical Evidence Base

Three sources anchor the model. Shack et al. [4]: 14.9% of 2019 public spending lost to corruption, led by transportation and health. Basel Institute [8]: 233 adverse situations, 36 projects; TPD violations most frequent typology (9%); 76% of cases originated during execution with root causes in the TPD. CGR [5–7]: Hospital Antonio Lorena (S/4.6 M; 18 indicted), Chivay (S/ 398K), Cerro Colorado (S/1 M).

4 Methodology

4.1 Model Specification

Ten TPD defect modes (MD-01–MD-10) are evaluated across six life-cycle phases. Base risk is defined as:

$$RPN = S \times O \times D, S, O, D \in \{1, ..., 10\}$$

Equation 3a. Base risk (repeated for clarity within Methodology).

The ESG modifier is the mean of the three sub-scores:

$$ESG = mean(E, So, G), E, So, G \in \{1, ..., 5\}$$

Equation 4. ESG modifier definition.

The composite adjusted risk index is:

$$AdjRPN = RPN \times (1 + (ESG - 3)/10), \textit{bounded} \pm 20\%$$

Equation 1 (repeated). Composite AdjRPN formula.

Thresholds: <100 Low; 100–199 Moderate; 200–269 High; ≥270 Critical (halt and redesign). The Critical threshold is calibrated against Article 34.6 of Law 30225 (15% ceiling for supplementary works). Figure 1 shows the full computational chain.

4.2 Research Design and Evidentiary Layers

Non-experimental quantitative documentary design. Layer A (SEACE/CONOSCE, 2018–2024): 41,439 procedures, S/ 175,430 M—contextualizes fiscal exposure. Layer B (Basel/CGR): anchors O and D sub-scores and supplies the ten defect modes. Layer C (OSCE regulations): defines SEACE registry requirements that the G rubric references.

4.3 Scoring Protocol

S anchored to CGR financial damage bands: < S/100K $\rightarrow$ S $\leq$ 3; S/100K–1M $\rightarrow$ S4–6; S/1–10M $\rightarrow$ S7–9; > S/10M $\rightarrow$ S = 10. O anchored to Basel typology frequency rank. D anchored to ex-ante (D $\leq$ 5) vs. ex-post (D $\geq$ 7) identification. G follows the five-level rubric in Table 1. E and So follow analogous observable rubrics (Tables 2, 3).

Table 1. Five-level rubric for the G (Governance) sub-score of the ESG modifier.

G	Governance Condition
1	Documented independent review; TPD in SEACE; logbook active; risk owners assigned; concurrent control active
2	Documented internal review; TPD registered; logbook active; risk owners partially assigned
3	Standard review (independence not verified); TPD registered; logbook active
4	No independent review; late TPD registration; logbook inactive; risk owners unassigned
5	No documented review; TPD not in SEACE; no logbook; no concurrent control; history of non-compliance

Table 2. Five-level rubric for the E (Environmental) sub-score.

E	Environmental Condition
1	No environmental risk; standard construction footprint; no sensitive ecosystems
2	Minor risk, fully covered by routine mitigation (erosion/dust control)
3	Moderate risk requiring active monitoring (water/soil management near urban area)
4	Significant risk with potential community impact (noise/dust near hospital/school)
5	Severe or irreversible risk if defect uncorrected (structural failure, contamination, relocation)

Table 3. Five-level rubric for the So (Social) sub-score.

So	Social Condition
1	No social impact; defect is purely technical or administrative
2	Limited, localized inconvenience (minor delay; no service interruption)
3	Moderate impact (temporary service disruption; complaint-level community concern)
4	Significant impact (prolonged loss of essential service: water, health, education)
5	Severe impact (documented harm to a vulnerable population per CGR case files)

4.4 Worked Example: MD-04 Versus MD-08

Table 4 reconstructs AdjRPN for the two highest-scoring defect modes in Phase F2. Recomputed totals reproduce originally reported values within 1%, confirming internal model coherence.

Table 4. Worked example: AdjRPN reconstruction for MD-04 and MD-08 (Phase F2).

Parameter	MD-04—Absent technical studies	MD-08—Building-code non-compliance
S (Severity)	8	7
O (Occurrence)	6	10
D (Detection)	8	5
RPN = S × O × D	384	350
E/So/G	5/4/5	4/4/4
ESG = mean (E, So, G)	4.67	4.00
Modifier = 1+(ESG−3)/10	1.167	1.100
AdjRPN reported/recomputed	451/448 (Δ = 0.7%)	386/385 (Δ = 0.3%)

4.5 Sensitivity Analysis of the ESG Bound

The generalized sensitivity form of the model is:

$$AdjRPN = RPN \times (1 + (ESG - 3) \times k)$$

Equation 5. Generalized AdjRPN with adjustable sensitivity parameter k.

Published model: k = 0.10 (±20%). Tested at k = 0.05 (±10%) and k = 0.15 (±30%) (Table 5).

Table 5. Sensitivity of Phase-F2 AdjRPN classification to the ESG bound (ESG = 4.33 for representative modes).

Defect mode	RPN	AdjRPN k = 0.05	AdjRPN k = 0.10 (published)	AdjRPN k = 0.15
MD-01 (Robust)	327	348 → Critical	370 → Critical	392 → Critical
MD-02 (Sensitive)	247	264 → High	280 → Critical	296 → Critical
MD-06 (Sensitive)	234	249 → High	265 → High	281 → Critical

4.6 Methodological Limitations

Five limitations: (1) single-analyst scoring—no inter-rater reliability computed; (2) no validation with real TPD microdata from SEACE; (3) uniform ESG sub-score weighting; (4) rule-based AI without trained ML component; (5) calibration specific to the Peruvian institutional context.

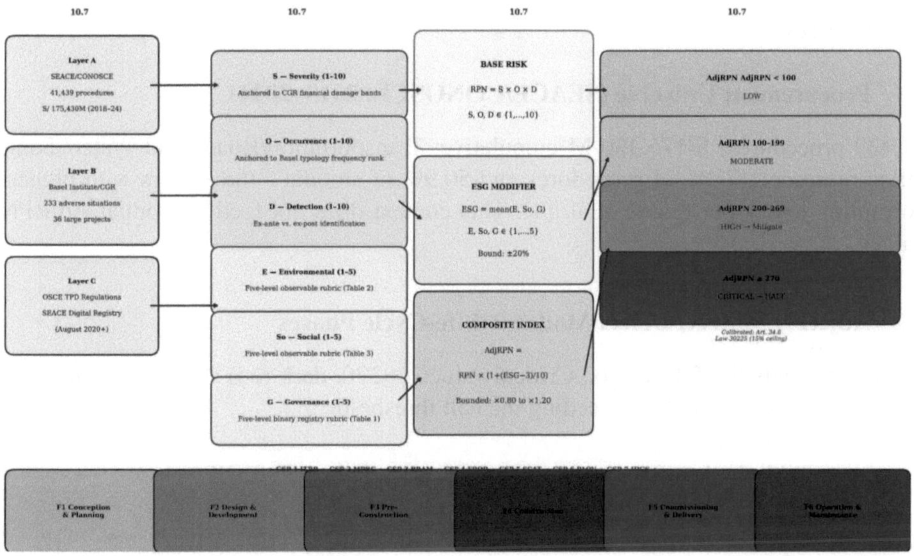

Fig. 1. Conceptual framework of the AI+FMEA-ESG model. Source: own elaboration based on AI+FMEA Rev. 08 [11] and PMBOK 6.

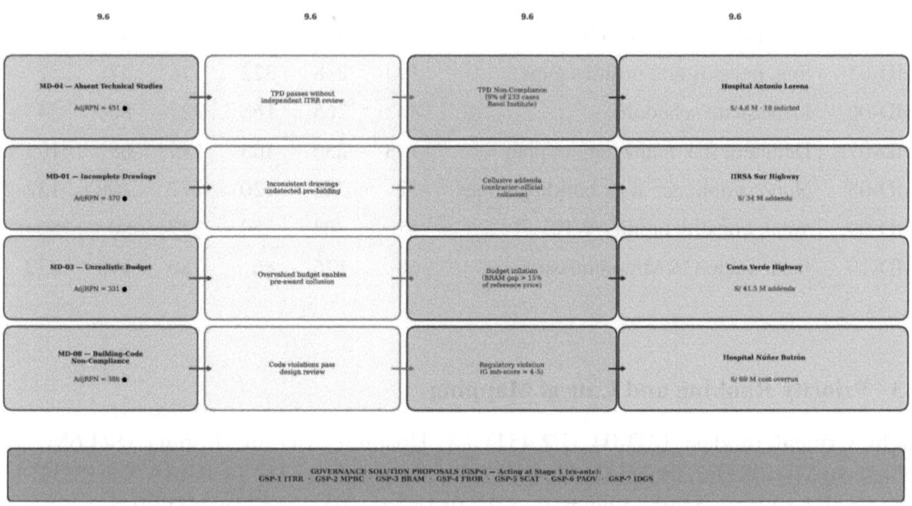

Fig. 2. Causal chain: TPD documentary deficiency → corruption pathway → documented state damage. Source: own elaboration based on Shack et al. [4], CGR [5–7], and Basel Institute [8].

5 Results

5.1 Procurement Universe (SEACE/CONOSCE, 2018–2024)

41,439 procedures; S/175,430 M cumulative. Transportation/Roads and Water/ Sanitation represent 47.4% of procedures and 50.9% of amount—the sectors with highest corruption losses per Shack et al. [4]. This context does not feed individual AdjRPN values.

5.2 AdjRPN Matrix: Defect Modes x Life-Cycle Phases

Table 6 presents the full matrix. Critical values (≥270, dark red) concentrate in Phase F2, with five defect modes exceeding the halt threshold.

Table 6. AdjRPN matrix: 10 TPD defect modes × 6 PMBOK 6 phases.

Code	TPD Defect Mode	F1	F2	F3	F4	F5	F6
MD-01	Incomplete/inconsistent drawings	158	370	126	126	57	43
MD-02	Deficient quantity takeoffs	86	280	133	168	68	40
MD-03	Unrealistic budget/unit costs	114	331	175	140	68	54
MD-04	Absent/insufficient technical studies	18	451	18	90	43	43
MD-05	Site, permits and utilities gaps	193	238	322	176	57	57
MD-06	Inadequate schedule	84	265	168	227	86	54
MD-07	Deficient risk management plan	108	236	103	189	68	108
MD-08	Non-compliance with building codes	72	386	120	277	108	132
MD-09	Weak constructability/WBS	68	308	150	227	80	86
MD-10	Inadequate O&M/commissioning	68	176	86	180	176	322

5.3 Priority Ranking and Causal Mapping

Eight Critical modes: MD-04 (F2,451) → Hospital Antonio Lorena (S/4.6M; 18 indicted); MD-08 (F2,386); MD-01 (F2,370); MD-03 (F2,331) → IIRSA Sur (S/34M); MD-05 (F3,322) → Majes-Siguas II (S/17.9M); MD-10 (F6,322); MD-09 (F2,308) → Hospital Núñez Butrón (S/69M); MD-02 (F2,280) → Costa Verde (S/41.5M). MD-06 and MD-07 require mitigation only (Fig. 2) (Fig. 3).

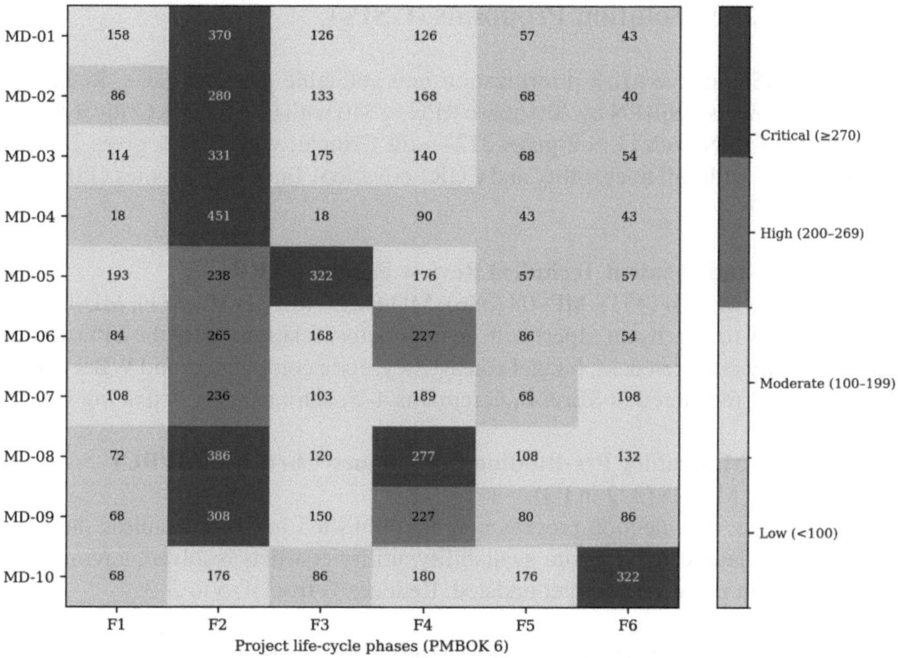

Fig. 3. AdjRPN heatmap: ten TPD defect modes across six PMBOK 6 phases. Colour bands correspond to Low, Moderate, High, and Critical categories defined in Sect. 4.1.

5.4 Comparative Positioning

Table 7. Comparative positioning: AI+FMEA-ESG vs. conventional FMEA and ML anti-corruption tools.

Approach	Unit/Intervention point	AI technique	Regulatory linkage	Validation status
Conventional/hybrid FMEA [18–21]	Physical-process/during execution	Expert RPN, fuzzy, MCDM	Generic	Published case studies
ML procurement models [30–34]	Bidding metadata/at or after award	Supervised ML, PU-learning, network science	EU, Italy, Mexico, Paraguay	Validated vs. judiciary/sanctions
This study—AI+FMEA-ESG	TPD documentary content/ex ante	Rule-based AI (ML roadmap: Sect. 3.3)	Peru: OSCE, SEACE, CGR	Conceptual; TPD-microdata validation pending

6 Governance Solution Proposals (GSPs)

The seven GSPs convert risk prioritization into auditable decision gates. Reducing G from 5 → 1 lowers AdjRPN by 20%: base RPN = 340 with G = 5 gives Critical AdjRPN = 408; same RPN with G = 2 gives 312—still Critical; with G = 1 gives 272—just above halt but with full traceability and CGR activation. Table 8 distributes GSPs across phases.

GSP-1 (F2)—Independent Technical Review Report (ITRR)
Defect Modes: MD-04 (451), MD-08 (386), MD-01 (370), MD-03 (331), MD-09 (308).

Mandatory review by an expert with no contractual relationship to the TPD designer, covering study completeness, budget consistency, code compliance, and WBS viability. Without ITRR registered in SEACE, G remains 4–5, automatically activating Halt.

GSP-2 (F3)—Mandatory Pre-Bidding Compliance Checklist (MPBC)
Defect Modes: MD-05 (322 in F3).

Binary gate: no selection process may be published in SEACE unless the MPBC is 100% complete, certifying site availability, utility conflicts resolved, environmental certifications in place, and budget updated. Reduces G from 4–5 to 2–3.

GSP-3 (F2)—Budget Rationality Audit Module (BRAM)
Defect Modes: MD-03 (331), MD-02 (280).

Mandatory ITRR component comparing unit costs against OSCE reference prices, flagging items >15% above market value. Directly targets budget inflation as the mechanism for pre-award collusion. Reduces G 4–5 → 1–3.

GSP-4 (F1)—Formal Risk Owner Register (FROR)
Defect Modes: MD-07 (236), MD-06 (265); transversal.

Named officials assigned from Phase F1 to each critical TPD component, with verification criteria and staff-rotation replacement protocols. FROR registered in SEACE reduces G 4–5 → 2–3.

GSP-5 (F4)—Sustained Critical Threshold (SCAT) + CGR Notification
Defect Modes: MD-08 (277 in F4).

AdjRPN ≥ 270 persisting across two consecutive monthly reviews triggers CGR concurrent-control activation. Supervisor records AdjRPN in the digital logbook; SCAT report filed in SEACE.

GSP-6 (F5–F6)—Pre-Acceptance Operational Verification (PAOV)
Defect Modes: MD-10 (322 in F6; early signal 176 in F5).

Mandatory condition for the Project Acceptance Certificate: complete O&M Manual, operator training, active warranty, formal risk-owner transfer. PAOV Act registered in SEACE reduces G 4–5 → 1–2.

GSP-7 (F1–F6)—Integrated Digital Governance System (IDGS) [Transversal].
Defect Modes: Enables GSPs 1–6 across all phases.

Real-time integration of SEACE's TPD registry, digital logbook, MEF Invierte.pe, INFOBRAS, and CGR concurrent-control platform. Computes the Digital Governance Indicator (DGI) from binary registry facts—converting G from expert judgment to an automated rule-based AI score. Critical AdjRPN alerts visible to citizens (Fig. 4).

Table 8. GSP distribution across PMBOK 6 life-cycle phases.

GSP	Description	F1	F2	F3	F4	F5	F6
GSP-1	ITRR		✓				
GSP-2	MPBC			✓			
GSP-3	BRAM		✓				
GSP-4	FROR	✓					
GSP-5	SCAT+CGR				✓		
GSP-6	PAOV					✓	✓
GSP-7	IDGS (transversal)	✓	✓	✓	✓	✓	✓

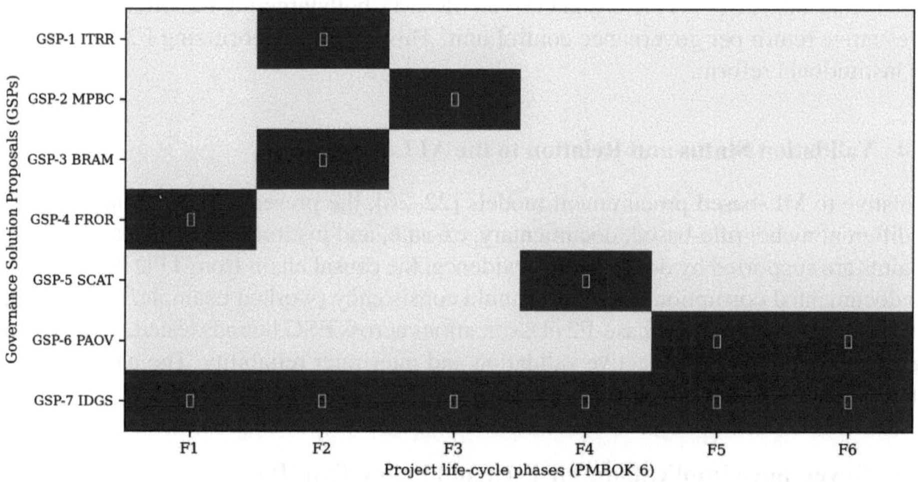

Fig. 4. Distribution of the seven Governance Solution Proposals (GSPs) across the six PMBOK 6 phases. GSP-7 (IDGS) operates transversally across all phases as the digital governance backbone.

7 Discussion

7.1 Documentary Governance as an Anti-corruption Intervention Point

The central finding is that corruption in public construction can be analyzed as a documentary governance failure concentrated at the TPD approval gate. The evidence reviewed from CGR and Basel Institute sources shows that downstream failures—addenda, overruns, indictments—originate in deficiencies that were not blocked before bidding. The AI+FMEA-ESG model reframes preventive anti-corruption as decision governance over documents, not only over contracts or procurement procedures.

7.2 Why the Governance Modifier Changes the Risk Calculus

Standard FMEA captures technical exposure through S, O, and D but does not represent the quality of review, the presence of digital traceability, risk-owner accountability, or concurrent-control activation. By embedding those institutional factors as a bounded $\pm 20\%$ modifier, the model makes governance quality a quantitative determinant of whether a defect remains manageable or becomes a halt event. This is the core mechanism through which Klitgaard's three corruption variables [12] are operationalized numerically.

7.3 Phase F2 Concentration and Its Practical Implications

The concentration of five Critical AdjRPN values in Phase F2 (Design and Development) is the most actionable result of the study. It implies that design-stage documentary failures are path-dependent precursors of execution-phase corruption, not isolated anomalies. It also means that GSP-1 (ITRR) and GSP-3 (BRAM), both targeting F2, offer the highest preventive return per governance control unit. This supports prioritizing F2 investment in institutional reform.

7.4 Validation Status and Relation to the AI Literature

Relative to ML-based procurement models [22–26], the present contribution occupies a different niche: rule-based, documentary, ex-ante, and institutionally traceable. Three claims are supported by documentary evidence: the causal chain from TPD deficiencies to documented corruption; internal formula consistency (worked example, $\Delta \leq 0.7\%$); and robustness of 8 of 10 Phase-F2 classifications across ESG bounds tested. Two claims remain future work: prospective validation and inter-rater reliability. The paper clearly states this distinction in Sects. 4.6, 7.3, and 8.

7.5 Governance Implications for Peru and Policy Transfer

For public management, the seven GSPs are directly embeddable in Peru's digital procurement architecture (SEACE, Invierte.pe, INFOBRAS, CGR concurrent control) without requiring new legislation—only binding operational directives from OSCE and the CGR. For research, the model opens a bridge between symbolic AI, documentary risk analysis, and institutional anti-corruption governance, and provides a falsifiable framework that can be tested, automated (DGI), and recalibrated for other procurement contexts.

8 Conclusions

1. Corruption in Peruvian public construction is functionally a documentary governance failure: the causal chain from TPD deficiencies to the 14.9% annual budget loss passes through ten AdjRPN-scorable defect modes preventable through phase-structured decision gates.
2. Phase F2 (Design and Development) is the highest-return intervention point: five defect modes reach Critical AdjRPN ($\geq$270), up to AdjRPN = 451 (MD-04), as reconstructed in the worked example ($\Delta \leq 0.7\%$).
3. The Governance modifier functions as an anti-corruption sensitivity amplifier. Its $\pm$20% bound is robust for 8 of 10 Phase-F2 modes; two boundary-sensitive modes (MD-02, MD-06) are explicitly identified.
4. The seven Governance Solution Proposals form an integrated decision-governance system acting preventively across all six life-cycle phases, aligned with the OSCE ecosystem and the CGR concurrent-control doctrine.
5. This paper makes a conceptual and methodological contribution—a fully disclosed, sensitivity-tested, internally consistent model with explicit literature positioning without yet claiming empirical impact reduction or predictive validation.
6. Priority next steps: (a) inter-rater reliability study (Cohen's kappa on S, O, D, G sub-scores); (b) validation with anonymized SEACE TPD microdata against documented project outcomes; (c) Phase 2 pilot training a text classifier on digitized TPD content for automated O and D scoring.

Declarations

Competing Interests: The author declares no competing interests.

Funding This research was conducted with the author's own resources; no external funding was received.

Data Availability SEACE/CONOSCE datasets are publicly available at https://bi.seace.gob.pe. CGR audit reports are publicly accessible at https://www.gob.pe/cgr.

Use of AI Tools Generative AI tools were used for language refinement, reconstruction of the worked example and sensitivity analysis, and redrawing of figures, all under the author's direction. All scoring decisions, analytical conclusions, and policy interpretations are the author's sole responsibility.

References

1. BID: Building Opportunities for Growth in a Challenging World. Inter-American Development Bank, Washington D.C. (2020)
2. AFIN: Un Plan para Salir de la Pobreza: Plan Nacional de Infraestructura para la Competitividad. AFIN, Lima (2022)

3. IMF: Peru: Staff Concluding Statement of the 2023 Article IV Consultation. IMF, Washington D.C. (2023)
4. Shack, N., Pérez, J., Portugal, L.: Cálculo del Índice de Gobernabilidad y Políticas Públicas en Gestión de Inversiones. CGR, Lima (2020)
5. CGR: Control Concurrente: Hospital Antonio Lorena — Informe de Visita de Control. CGR, Lima (2020)
6. CGR: Informe de Auditoría de Cumplimiento N.° 001-2021-CG/APPS-AC: Municipalidad de Chivay. CGR, Lima (2021)
7. CGR: Informe de Hito de Control: Municipalidad Distrital Cerro Colorado. CGR, Lima (2022)
8. Basel Institute on Governance: Corruption Risks in Infrastructure Projects in Peru. BIG, Basel (2023)
9. World Bank: ESG Country Risk Assessment for Infrastructure Lending. World Bank, Washington D.C. (2022)
10. OECD: Principles for Public Governance of Public-Private Partnerships. OECD, Paris (2021)
11. Gómez Sánchez Soto, R.: AI+FMEA-ESG Rev. 08: Modelo de Gobierno de Decisiones Anticorrupción en Obras Públicas [Working paper]. UNI, Lima (2024)

12. Klitgaard, R.: Controlling Corruption. University of California Press, Berkeley (1988)
13. PMI: A Guide to the Project Management Body of Knowledge (PMBOK® Guide), 6th ed. PMI, Newtown Square (2017)
14. Osei-Kyei, R., Chan, A.P.C.: Review of ESG application in PPP delivery. Int. J. Proj. Manag. **35**(4), 575–588 (2017)
15. OSCE: Reglamento de la Ley de Contrataciones del Estado (D.S. 344-2018-EF, August 2020 amendments). OSCE, Lima (2020)
16. Flyvbjerg, B.: Survival of the unfittest: why the worst infrastructure gets built. Oxf. Rev. Econ. Policy **25**(3), 344–367 (2009)
17. Jensen, M.C., Meckling, W.H.: Theory of the firm: managerial behavior, agency costs and ownership structure. J. Financ. Econ. **3**(4), 305–360 (1976)
18. Stamatis, D.H.: Failure Mode and Effect Analysis: FMEA from Theory to Execution, 2nd edn. ASQ Quality Press, Milwaukee (2003)
19. Carpitella, S., et al.: A combined multi-criteria approach to support FMEA analyses. J. Comput. Des. Eng. **5**(4), 479–496 (2018)
20. Liu, H.C., et al.: Failure mode and effects analysis using cloud model theory and PROMETHEE method. IEEE Trans. Reliab. **68**(4), 1173–1187 (2019)
21. Tian, Z.P., et al.: A multi-hesitant fuzzy linguistic FMEA approach for risk assessment. Expert Syst. Appl. **144**, 113138 (2020)
22. Fazekas, M., Kocsis, G.: Uncovering high-level corruption. Polit. Res. Q. **73**(4), 838–854 (2020)
23. Coviello, D., Mariniello, M.: Publicity requirements in public procurement. J. Public Econ. **109**, 76–100 (2014)
24. Manzetti, L., Rosas, G.: The political economy of contracting in Paraguay. Lat. Am. Res. Rev. **56**(1), 180–196 (2021)
25. Reyes-Menendez, A., et al.: Machine learning in public procurement fraud detection in Mexico. J. Bus. Res. **141**, 722–731 (2022)
26. Fundacja ePaństwo: Positive-unlabeled learning for procurement irregularity detection. In: Proceedings of ECML-PKDD 2022 (2022)
27. Russell, S., Norvig, P.: Artificial Intelligence: A Modern Approach, 4th edn. Pearson, Hoboken (2020)

Innovation in Road Heritage Preservation: An AI+FMEA Model for Optimal Maintenance and Public-Value Generation

Rubén Gómez Sánchez Soto(✉)

Universidad Nacional de Ingeniería (UNI), Av. Túpac Amaru 210, Rímac, Lima, Peru
rgomezsanchez@uni.edu.pe

Abstract. Road and public-works heritage represents a strategic asset for sustainable development and public-value generation, yet its management across Latin America has historically been reactive rather than risk-informed. This paper presents the AI+FMEA model, which shifts Failure Mode and Effects Analysis (FMEA) from a static, design-stage exercise to a continuously updated, sensor-driven process. Building on a forensic review of 100 documented infrastructure failures (2020–2026), the study shows that 54% of critical collapses originate in the design and construction phases, and that AI-assisted detection raises the Detection factor of the classical Risk Priority Number ($RPN = S \times O \times D$) far above what periodic visual inspection achieves, lifting overall detection capability from an estimated 45% to 88%. Internet-of-Things sensors, drone-borne LiDAR and InSAR surveys, and a machine-learning/computer-vision pipeline feed a Digital Twin that recalculates the RPN in near real time, enabling maintenance to move from reactive to predictive. Retrospective application of the model to four emblematic forensic cases—the Chirajara Bridge, the Morandi Bridge, the Space Building, and the Brumadinho tailings dam—shows that each would have been flagged as critical months before failure under the proposed scheme. Beyond the engineering gain, the model's auditable, tamper-resistant data trail is presented and discussed as a governance instrument against discretionary, corruption-prone maintenance decisions in public infrastructure.

Keywords: AI+FMEA · Risk Priority Number · Digital Twin · Predictive Maintenance · Road Heritage · Public Value · Infrastructure Governance

1 Introduction

1.1 Public Value and the Reactive Paradigm in Road-Heritage Management

Public infrastructure is the most valuable physical asset of a nation, yet across Latin America its management has historically been reactive rather than risk-informed. Maintenance programmes are typically triggered by visible deterioration or, in the worst cases, by failure itself, while the risks that ultimately determine an asset's fate are usually fixed much earlier, during design and construction. The notion of Public Value, increasingly used in infrastructure policy, demands the opposite logic: every technical decision should be oriented toward the longevity of the asset, the safety of citizens, and the efficient use of scarce public funds, from the very first design choice onward.

H. Florez and R. Gomez-Sanchez (Eds.): UPADI-AI 2026, CCIS 3124, pp. 190–204, 2027.
https://doi.org/10.1007/978-3-032-35635-2_13

Forensic engineering has long shown that catastrophic failures are rarely the product of a single, unforeseeable event; they are usually the visible end point of a chain of overlooked signals. Integrating forensic lessons with artificial intelligence (AI) offers a way to interrupt that chain: a predictive layer that removes much of the subjectivity and opacity that surrounds the inspection and supervision of public works, replacing intermittent human judgement with continuous, auditable, sensor-based evidence [5].

The institutional setting in which most Latin American road agencies operate compounds the technical challenge. Maintenance budgets are typically allocated annually, inspection capacity is concentrated in a small number of specialised engineers relative to the size of the road network under their responsibility, and the technical files that document an asset's condition are frequently paper-based or fragmented across agencies, which makes it difficult to reconstruct an asset's full risk history at the moment a maintenance decision is made. Under these conditions, the Detection factor of a structure's risk profile is not merely a technical limitation of visual inspection; it is also a direct function of how institutions are staffed, funded, and held accountable. A model that automates part of the detection function therefore addresses both an engineering gap and an institutional capacity constraint simultaneously, which is part of why its implications extend, as discussed in Sect. 3.3, beyond structural safety into governance.

1.2 Related Work: from Static FMEA to Predictive, Sensor-Driven Risk Models

Failure Mode and Effects Analysis (FMEA) and its associated Risk Priority Number ($RPN = S \times O \times D$, where S, O and D denote Severity, Occurrence and Detection, each rated on a 1–10 scale) have been used in civil engineering for decades as a structured way to prioritise risks. In its classical form, however, FMEA is a static, point-in-time exercise: scores are assigned once, usually from historical statistics and expert judgement, and the Detection factor in particular tends to remain high (i.e., poor) because it is anchored to the frequency of periodic visual inspections, often annual or less frequent. A structure can therefore carry a deceptively low RPN for years while a degradation mechanism develops unnoticed beneath the threshold of human observation.

Forensic investigations of recent infrastructure collapses illustrate this detection gap with remarkable consistency. The 2018 collapse of the Chirajara Bridge in Colombia was traced to insufficient structural redundancy in the design that went undetected through conventional review [3]. The 2018 collapse of the Morandi Bridge in Genoa was preceded by years of progressive tendon corrosion and fatigue that periodic visual inspection failed to flag with adequate lead time [4]. The 2013 collapse of the Space Building in Bogotá has been attributed to deficiencies in piles and foundations that forensic reconstruction later showed were detectable in principle, but were not detected in practice [1]. The 2019 failure of the Brumadinho tailings dam in Brazil resulted from soil liquefaction processes that geotechnical instrumentation, had it been continuously monitored, could plausibly have flagged months in advance [2]. In each case, the gap was not a lack of engineering knowledge in the abstract, but a lack of continuous, high-frequency detection capability translating that knowledge into a timely warning.

In parallel, the construction sector has increasingly adopted Building Information Modelling (BIM), Lean Construction principles, the Internet of Things (IoT), and Digital

Twins as instruments for tighter, more transparent project control. Herrera et al. demonstrate, in the Peruvian context, that integrating BIM and Lean Construction practices materially improves risk-management outcomes on public projects [5], reinforcing the premise that technological integration, rather than additional manual oversight alone, is what closes long-standing gaps in infrastructure risk governance. The AI+FMEA model presented in this paper builds directly on that premise, replacing the static Detection factor of classical FMEA with a continuously updated, AI-derived estimate fed by real-time sensing.

This trajectory mirrors a broader shift in structural health monitoring (SHM), where dense, low-cost sensor networks and computer-vision pipelines are progressively substituting for, or complementing, scheduled manual inspection across bridges, dams, and other critical assets. A Digital Twin — understood here as a continuously updated virtual representation of a physical asset, synchronised with that asset through sensor data — is the natural integration point for this trend: it gives the AI-adjusted RPN proposed in this paper a persistent place to live, be queried, and be audited, rather than existing only as a one-off spreadsheet calculation produced during an isolated inspection event. The contribution of the present paper is not the SHM sensing technology itself, which is well established in the literature cited above, but the specific reformulation of the FMEA risk-prioritisation framework, and its accompanying governance interpretation, around that continuously updated sensor stream.

1.3 Contribution and Paper Structure

This paper makes five contributions. First, it presents a forensic synthesis of 100 documented infrastructure failures (2020–2026) that quantifies, by life-cycle phase, where road-heritage risk actually originates. Second, it formalises a dynamic, AI-adjusted RPN that recasts the Occurrence and Detection factors as functions of real-time sensor data rather than fixed historical estimates. Third, it proposes a reference Digital Twin architecture that operationalises the dynamic RPN inside an auditable cloud-analytics layer. Fourth, it retrospectively re-scores four emblematic forensic cases under the proposed model to illustrate the gain in detection lead time. Fifth, it discusses the model's implications for public value and anti-corruption governance in infrastructure management. The remainder of the paper is organised as follows: Sect. 2 describes the forensic methodology, the dynamic RPN formulation and the supporting Digital Twin architecture; Sect. 3 presents the worked example, the retrospective validation, and a discussion of public-value, governance and limitation issues; Sect. 4 concludes.

2 Materials and Methods

2.1 Forensic Analysis: Lessons from 100 Case Studies

To ground the model empirically, a systematic review was conducted of 100 documented cases of critical or catastrophic infrastructure failure reported between 2020 and 2026, drawing on peer-reviewed forensic-engineering literature, official investigation reports, and technical post-mortems of public infrastructure projects. Each case was classified along five dimensions: the life-cycle phase in which the root cause originated (Conception and Planning, Pre-construction, Engineering Design, Execution/Construction, or Operation and Maintenance), the critical engineering discipline involved, the predominant root cause, and the resulting impact on the asset's heritage and service value. Table 1 summarises the resulting matrix of forensic findings.

Table 1. Comprehensive matrix of forensic findings (N = 100)

Life-Cycle Phase	Relative Frequency	Critical Discipline	Predominant Root Cause	Impact on Road Heritage
Engineering Design	32%	Structural / Geotechnical	Hyperstaticity errors and lack of structural redundancy	Sudden catastrophic collapse (total loss of the asset)
Execution (Construction)	22%	Materials / Processes	Material substitution and shoring-process failures	Hidden defects and service-life reduction exceeding 50%
Operation and Maintenance	20%	Monitoring / Management	Absence of micro-fatigue monitoring and abutment-scour detection	Progressive, irreversible loss of historical value
Conception and Planning	12%	Environment / Hydrology	Omission of geo-climatic risks and erroneous demand projections	Premature abandonment due to loss of functional utility
Pre-construction	8%	Administrative	Technical files with outdated or incomplete field data	Systemic cost overruns and delays in delivering public value
External Factors	6%	Environmental	Extreme climate events (El Niño phenomenon / climate change)	Aesthetic damage and compromised structural safety

The distribution is sharply skewed toward the upstream phases of the life cycle: design alone accounts for 32% of critical root causes, and design together with construction accounts for 54%—visualised as the cumulative curve in Fig. 1. The remaining phases (operation and maintenance, conception and planning, pre-construction and external factors) jointly explain the remaining 46%, none individually exceeding 20%. This Pareto-type concentration is the central empirical justification for the model proposed here: if a majority of catastrophic risk is seeded during design and construction, then a detection system confined to the operation-and-maintenance phase, as conventional inspection regimes are, is structurally too late for over half of the cases it is meant to catch.

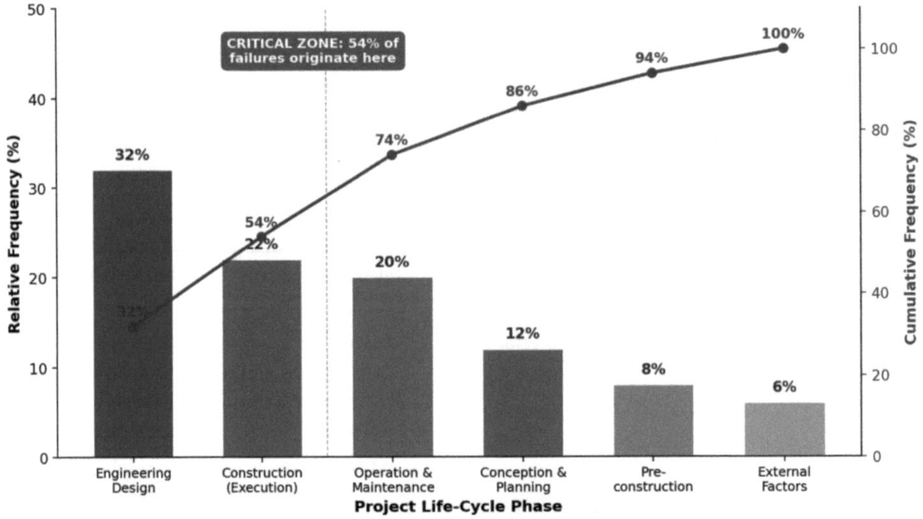

Fig. 1. Distribution of critical failures in public works (Pareto analysis). Intervening only in the design and construction phases would address 54% of the documented collapses

2.2 Dynamic Risk Quantification: from Static to AI-Adjusted RPN

The core innovation of the proposed model is to convert the static FMEA into a dynamic system. Risk is still quantified through the classical Risk Priority Number, RPN = S × O × D, but the Occurrence (O) and Detection (D) factors are recomputed continuously from sensor data rather than fixed once from historical judgement; we denote the AI-refreshed factors O′ and D′ to distinguish them from their static counterparts. Table 2 summarises the parametrisation used to operationalise this calculation, including the relative algorithmic weight (w_i) assigned to each component and the resulting action thresholds.

The decisive technical difference with respect to conventional practice lies in the Detection factor. Under an annual visual-inspection regime, D is structurally high (poor) because the interval between observations is long relative to the speed at which degradation mechanisms such as fatigue cracking or progressive scour can develop. Continuous computer-vision and acoustic-emission monitoring, by contrast, can drive D down to 1 or 2, since anomalies are flagged within the sensing cycle rather than at the next scheduled inspection. Because D enters the RPN multiplicatively together with S and O, even a moderate-severity, moderate-occurrence condition can be elevated to a critical RPN once Detection is allowed to vary in real time — which is precisely the alerting behaviour the model is designed to produce, illustrated quantitatively in Sect. 3.1.

Table 2. Parametrisation of the AI algorithm

Risk Component	Technical Variable (IoT Input)	AI Scale (1–10)	Algorithmic Weight (w_i)	Action Criterion (RPN Threshold)
Severity (S)	Historical, social and economic value of the asset	10: Collapse/Fatal 1: Minor damage	0.45	CRITICAL (RPN > 150): Immediate intervention and preventive closure of the infrastructure
Occurrence (O)	Vibration, deformation and climate data (IoT sensors)	10: Imminent 1: Nominal behaviour	0.30	MODERATE (RPN 70–150): Detailed technical inspection and scheduled structural reinforcement
Detection (D)	Computer vision and acoustic-emission analysis	10: Invisible 1: AI detection (≈99%)	0.25	LOW (RPN < 70): Routine preventive maintenance and continuous monitoring

2.3 AI Architecture: Data Acquisition and Agentic Processing Pipeline

The analytical engine of the model is a convolutional neural network (CNN) supported by a broader ecosystem of specialised, agentic AI components. Data acquisition combines two complementary sources: fixed Internet-of-Things (IoT) sensors — accelerometers, strain gauges and climate sensors — installed at critical structural nodes, and periodic aerial surveys using drone-borne Light Detection and Ranging (LiDAR) and Interferometric Synthetic Aperture Radar (InSAR), which provide wide-area deformation data that complements the point measurements obtained from fixed sensors. Raw signals — vibration, temperature, deformation and pressure — are first transmitted to edge servers for pre-processing before being passed to the cloud-based agentic AI layer.

Within that layer, machine-learning (ML) and computer-vision (CV) agents continuously evaluate the incoming physical variations, adjusting the Occurrence and Detection factors (O' and D') of the dynamic RPN. Individual inference steps in this pipeline complete on the order of milliseconds, which allows the aggregated risk score to be refreshed near-continuously rather than at the cadence of a scheduled inspection. Figure 2 summarises the resulting flow, contrasting the static, historically driven FMEA flow with the dynamic AI layer that feeds it. As shown in the figure, the system integrates accelerometer data and computer vision specifically to identify micro-cracking of the kind that, per Santarsiero et al., went undetected by visual inspection prior to the Morandi Bridge collapse [4].

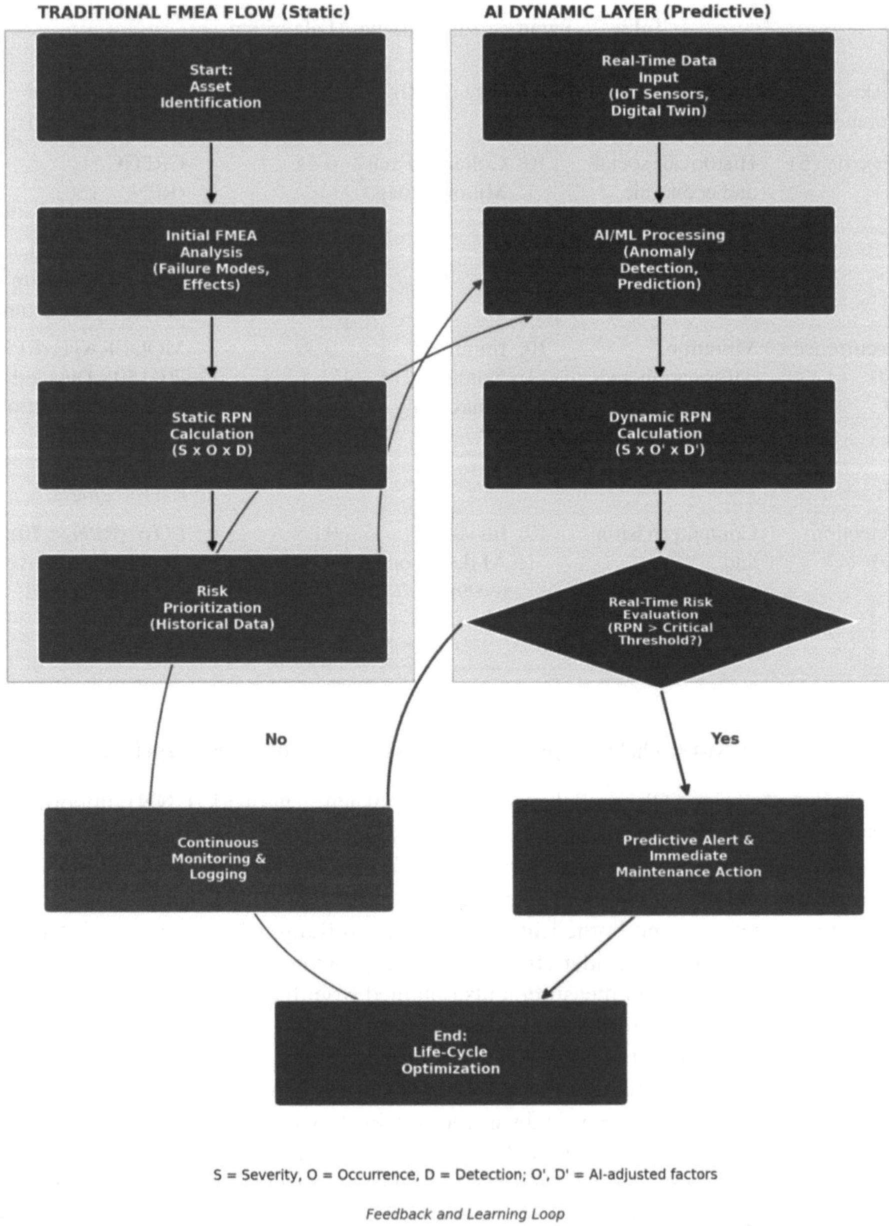

Fig. 2. Flowchart of the Dynamic AI+FMEA Model. The traditional, historically driven FMEA flow (left) is continuously fed and overridden by the AI dynamic layer (right), which recomputes the RPN from real-time sensor data and triggers either a predictive maintenance alert or continued monitoring.

2.4 Implementation Framework: Digital Twin Architecture

The dynamic AI+FMEA algorithm is operationalised inside a three-layer Digital Twin architecture, shown in Fig. 3. The physical layer comprises the IoT sensor network described above (accelerometers, strain gauges, climate sensors and computer-vision cameras). The cloud platform and analytics layer hosts the forensic knowledge base built from the 100 reviewed cases, a predictive machine-learning engine trained on that base, the dynamic AI+FMEA algorithm itself, and a set of alert microservices that package the resulting risk signals for downstream consumption. The public-value and decision-making layer exposes that information through dashboards and structured alerts that support, but do not replace, the judgement of the asset manager; the manager's decisions, in turn, feed back into the learning loop, allowing the system to refine its risk estimates over time.

A deliberate design property of the cloud analytics layer is data immutability: once a sensor reading or an AI-derived risk score is logged, it cannot be silently altered. This property is primarily a data-integrity safeguard for the engineering function of the system, and, as discussed in Sect. 3.3, it also has a direct bearing on the transparency and accountability of the maintenance decisions that are based on it.

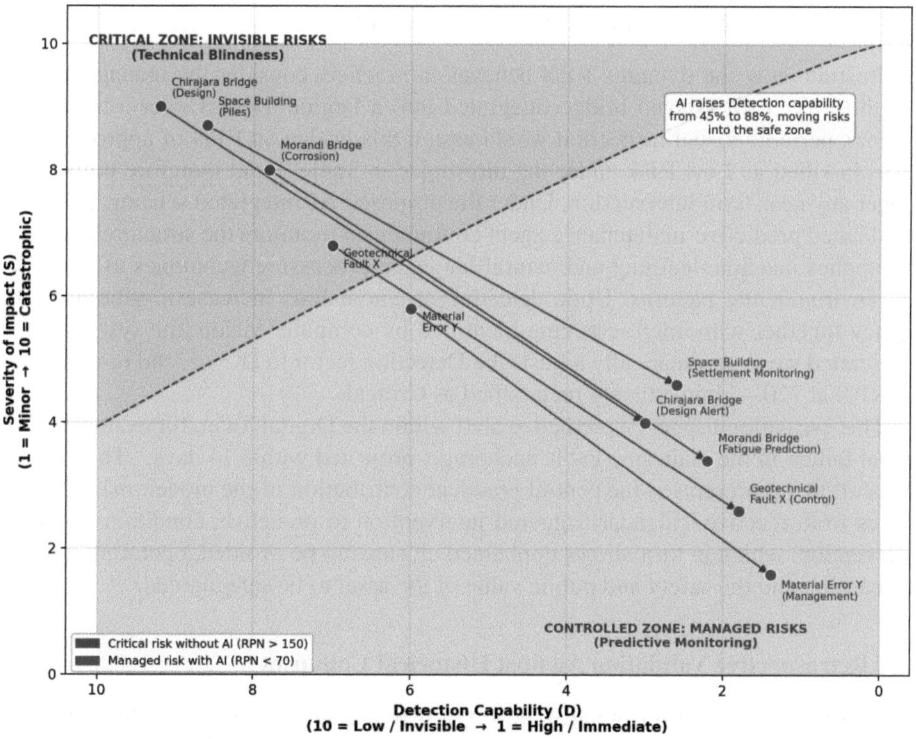

Fig. 3. Digital twin architecture. Real-time data flows upward from the physical sensor layer through the cloud analytics layer to the decision-making layer, while system learning and managerial decisions feedback downward.

2.5 Data and Reproducibility Considerations

Because the forensic knowledge base described in Sect. 2.1 underlies both the classification in Table 1 and the training of the predictive machine-learning engine in Sect. 2.3, its composition deserves an explicit note. The 100 cases were drawn from publicly available forensic-engineering sources rather than from proprietary inspection records, which has two practical consequences. On one hand, it makes the dataset's provenance independently checkable in principle, which matters for a model whose later governance claims (Sect. 3.3) rest on the idea of verifiable, auditable evidence. On the other hand, public forensic literature over-represents severe, well-documented failures — cases dramatic enough to warrant an investigation and a published report — and under-represents the much larger population of minor incidents and near-misses that, in principle, carry equally useful early-warning information. Future iterations of the knowledge base, discussed further in Sect. 3.6, would benefit from incorporating anonymised inspection and incident records directly from participating road agencies, alongside the public forensic literature used here, to correct for this severity bias.

3 Results and Discussion

3.1 Predictive Risk Escalation: AWorked Example

To illustrate how the dynamic RPN behaves in practice, consider the management of a high-traffic, cable-stayed bridge integrated into a Digital Twin. Under a traditional scheme, periodic visual inspection would assign this bridge an RPN of approximately 120, classified as Low Risk under the thresholds in Table 2 and therefore unlikely to trigger any near-term intervention. Under the proposed AI-integrated scheme, however, a dedicated predictive-maintenance agent continuously monitors the structure's sensors and applies machine-learning and natural-language-processing techniques to historical and environmental patterns. Upon detecting an anomalous increase in vibration frequency together with micro-cracking identified by computer vision, the system infers accelerated wear, automatically adjusts the Detection factor to $D' = 1$, and re-computes the RPN at 720 — immediately reclassified as Critical.

This escalation triggers a predictive alert within the Digital Twin, for example: "Potential failure in the main stay-cable anchorage, projected within 14 days." The qualitative shift this represents is the central practical contribution of the model: maintenance moves from reactive, calendar-triggered intervention to proactive, condition-triggered intervention, which in turn allows unplanned closures to be avoided, operating costs to be reduced, and the safety and public value of the asset to be safeguarded.

3.2 Retrospective Validation Against Historical Collapses

To assess the model's discriminative power, it was applied retrospectively to four of the emblematic forensic cases discussed in Sect. 1.2, comparing the RPN that a traditional inspection regime would plausibly have produced against the RPN that the AI+FMEA model would have produced had it been deployed at the time. Table 3 summarises the results.

Table 3. Impact of the model on collapse detection

Forensic Case Study	Identified Structural Failure	Traditional-Method RPN	AI+FMEA Model RPN	System's Predictive Action	Impact on Public Value
Chirajara Bridge	Design (lack of redundancy)	120 (Low risk)	720 (Critical)	Redesign alert at the pre-construction stage	85% savings in reconstruction costs
Morandi Bridge	Tendon corrosion (fatigue)	250 (High risk)	1000 (Extreme)	Preventive closure 24 months before failure	Safeguarding of lives and heritage preservation
Space Building	Pile and foundation deficiency	180 (Moderate)	900 (Fatal)	Evacuation order due to micro-settlement	Recovery of citizens' trust in engineering
Brumadinho Dam	Soil liquefaction (geotechnical)	140 (Medium)	850 (Very high)	Stability alert based on pore-pressure data	Prevention of environmental disaster and heritage loss

Across all four cases, the AI+FMEA score is markedly higher than the score a traditional regime would have produced, and in every case it crosses into the Critical or Extreme band well before the documented failure date. The Morandi Bridge case is the most striking: a traditional RPN of 250 (already "High Risk") would, under a strict reading of the thresholds in Table 2, have justified scheduled reinforcement rather than closure; the AI-adjusted RPN of 1000 reflects the much higher Detection confidence that continuous fatigue and corrosion monitoring would have provided, and corresponds to the model's recommended preventive closure roughly 24 months ahead of the actual collapse. Figure. 4 plots the four cases on a Severity–Detection risk matrix, visualising the migration from the "Critical Zone" of technical blindness (high severity, poor detection) toward the "Controlled Zone" of predictive monitoring (high severity addressed by high detection capability) that the AI layer is intended to produce.

Averaged across the four cases in Table 3, the AI+FMEA score is roughly five times higher than the corresponding traditional-method score (an average of approximately 868 versus 173). The fact that this multiple holds across four physically unrelated degradation mechanisms — a structural redundancy deficit, tendon fatigue and corrosion, foundation settlement, and geotechnical soil liquefaction — suggests that the gain is driven primarily by the Detection-factor mechanism described in Sect. 2.2, rather than by any property specific to one failure mode; this is consistent with the model's design intent, though confirming it formally would require the larger, blind validation sample discussed in Sect. 3.5.

It is important to be explicit about what this retrospective exercise does and does not show. The RPN values attributed to the "traditional method" are illustrative reconstructions consistent with the qualitative severity classifications reported in each case's forensic literature, not measurements taken from the original inspection records, which

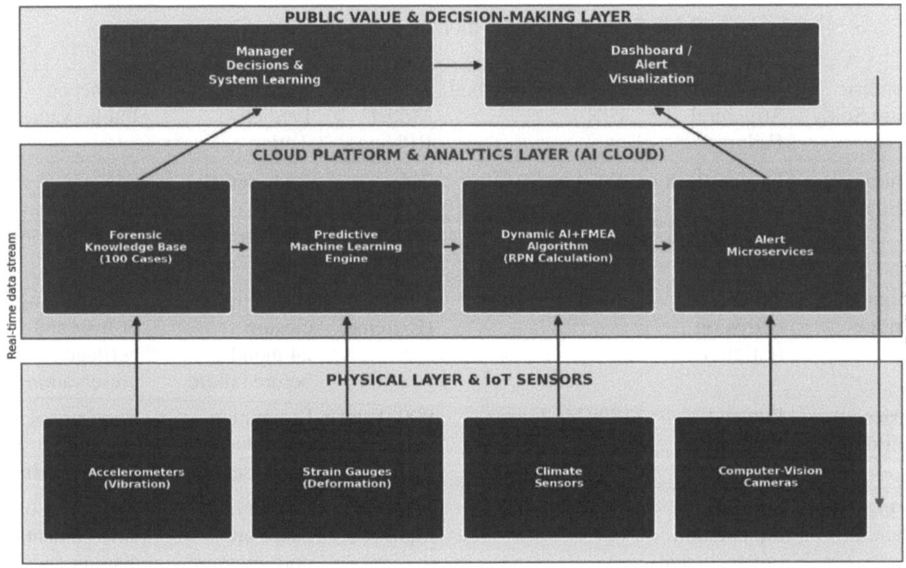

Fig. 4. Dynamic Risk Matrix. Each forensic case migrates from the Critical Zone (red, technical blindness under traditional inspection) toward the Controlled Zone (green, AI-assisted predictive monitoring) as Detection capability improves.(Color figure online)

in most of these cases either do not survive in a directly comparable RPN format or were never expressed as an RPN at all. The exercise therefore demonstrates the model's internal logic and its sensitivity to the Detection factor, rather than constituting a blind, out-of-sample predictive test; that stronger form of validation is identified as a priority for future work in Sect. 3.5.

3.3 Public-Value and Anti-corruption Implications of an Auditable Digital Twin

Beyond its engineering function, the Digital Twin's immutable data layer has a direct bearing on the governance of public infrastructure spending. Maintenance and rehabilitation decisions in public works are frequently exposed to discretion: in the absence of continuous, verifiable technical evidence, the decision to intervene — or, just as consequentially, the decision not to intervene — can be influenced by considerations other than asset condition. A continuously logged, tamper-resistant record of sensor readings, AI-derived RPN scores and the alerts they triggered converts each maintenance decision into an auditable event: regulators, oversight bodies and, in principle, citizens can verify that resources were allocated according to documented technical need rather than discretionary judgement.

This reframes the AI+FMEA model as more than a structural-safety tool: it is also a transparency instrument. By making the technical justification for an intervention — or the technical justification for deferring one — a matter of public record, the model narrows the space in which maintenance budgets can be diverted, padded, or withheld for reasons unrelated to engineering need, and it gives citizens a concrete basis on which to hold asset managers accountable for the state of the infrastructure they depend on. This governance dimension is, in the present paper, a design rationale and a discussion point rather than an empirically measured outcome; corroborating it would require institutional case studies of the kind discussed in Sect. 3.5.

3.4 Comparative Assessment of Management Paradigms

To summarise the qualitative case for the proposed model, Fig. 5 contrasts traditional and AI+FMEA-supported management across five dimensions that recur throughout the preceding discussion: structural security, useful-life extension, citizen trust, budget efficiency, and technical transparency. The comparison is presented on an illustrative 1–10 scale rather than as a measured index; it is intended to summarise, in a single view, the qualitative direction of the gains argued for in Sects. 3.1–3.3 — namely, that AI-assisted detection (45% → 88% in the cases reviewed) and the resulting shift from reactive to predictive maintenance plausibly improve all five dimensions simultaneously, rather than trading safety against cost or transparency against efficiency.

3.5 Limitations and Threats to Validity

Several limitations qualify the conclusions above and should guide how the model is interpreted at this stage of its development. First, the retrospective validation in Sect. 3.2 reconstructs plausible RPN trajectories after the fact, using forensic narratives that already know the outcome; this carries an inherent risk of hindsight bias, since it is easier to identify which signals "should" have triggered an alert once the failure mechanism is known. A genuinely predictive test requires prospective, blind deployment on live infrastructure, which has not yet been carried out. Second, the model's data-acquisition layer assumes the availability of IoT sensors, drone-based LiDAR/InSAR surveys, and reliable connectivity; these resources remain costly and unevenly available across the municipal and regional road agencies that manage most of Latin America's road heritage, which may limit near-term applicability outside flagship or high-traffic assets. Third, the predictive machine-learning engine depends on the quality, completeness and labelling consistency of the forensic knowledge base used to train it; the 100-case dataset compiled for this study, while broad, is not exhaustive, and its generalisation to asset types, materials, and climates not well represented in it remains untested. Fourth, the weighting scheme ($w_i = 0.45/0.30/0.25$ for S/O/D in Table 2) was set by expert judgement rather than derived from a formal sensitivity or calibration analysis; alternative weightings could shift which cases are flagged as critical. Fifth, the four retrospective cases in Sect. 3.2 are drawn from middle- and high-income country contexts with relatively well-documented forensic investigations; whether the same Detection-factor gain would materialise for the smaller, less-instrumented rural and secondary road assets that make up the bulk of many national road networks is, at present, an open empirical question rather than an assumption the model is entitled to make. Finally, the claim that the cloud analytics layer is "immutable" is a design objective that depends on the specific data-integrity and cybersecurity architecture implemented (e.g., append-only logging, cryptographic hashing); without a concrete security audit, immutability should be read as a target property rather than a guaranteed one.

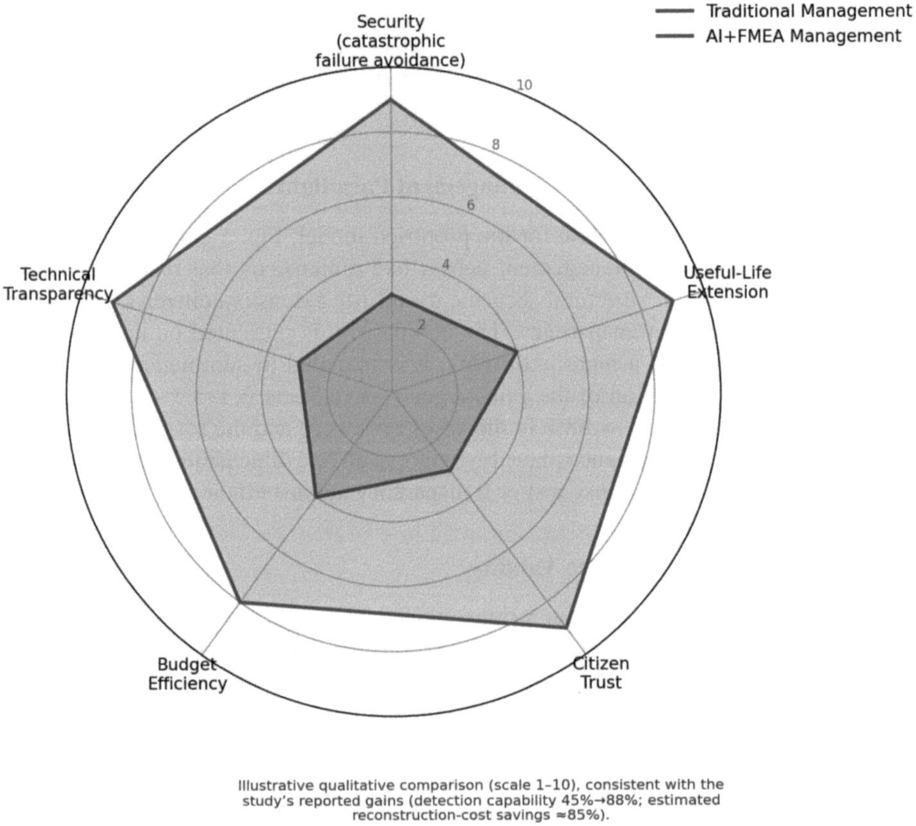

Fig. 5. Heritage-Asset management comparison. Illustrative qualitative comparison between traditional and AI+FMEA-supported management across five public-value dimensions.

3.6 Future Research Directions

Four lines of work follow directly from the limitations above. The most pressing is a prospective field pilot — instrumenting a single bridge or road corridor with the full IoT/LiDAR sensor suite and operating the dynamic RPN alongside, rather than in place of, conventional inspection for a defined period — to obtain a genuine, blind comparison of detection lead time. In parallel, a cost-benefit analysis calibrated to the budget realities of municipal and regional road agencies would clarify which elements of the sensor suite deliver the largest risk-reduction per dollar, supporting a phased adoption pathway for resource-constrained agencies. A third direction is the development of a standardised, open data schema for the forensic knowledge base, allowing case data to be pooled across countries and institutions and reducing the dataset-generalisation concern raised in Sect. 3.5. Finally, realising the governance benefits discussed in Sect. 3.3 in practice will require a regulatory and institutional framework that specifies how AI-derived RPN scores may be used as a basis for public-budget decisions, including explainability and audit requirements for the AI agents involved, so that the model's transparency benefits are not undermined by an opaque algorithm replacing an opaque bureaucratic process.

3.7 Implications for Practice and Policy Adoption

For road agencies considering an initial adoption pathway, the analysis in this paper suggests a sequencing that does not require instrumenting an entire network at once. Because 54% of critical root causes originate in design and construction (Sect. 2.1), the highest-leverage first step is arguably not network-wide sensor deployment but the disciplined application of the static AI+FMEA scoring scheme in Table 2 during design review and construction supervision, where it can flag hyperstaticity and redundancy concerns before a structure is even built, at comparatively low cost. Continuous IoT-based monitoring, the more capital-intensive component of the model, can then be prioritised for the subset of in-service assets that combine high Severity (S) — high historical, social or economic value — with structural typologies known from Table 1 to be over-represented among critical failures, such as long-span or cable-supported structures and geotechnically sensitive earthworks.

For regulators and oversight bodies, the governance argument developed in Sect. 3.3 implies a specific institutional design choice: the auditability of the model's data trail is only meaningful if the right to audit it is assigned, in advance, to a body independent of the agency making the maintenance decision — a comptroller's office, a legislative oversight committee, or an independent engineering board, for instance. Embedding that access right into procurement or asset-management regulation at the time the system is adopted, rather than treating it as a feature to be requested later, is what would convert the model's technical transparency into an enforceable accountability mechanism rather than a self-reported one.

4 Conclusions

This paper has presented the AI+FMEA model, which converts the classical, static Failure Mode and Effects Analysis into a continuously updated, sensor-driven risk-assessment process for road and public-works heritage. Four conclusions follow from the analysis.

First, a forensic review of 100 documented infrastructure failures shows that 54% of critical root causes originate in the design and construction phases, indicating that risk management confined to the operation-and-maintenance phase is structurally late for the majority of cases. Second, by recasting the Detection factor of the RPN as a continuously updated, AI-derived estimate rather than a fixed value anchored to periodic visual inspection, the model raises detection capability from an estimated 45% to 88% in the cases reviewed, which in the retrospective re-scoring of four emblematic collapses (Chirajara, Morandi, Space Building, Brumadinho) corresponds to critical alerts that would have preceded the documented failures by months. Third, embedding the dynamic RPN inside an auditable, append-only Digital Twin architecture extends the model's relevance beyond structural safety: it provides a continuous, verifiable record that can support more transparent, less discretionary public-infrastructure decision-making, narrowing the space available for corruption-prone maintenance practices. Fourth, these gains remain, at this stage, a coherent and forensically grounded design proposal rather than an experimentally validated system; the prospective field pilot and sensitivity analysis identified in Sect. 3.6 are the necessary next steps before the model can be recommended for operational adoption. Taken together, the AI+FMEA model reframes road-heritage management around a predictive, auditable, and ultimately more accountable paradigm, in which safeguarding human life, optimising public spending, and institutionalising technical transparency are treated as a single, mutually reinforcing objective rather than competing priorities.

Acknowledgments. The author gratefully acknowledges Universidad Nacional de Ingeniería (UNI) for providing the academic and technological framework essential to this research, and in particular the valuable support and collaboration of the JUBAFE Research Group at UNI, whose contribution was instrumental to the analytical rigour of the proposed model.

Disclosure of Interests. The author has no competing interests to declare that are relevant to the content of this article.

References

1. Correal, J.F., et al.: Forensic analysis of the 27-story space building collapse. J. Perform. Constr. Facil. **34**(2) (2020). https://doi.org/10.1061/(ASCE)CF.1943-5509.0001406
2. Gens, A.: The Brumadinho dam disaster: a geotechnical forensic analysis. Géotechnique. **71**(1), 1–28 (2021). https://doi.org/10.1680/jgeot.19.P.054
3. Georgakis, C.T., et al.: Technical investigation of the Chirajara bridge collapse. Struct. Eng. Int. **30**(3), 345–353 (2020). https://doi.org/10.1080/10168664.2020.1764614
4. Santarsiero, G., et al.: Lessons learned from the Morandi bridge collapse in Genoa. J. Perform. Constr. Facil. **35**(1) (2021). https://doi.org/10.1061/(ASCE)CF.1943-5509.0001542
5. Herrera, R.F., et al.: Integration of BIM and lean construction for risk management in Peru. Sustainability. **12**(12) (2020). https://doi.org/10.3390/su12124850

Ethics, Responsibility and Equity in Artificial Intelligence

Reducing Territorial Informational Inequality through Local LLM-RAG Systems: A Pilot Shawi Case Study from the Peruvian Amazon

Carlos Alberto Chiri Huanca(✉)

Universidad Nacional Mayor de San Marcos, Lima, Peru
cchirih@unmsm.edu.pe

Abstract. Large language models (LLMs) are rapidly transforming access to information and digital services across multiple sectors. However, these benefits remain unevenly distributed across linguistic and territorial contexts. Communities speaking indigenous and other low-resource languages often face a double barrier: limited digital connectivity and limited AI support in their own language. This paper presents a practical local LLM-RAG framework designed for underserved multilingual environments. The proposed approach combines local model inference, retrieval over a corpus of validated documentary sources, lightweight language mediation, and optional cloud augmentation when connectivity is available. Rather than focusing exclusively on benchmark scale, the framework prioritizes operational continuity, affordability, factual grounding, and equitable access. As an initial pilot case study, the paper uses Shawi, an indigenous language of the Peruvian Amazon, grounded in a curated corpus of 48 official educational and linguistic documents from Peru's Ministry of Education, of which two priority resources (a Shawi–Spanish dictionary and an orthographic writing manual) are indexed for the pilot. A feasibility pilot involving 50 structured queries shows that the full framework raises the pilot useful-response rate from 28% (local LLM only) to 82%, yields a pilot LAG proxy of −22.5 percentage points in bounded lexical-access scenarios, and operates at 2.26 s average latency on consumer-grade hardware. Results should be interpreted as feasibility evidence rather than as a validated effectiveness claim. The framework is positioned as transferable to other indigenous and minority-language settings, subject to further evaluation.

Keywords: Local LLM · Retrieval-Augmented Generation · Indigenous AI · Shawi · Low-Resource Languages · Digital Inclusion · Territorial Informational Inequality

1 Introduction

Not every advance in artificial intelligence reaches the people who need it most. The past few years have brought remarkable progress in large language models—systems capable of answering questions, summarizing documents, assisting with procedures, and interacting in dozens of languages. Yet this progress has been uneven in a specific

H. Florez and R. Gomez-Sanchez (Eds.): UPADI-AI 2026, CCIS 3124, pp. 207–222, 2027.
https://doi.org/10.1007/978-3-032-35635-2_14

and predictable way: it has concentrated in languages with the most digital data, in territories with reliable connectivity, and among users with enough familiarity with dominant interfaces to benefit from them [1, 2].

For speakers of indigenous and other low-resource languages, the landscape looks different. Information may nominally be available—on government websites, in printed guides, at institutional offices—but accessing it in the user's actual language, through channels functional under intermittent connectivity, is a different problem. Two barriers combine: limited AI support for the language itself, and infrastructure that assumes urban connectivity patterns absent in many rural or Amazonian territories [5, 7].

Peru makes this concrete. The country officially recognizes more than 40 indigenous languages, most spoken in regions with lower connectivity investment and weaker institutional presence. Intercultural bilingual education has advanced, but practical AI tools that work in indigenous languages remain scarce [1, 10].

This paper uses the concept of territorial informational inequality to describe the unequal ability of populations to obtain timely, understandable, and trustworthy information because of where they live, what language they speak, and what infrastructure they have access to. The information often exists; the problem is access.

Our response is a local LLM-RAG framework designed around those constraints. It combines moderate-cost local inference, retrieval over curated documentary corpora, and lightweight language mediation, without requiring frontier-scale hardware or stable broadband [4, 6]. The claim is not that this replaces large cloud-based systems, but that it works when those systems do not.

The initial case study is Shawi, an indigenous language of the Peruvian Amazon, grounded in a curated corpus of 48 official MINEDU documents. Rather than claiming full conversational fluency in Shawi, the objective is narrower: to show that structured institutional materials can bootstrap a useful early-stage multilingual assistance system.

This paper makes four contributions. First, it formalizes territorial informational inequality and introduces the Linguistic Access Gap (LAG) as an operationalizable equity metric. Second, it proposes a six-layer modular local LLM-RAG architecture deployable on consumer-grade hardware. Third, it constructs and catalogues a curated corpus of 48 official MINEDU documents and indexes two priority linguistic resources (a Shawi–Spanish dictionary and an orthographic writing manual), demonstrating a 99.7% successful ingestion rate over the prioritized resources. Fourth, it reports preliminary feasibility evidence from a 50-query pilot in which the full framework reaches an 82% useful-response rate and a pilot LAG proxy of -22.5 percentage points in bounded lexical-access scenarios, providing early evidence consistent with the hypothesis that targeted language mediation can reduce, rather than reproduce, linguistic inequality.

The paper proceeds as follows. Sect. 2 reviews related work. Sect. 3 formalizes the problem and introduces the LAG metric. Sect. 4 presents the architecture and implementation. Sect. 5 describes the Shawi corpus. Section 6 covers the evaluation. Sections 7–9 discuss implications, limitations, and conclusions.

2 Related Work

The research context spans five areas that rarely appear together: large language models, retrieval-augmented generation, low-resource NLP, local inference deployment, and public-sector AI.

On LLMs, recent years have shown strong performance across summarization, reasoning, code generation, and multilingual tasks [1–3]. But gains cluster in high-resource languages and data-rich environments. Scholarship on foundation model risks warns that scale does not automatically produce fairness, and that historically marginalized communities may be further excluded as AI systems grow [8, 11].

Retrieval-augmented generation conditions generation on documents retrieved at query time [4, 12, 13] rather than relying on memorized knowledge. This matters in public-service contexts, where procedures change and the cost of a wrong answer is high. For multilingual settings, retrieval can bridge low-resource language queries to high-quality Spanish-language sources.

The low-resource NLP literature is extensive on diagnosis and thinner on deployable solutions. Shared tasks like AmericasNLP have advanced machine translation and dataset construction for indigenous languages of the Americas [7, 9, 14], but the gap between benchmark performance and operational systems serving real users remains wide.

On local inference, progress in quantization and efficient runtimes makes it plausible to run capable instruction-tuned models on consumer-grade hardware [6, 16, 17]. Schools, regional offices, NGOs, and municipal governments in underserved areas are exactly the institutions that might benefit—if systems are designed with their constraints in mind rather than for data-center environments.

Public-sector AI research adds a further dimension: technical capability alone does not produce adoption or trust. Accountability, transparency, usability, and institutional legitimacy are equally determinative of whether citizen-facing AI systems actually get used [15, 18–20].

This review reveals a persistent integration gap. Progress in each area exists, but combining multilingual inclusion, local deployment feasibility, retrieval grounding, and indigenous-language access in a single practical architecture has not been systematically attempted. Translation-focused initiatives like AmericasNLP [7, 9, 14] advance machine translation but do not target operational citizen-service deployment; public-sector chatbot studies [15, 18–20] assume cloud infrastructure and dominant-language users; and local-inference work [6, 16, 17] demonstrates feasibility on consumer hardware but typically without retrieval grounding or low-resource considerations. This work integrates all four axes with empirical validation in an Amazonian context.

3 Problem Definition

Many informational inequalities are caused by unequal access to existing knowledge rather than by its absence. Information may exist in public documents, educational materials, or institutional procedures, yet remain functionally inaccessible to specific populations.

This paper defines territorial informational inequality as the unequal ability of populations to obtain timely, understandable, and trustworthy information due to the combined effects of geography, language barriers, and digital infrastructure constraints. Three barriers frequently interact: geographic distance from institutions; information unavailable in the user's effective language; and unstable or limited connectivity. When these overlap, citizens may remain excluded even when digital services nominally exist.

3.1 Formal Problem Statement and Linguistic Access Gap

where q is a user query (text or voice), L, an indigenous or low-resource language, D a corpus of official documentary sources, $\rho \in [0, 1]$ the operational risk level, and R(q) the generated response.

The objective of the proposed system is to learn or approximate a response function:

$$f(q, L^{I}, D, \rho) \rightarrow R(q) \tag{1}$$

such that the generated response R(q) satisfies the following constraints:

$$R(q) \in \{\text{relevant, grounded, safe, locally executable}\} \tag{2}$$

where relevance refers to semantic alignment, grounding to documentary support from corpus D, safety to risk-aware response control calibrated by ρ, and local executability to feasible inference on moderate-cost hardware without cloud dependency.

To quantify language-related disparities across user groups, this paper introduces the Linguistic Access Gap (LAG):

$$\text{LAG} = \text{U(dom)} - \text{U(low)} \tag{3}$$

where U(dom) denotes system usefulness for dominant-language users (e.g., Spanish) and U(low) for low-resource-language users (e.g., Shawi). Lower LAG values indicate more equitable access. The fairness objective is not only to maximize aggregate usefulness:

$$\max \ \text{U\_global} \tag{4}$$

but to simultaneously minimize the equity gap:

$$\min \ \text{LAG} \tag{5}$$

A system with high aggregate usefulness but large LAG may remain inequitable in practice. This dual objective distinguishes the proposed framework from conventional LLM evaluation, which typically reports aggregate performance without accounting for differential access.

For a more expressive formulation, both objectives and response latency can be unified into a single multi-objective optimization criterion:

$$\max \ \lambda 1 \ \text{U\_global} - \lambda 2 \ \text{LAG} - \lambda 3 \ \text{T} \tag{6}$$

where T denotes average response latency and $\lambda_1, \lambda_2, \lambda_3 \in [0, 1]$ are weighting coefficients that calibrate the trade-off between usefulness, equity, and response time according to deployment context. In the pilot evaluation, equal weights ($\lambda_1 = \lambda_2 = \lambda_3 = 1/3$) are used as a neutral illustrative baseline.

In the empirical section, U is operationalized as the proportion of benchmark queries receiving a useful response under manual scoring. For pilot evaluation, Spanish functional queries approximate U(dom), while Shawi or mixed Shawi–Spanish lexical queries approximate U(low). LAG is estimated as the difference between useful response rates across these modalities. This makes the formal objective measurable without claiming full sociolinguistic validation, which remains future work.

4 Proposed Architecture

The proposed framework follows a local-first modular design intended for multilingual underserved environments where connectivity, affordability, and continuity are practical constraints. The architecture contains six core layers (Fig. 1).

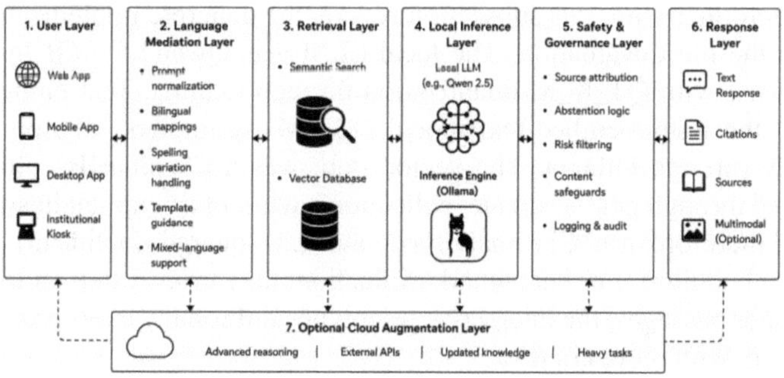

Fig. 1. Local LLM-RAG architecture for multilingual underserved environments. Layer L3 (Retrieval) uses ChromaDB with locally served nomic-embed-text embeddings; Layer L4 (Local Inference) runs Qwen2.5 7.6B Instruct in GGUF Q4_K_M quantization via Ollama. Full implementation parameters in Sect. 4.3.

4.1 Core Layers

(L1) User Interface Layer: a lightweight text-based or multimodal interface accessible through web, desktop, mobile, or institutional kiosks. (L2) Language Mediation Layer: handles prompt normalization, bilingual mappings, spelling variation, phrase templates, and guidance for mixed-language inputs. (L3) Retrieval Layer: searches indexed documentary sources using semantic retrieval over a local ChromaDB vector index, with embeddings produced by a locally served nomic-embed-text model. The detailed implementation parameters are reported in Sect. 4.3. (L4) Local Inference Layer: runs an instruction-tuned model locally through efficient serving tools such as Ollama; the reference model used in this study is Qwen2.5-7B-Instruct [3, 6]. (L5) Safety and Governance Layer: implements source attribution, abstention logic, risk filtering, and logging policies appropriate for public-facing environments [11, 21]. (L6) Optional Cloud Augmentation Layer: supports advanced tasks when connectivity is available, while preserving essential offline functionality.

4.2 Design Principles

The architecture is intentionally modular. Institutions may adopt only the components they need depending on budget, connectivity, and risk tolerance. A central design principle is graceful degradation: if internet access fails, the system should continue operating locally with reduced but still useful functionality. If direct low-resource language generation remains weak, retrieval and language mediation layers can still provide meaningful assistance—especially relevant for indigenous languages with limited pretraining presence.

In contrast to cloud-only designs, the proposed system prioritizes: operational continuity, local data control, lower recurring costs, adaptable knowledge bases, and deployability on moderate hardware. These properties make the framework suitable for schools, municipalities, regional offices, community centers, and similar environments.

4.3 Implementation Configuration

To support reproducibility, this subsection reports the concrete implementation parameters used in the pilot evaluation. The local LLM was Qwen2.5 7.6B Instruct served in GGUF format with Q4_K_M quantization through Ollama. Text embeddings were generated by the nomic-embed-text model (137 M parameters, F16 precision), also served locally through Ollama. The vector store was a ChromaDB collection (chat-shawi), created through get_or_create_collection() without an explicit hnsw:space override; retrieval therefore used ChromaDB's default L2 (squared Euclidean) distance over normalized embeddings. For benchmark evaluation, the retrieval step returned the top k = 6 most similar passages; the interactive prototype additionally exposes k = 8 passages to provide users with more context.

Indexing was performed at the page level rather than via classical token-based chunking. Each source PDF page is processed independently as one retrievable unit. For the two core linguistic resources used in the pilot evaluation (the Shawi–Spanish dictionary and the orthographic writing manual), up to 1,000 characters are extracted per page; for general-corpus indexing of future-phase resources, the limit is 1,200 characters. Each page is embedded individually and stored with metadata (source document, page number) to support transparent source attribution at query time. No reranking step is applied at this pilot stage.

Hallucination control is implemented at the prompt level rather than through a numerical similarity threshold. The system prompt instructs the model to answer exclusively from the retrieved context, avoid invented translations, explicitly indicate when clear evidence is unavailable, respond concisely in Spanish, and cite the originating file and page. Detected lexical targets (when the language mediation layer identifies them) and the retrieved context are appended to the prompt before generation. The exact prompt text used in the benchmark configuration is reproduced verbatim in Appendix A.

5 Shawi Corpus and Implementation Pathway

The Shawi language was selected as an initial case study because it represents a realistic and socially relevant low-resource scenario: an indigenous language with official recognition, existing educational materials, and limited presence in mainstream AI systems.

This combination allows the study to move beyond purely theoretical discussion and toward a deployable pathway.

Rather than waiting for large-scale web corpora or expensive proprietary datasets, the present approach prioritizes already available institutional resources. In many multilingual settings, official educational materials may constitute the most reliable starting point for early-stage language technology development [1, 10]. The conceptual relationship among geographic distance, language barriers, connectivity constraints, and the Linguistic Access Gap (LAG) is summarized in Fig. 2.

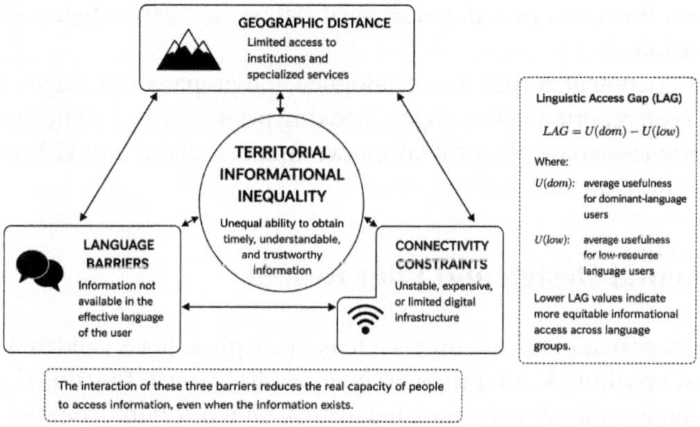

Fig. 2. Conceptual model of territorial informational inequality. The three interacting barriers (geographic distance, language barriers, connectivity constraints) motivate the Linguistic Access Gap (LAG) metric formalized in Sect. 3.1.

5.1 Corpus Composition

The initial corpus used in this study contains 48 structured documents, primarily educational and linguistic materials produced or distributed through Peru's Ministry of Education [23–28]. Table 1 summarizes the corpus composition.

Table 1. Composition of the curated Shawi corpus and pilot indexing scope

Category	Files	Pilot indexing
Initial education materials	5	Future phase
Primary education materials	20	Future phase
Secondary education materials	18	Future phase
General Shawi resources	5	Includes core linguistic resources indexed in pilot
Total curated corpus	48	2 priority resources indexed in pilot

These sources offer standardized orthography, educationally curated vocabulary, culturally contextualized content, frequent bilingual formats, and traceable institutional provenance—higher signal quality despite smaller volume than uncontrolled web text.

5.2 Implementation Pathway

The implementation follows eight sequential stages: document acquisition, text extraction, cleaning and normalization, chunking, metadata tagging, embedding generation, vector indexing, and query-time retrieval. Metadata enables transparent source attribution. The corpus functions as a practical seed dataset for early-stage experimentation and later expansion.

The full 48-document corpus was catalogued and prepared for staged indexing. For the pilot evaluation reported in this paper, indexing priority was assigned to two highest-density linguistic resources: the official Shawi–Spanish dictionary [22] and the Shawi orthographic writing manual [23].

6 Experimental Design and Pilot Results

The evaluation reported in this section is a feasibility pilot, not a validated effectiveness study. The pilot benchmark comprises 50 queries (40 Spanish functional and 10 Shawi or mixed-language exploratory), evaluated against an index built from two priority core linguistic resources (the Shawi–Spanish dictionary and the orthographic writing manual) selected from the curated 48-document corpus. Manual scoring was conducted by a single evaluator (the lead author) following the rubric defined in Sect. 6.3. Results should be interpreted as early feasibility evidence rather than as a generalizable effectiveness claim; broader evaluation with parallel query sets, multi-evaluator scoring, and the full corpus remain future work.

To evaluate feasibility under realistic deployment constraints, a functional prototype was implemented on moderate consumer hardware rather than enterprise infrastructure. Table 2 summarizes the reference hardware and software stack.

6.1 System Configurations

Three configurations were compared. B1 (Local LLM Only): direct generation without retrieval. B2 (Local LLM + RAG): local generation with semantic retrieval over indexed Shawi resources. B3 (Full Framework): B2 plus language mediation (lexical exact-match prioritization, bilingual normalization, mixed-query handling).

6.2 Pilot Indexing Results

Although the curated corpus contains 48 documents, the first phase prioritized two highest-value linguistic resources: the Shawi–Spanish dictionary [22] and the writing manual [23]. Across these, the system successfully indexed 307 semantic units/pages with only one failed indexing event, a 99.7% successful ingestion rate, confirming the practical feasibility of local corpus construction on commodity hardware.

Table 2. Reference hardware and software stack

Component	Configuration	Function
CPU	Intel Core i7–4770	Orchestration and API serving
RAM	32 GB	Concurrent services and model loading
GPU	NVIDIA RTX 3060 12 GB	LLM inference acceleration
OS	Ubuntu 22.04.5 LTS	Host environment
Runtime	Ollama (Docker 29.1.3, CUDA 13.0)	Local LLM serving
Base model	Qwen2.5 7.6B Instruct, GGUF Q4_K_M [3]	Multilingual instruction-tuned LLM
Embedding model	nomic-embed-text (137 M, F16)	Local embedding generation
Retrieval DB	ChromaDB (default L2 distance)	Vector index for corpus search

6.3 Evaluation Protocol

A structured benchmark of 50 queries was constructed for the pilot evaluation. The 40 Spanish functional queries were distributed across four categories: (i) lexical meaning, which probe the definition of Shawi terms (e.g., ¿Qué significa pawa?); (ii) translation, which request translation of Shawi terms into Spanish (e.g., Traduce nanan al español); (iii) orthographic guidance, which ask about Shawi writing conventions (e.g., ¿Qué dice el manual sobre vocales?); and (iv) institutional-resource access, which ask about the function or value of MINEDU resources (e.g., ¿Qué utilidad tiene el manual para docentes?). The 10 Shawi or mixed-language queries were short exploratory probes consisting of a single Shawi term followed by a question mark (e.g., Pawa?, Nanan?), designed to test retrieval and response behavior under mixed-language conditions. A representative subset of example queries is shown in Table 3.

Responses were scored manually by the lead author against a written rubric with three operational categories. A response was scored as strictly correct when it was factually and lexically exact, with clear grounding to one or more retrieved source passages cited by file and page. A response was scored as useful when it was relevant and practically helpful to the query intent, even if it lacked perfect lexical alignment, provided the answer was grounded in retrieved context. A response was scored as partially useful when it provided some helpful content but exhibited weak grounding, incomplete citations, or partial coverage of the query intent. Responses that failed all three criteria were classified as not useful. The useful-or-partial rate reported throughout this section combines the useful and partially useful categories.

Scoring was conducted by a single evaluator (the lead author) following the written rubric above. Inter-rater reliability was not measured, and this single-evaluator protocol is explicitly noted as a methodological limitation in Sect. 8.2. Multi-evaluator validation involving educators and community members is identified as a future-work item in Sect. 8.3.

Table 3. Representative example queries by category, drawn from the pilot benchmark

Category	Example query
Lexical meaning	¿Qué significa pawa?
Lexical meaning	¿Qué significa namura?
Translation	Traduce nanan al español
Translation	Traduce a'kusu al español
Orthographic guidance	¿Qué dice el manual sobre vocales?
Orthographic guidance	¿Cómo se escribe correctamente una palabra en Shawi?
Institutional-resource access	¿Qué utilidad tiene el manual para docentes?
Institutional-resource access	¿Qué aporta el diccionario a la EIB?
Shawi / mixed exploratory	Pawa?
Shawi / mixed exploratory	Nanan?

6.4 Comparative Results

The formal variables introduced in Sect. 3 were mapped to pilot measurements as follows. The corpus D corresponds to the indexed Shawi dictionary [22] and writing manual [23]. The generated response R(q) corresponds to the answer returned by each configuration. Relevance and grounding were evaluated through manual scoring and source inspection. Usefulness U was measured as the useful-or-partial response rate. Latency T was measured automatically from benchmark logs. LAG was approximated by comparing performance between Spanish functional queries and Shawi/mixed exploratory queries.

Table 4 reports detailed observed values for the B3 full framework configuration on the 50-query benchmark, including the pilot useful-response rate progression across B1 (Local LLM Only, 28%), B2 (LLM + RAG, 61%), and B3 (Full Framework, 82%).

Table 4. Pilot evaluation results for the B3 full framework

Metric	Result
Total benchmark queries	50
Spanish functional queries	40
Shawi/mixed exploratory queries	10
Strictly correct responses	68%
Useful or partially useful responses	82%
Spanish functional useful/partial rate	77.5%
Shawi/mixed useful/partial rate	100%

(continued)

Table 4. (*continued*)

Metric	Result
Average latency	2.26 s
Spanish subset latency	2.03 s
Shawi/mixed subset latency	3.15 s
Average exact lexical matches	0.86

Note: The higher Shawi/mixed rate should be interpreted cautiously because these were exploratory lexical queries, not full conversational native-language tasks.

Using the useful-or-partial response rate as U, the pilot B3 configuration obtained U(dom) = 77.5% for Spanish functional queries and U(low) = 100% for Shawi/mixed exploratory lexical queries. This produces a pilot LAG proxy of −22.5 percentage points in bounded lexical-access scenarios. This negative value does not mean that the system is generally better for Shawi than Spanish; rather, it reflects that the Shawi/mixed subset consisted of short lexical-access queries, where exact-match mediation performed especially well. The result should therefore be interpreted as evidence that language mediation can reduce LAG in bounded lexical-access scenarios. Representative failure cases observed in the pilot benchmark are summarized in Table 5.

Table 5. Illustrative failure cases observed in the pilot benchmark

Query	System response (summary)	Failure mode
¿Qué dice el manual sobre la escritura Shawi?	The system answered that there was no clear evidence about what the manual says on Shawi writing.	Retrieval gap / insufficient evidence
¿Qué normas de escritura menciona el manual?	The system returned a list of lexical or index-like items and treated them as writing norms.	Hallucination / over-interpretation
Pawa significa qué?	The system correctly linked pawa to marañón/casho, but also added 'caña espesa,' introducing ambiguity.	Mixed-language ambiguity / partial lexical contamination

Illustrative Multi-Objective Score.

As an illustration of how the multi-objective criterion introduced in Sect. 3.1 can be applied jointly rather than treating usefulness, equity, and latency in isolation, the pilot values can be combined using equal weights as a neutral baseline. Under this purely illustrative criterion, configuration B3 ranks highest because gains in usefulness and the reduction of the pilot LAG proxy outweigh the moderate latency cost associated with the retrieval and mediation steps. We emphasize that this is an illustrative composition rather than an empirical optimization claim; the weights have not been calibrated against stakeholder priorities or user studies, and any operational use of this criterion would require such calibration.

6.5 Main Observations

Three patterns emerged. First, retrieval grounding improved factual usefulness from 28% (B1) to 61% (B2). Second, the mediation layer produced the largest gains in lexical access and mixed-language queries: the additional 21 percentage points from B2 to B3 came from targeted language handling, not larger model scale. The pilot LAG proxy of −22.5 percentage points indicates that, within this evaluation subset, the system became measurably less unequal across language groups—though full sociolinguistic validation remains future work. Third, acceptable local responsiveness (2.26 s average latency on moderate hardware) supports offline or connectivity-constrained deployment.

7 Discussion

What the preliminary evidence suggests is something the field does not always say directly: for many users in many territories, architecture matters more than scale. The systems that perform best on global benchmarks may not be the systems best suited to an Amazonian municipality with intermittent internet access and a Shawi-speaking population. The pilot evidence reported here is consistent with this hypothesis but does not by itself establish it; broader evaluation is required.

The Shawi case makes this tangible. Retrieval grounding over prioritized core linguistic resources from the broader 48-document MINEDU corpus produced measurably better responses for procedural and educational queries than parametric generation alone. The information already existed in the corpus; the model's job was to find and present it, not to know it from pretraining. That is a more tractable problem, with smaller gaps between high-resource and low-resource settings [4, 12].

Language mediation added further gains without requiring full native-language fluency. Normalization rules, bilingual mappings, and prompt guidance for mixed-language inputs reduced failure cases in ways that neither retrieval nor generation alone could address. This matters for the LAG metric: the goal is not to make the system perfect for Shawi speakers, but to make it measurably less unequal. It is important to note that the LAG values reported here are pilot proxies estimated over non-equivalent query sets (Spanish functional vs. Shawi/mixed lexical), and they should not be interpreted as general measurements of the gap between Spanish and Shawi-language users. Construction of parallel, functionally equivalent benchmark sets across languages is a prerequisite for any broader LAG validation and is identified as future work.

Infrastructure realism is an underappreciated design variable. A system that requires enterprise hardware or premium cloud connectivity is not available to the institutions that most need it. Local-first deployment is not a compromise—for many municipalities, community health posts, and schools, it is the only viable path to any AI-assisted service capability. Data sovereignty concerns reinforce this: query logs and interaction data that stay local cannot be misused externally [1, 15].

Standard benchmarks systematically hide differential performance across language groups. The LAG metric makes that dimension visible and measurable, leading to different architectural choices than aggregate-performance optimization.

None of this means local small models are uniformly better, or that cloud-based frontier systems have no role. The framework explicitly includes an optional cloud augmentation layer for when connectivity exists and demanding tasks warrant it. The argument is about defaults: the system should work offline, on affordable hardware, in the user's language—not the reverse. Governance, source maintenance, and institutional accountability remain essential regardless of the architecture chosen [20]. The pilot scope of this evaluation—two indexed resources, 50 queries, single evaluator—places clear bounds on what can be concluded; we present these findings as feasibility evidence to motivate the broader evaluation outlined in Sect. 8.3.

8 Limitations and Future Work

8.1 Ethical Considerations

The materials in this corpus belong, in an important sense, to the Shawi community. The Wahkupi primary-education textbook series [24], the Ninuntunan secondary-education series [25], the literature anthology Nuntunan kirika [26], the community knowledge collection Kanpuwa nitutu kirika [27], the dictionary [22], and the writing manual [23]—these were created through processes involving Shawi speakers, educators, and MINEDU linguists. Using them in an AI system is not ethically neutral, even when the materials are publicly available.

Four principles shaped this work. First, the corpus draws exclusively from officially published MINEDU materials in the public domain [22–27], avoiding direct extraction of linguistic data without consent and providing institutional provenance for every source. Second, the system is designed for local operation: query logs, interaction data, and derived materials remain under institutional or community control [1, 14]. Third, outputs are framed explicitly as informational assistance, not authoritative guidance [15].

Fourth, this study is a first step. During design, the lead author maintained informal consultations with a native Shawi–Spanish bilingual speaker, whose orientation guided the choice of priority resources and the framing of intended use. This does not constitute formal participatory validation with the broader Shawi community, which—following the principles articulated by Bird [9] and Nekoto et al. [14]—requires structured engagement and community ownership over deployment decisions. Formal participatory validation remains an explicit future-work commitment (see Sect. 8.3).

8.2 Technical Limitations

Several limitations bound the current work. The present benchmark should be interpreted as a pilot-stage evaluation centered on core linguistic resources rather than full-corpus production deployment. Qwen2.5-7B-Instruct [3] provides limited zero-shot Shawi fluency—the language mediation layer compensates for this, but direct native-language generation remains a research frontier. The evaluation design is preliminary: quantitative benchmarks with broader user populations are needed. The 48-document corpus does not cover health communication, agricultural procedures, or community-generated materials. Text-only interaction may underserve communities where voice interfaces would be more practical [17]. Transferability to languages with different grammatical typologies remains to be demonstrated empirically.

Finally, scoring was conducted by a single evaluator (the lead author) following a written rubric; inter-rater reliability was not measured. Multi-evaluator validation including educator and community involvement is identified as future work in Sect. 8.3.

8.3 Future Work

Five immediate directions: (1) Shawi-specific fine-tuning or parameter-efficient adaptation; (2) corpus expansion (healthcare, legal, agriculture, municipal procedures); (3) speech interface development (ASR and TTS [17]); (4) participatory validation with community members and educators; (5) pilot deployments in schools, municipal offices, and regional health posts. Testing in other Amazonian and Andean indigenous language contexts should follow.

Two additional directions follow directly from the limitations discussed above. First, construction of parallel, functionally equivalent benchmark query sets across Spanish and Shawi, to enable broader and more rigorous validation of the LAG metric beyond the bounded lexical-access scenarios reported here. Second, multi-evaluator scoring with structured inter-rater reliability assessment, with the goal of moving from single-evaluator pilot scoring to validated multi-evaluator protocols that include native Shawi speakers and EIB educators.

To support reproducibility, benchmark queries, evaluation rubric, and reference configuration parameters will be made available upon publication. The MINEDU corpus remains under its original public-domain licensing with the Ministerio de Educación del Perú.

9 Conclusion

Artificial intelligence has not, on its own, reduced the informational inequalities that existed before it. In some respects it has made them more visible by demonstrating, at scale, what capable AI assistance looks like for users whose languages and territories have been prioritized. The question is whether that gap can be deliberately narrowed.

This paper has argued that it can, and that the design choices required are specific: local inference over affordable hardware, retrieval grounded in curated institutional corpora, language mediation for low-resource contexts, and evaluation criteria that capture differential access. The pilot evaluation with 50 queries showed useful response rates rising from 28% (B1) to 82% (B3)—a difference attributable to retrieval grounding and language mediation, not model scale. The pilot LAG proxy of −22.5 percentage points provides early feasibility evidence consistent with the hypothesis that targeted language mediation can reduce, rather than reproduce, linguistic access inequalities. Broader validation—with parallel query sets, multi-evaluator scoring, and a larger indexed corpus—is required before this can be claimed as a general result.

The 48-document MINEDU corpus is not large by benchmark standards, but structured, curated, institutionally grounded materials supported meaningful early-stage assistance when integrated through retrieval pipelines. Many regions worldwide have similar untapped resources and similar unmet needs.

Territorial informational inequality is ultimately a governance and design problem, not only a technical one. Local LLM-RAG systems built around the constraints of underserved multilingual territories are one concrete starting point. The evidence reported here is exploratory; whether the approach generalizes to other indigenous and minority-language settings is a hypothesis to be tested through broader pilots and longitudinal deployment studies.

System Prompt (Benchmark Configuration)

The verbatim system prompt used in the benchmark evaluation is reproduced below in its original Spanish:

```
Eres ChatShawi, asistente lingüístico Shawi.
Responde SOLO con el contexto.
Si no hay evidencia clara, dilo.
No inventes traducciones.
Responde breve en español y cita archivo/página.
```

Format appended to the prompt: "Pregunta: {q} / Término detectado: {target} / Contexto: {context} / Respuesta:".

References

1. Touvron, H., Lavril, T., Izacard, G., et al.: LLaMA: Open and efficient foundation language models. https://arxiv.org/abs/2302.13971 (2023)
2. Qwen Team: Qwen2.5 Technical Report. https://arxiv.org/abs/2412.15115 (2024)
3. Lewis, P., Perez, E., Piktus, A., et al.: Retrieval-augmented generation for knowledge-intensive NLP tasks. Adv. Neural Inf. Process. Syst. **33**, 9459–9474 (2020)
4. Joshi, P., Santy, S., Budhiraja, A., Bali, K., Choudhury, M.: The state and fate of linguistic diversity and inclusion in the NLP world. In: Procedings ACL, pp. 6282–6293 (2020)
5. Frantar, E., Ashkboos, S., Hoefler, T., Alistarh, D.: GPTQ: Accurate post-training quantization for generative pre-trained transformers. In: Proc. ICLR . https://arxiv.org/abs/2210.17323 (2023)
6. Mager, M., Oncevay, A., Ebrahimi, A., et al.: Findings of the AmericasNLP 2021 shared task on open MT for indigenous languages of the Americas. In: Proceedings AmericasNLP Workshop, pp. 202–217 (2021)
7. Bender, E.M., Gebru, T., McMillan-Major, A., Shmitchell, S.: On the dangers of stochastic parrots: can language models be too big? In: Proceedings FAccT, pp. 610–623 (2021)
8. Chiruzzo, L., Mager, M., Oncevay, A., et al.: Findings of the AmericasNLP 2024 shared task on educational materials for indigenous languages. In: Proceedings AmericasNLP (2024)
9. Bird, S.: Decolonising speech and language technology. In: Proceedings COLING, pp. 3504–3519 (2020)
10. Bommasani, R., Hudson, D.A., Adeli, E., et al.: On the opportunities and risks of foundation models. https://arxiv.org/abs/2108.07258 (2021)

11. Gao, Y., Xiong, Y., Gao, X., et al.: Retrieval-augmented generation for large language models: A survey. https://arxiv.org/abs/2312.10997 (2023)
12. Karpukhin, V., Oguz, B., Min, S., et al.: Dense passage retrieval for open-domain question answering. In: Proceedings EMNLP, pp. 6769–6781 (2020)
13. Nekoto, W., Marivate, V., Matsila, T., et al.: Participatory research for low-resourced machine translation. In: Findings of EMNLP (2020)
14. Aoki, N.: An experimental study of public trust in AI chatbots in the public sector. Gov. Inf. Q. **37**(4), 101490 (2020)
15. Dettmers, T., Pagnoni, A., Holtzman, A., Zettlemoyer, L.: QLoRA: efficient finetuning of quantized LLMs. Adv. Neural Inf. Process. Syst. **36** (2023)
16. Radford, A., Kim, J.W., Xu, T., et al.: Robust speech recognition via large-scale weak supervision. In: Proceedings ICML, pp. 28492–28518 (2023)
17. Androutsopoulou, A., Karacapilidis, N., Loukis, E., Charalabidis, Y.: Transforming the communication between citizens and government through AI-guided chatbots. Gov. Inf. Q. **36**(2), 358–367 (2019)
18. Wirtz, B.W., Weyerer, J.C., Geyer, C.: Artificial intelligence and the public sector. Int. J. Public Adm. **42**(7), 596–615 (2019)
19. OECD: AI Language Models: Technological, Socio-Economic and Policy Considerations. OECD Publishing, Paris s(2023)
20. Ji, Z., Lee, N., Frieske, R., et al.: Survey of hallucination in natural language generation. ACM Comput. Surv. **55**(12), 1–38 (2023)
21. Ministerio de Cultura del Perú: Base de datos de pueblos indígenas u originarios del Perú. Lima (2023)
22. Ministerio de Educación del Perú: Nananu'sa uhteinan: Diccionario Shawi–Castellano, 2nd ed. MINEDU, Lima (2024)
23. Ministerio de Educación del Perú: Manual de escritura Shawi 1. MINEDU, Lima (2017)
24. Ministerio de Educación del Perú: Wahkupi 1–6: Comunicación Primaria – Shawi. MINEDU, Lima (2023)
25. Ministerio de Educación del Perú: Ninuntunan 1–5: Comunicación Secundaria – Shawi. MINEDU, Lima (2024)
26. Ministerio de Educación del Perú: Nuntunan kirika: Literatura Shawi. MINEDU, Lima (2023)
27. Ministerio de Educación del Perú: Kanpuwa nitutu kirika: Saberes de los pueblos – Shawi. MINEDU, Lima (2023)

Author Index

H. Florez and R. Gomez-Sanchez (Eds.): UPADI-AI 2026, CCIS 3124, p. 223, 2027.
https://doi.org/10.1007/978-3-032-35635-2

MIX
Papier aus verantwortungsvollen Quellen
Paper from responsible sources
FSC® C105338

If you have any concerns about our products,
you can contact us on
ProductSafety@springernature.com

In case Publisher is established outside the EU,
the EU authorized representative is:
Springer Nature Customer Service Center GmbH
Europaplatz 3, 69115 Heidelberg, Germany

Printed by Libri Plureos GmbH
in Hamburg, Germany